JEWS IN CHINA:
CULTURAL CONVERSATIONS,
CHANGING PERCEPTIONS

T0392365

Jews in China: Cultural Conversations, Changing Perceptions

IRENE EBER

EDITED WITH AN INTRODUCTION
BY KATHRYN HELLERSTEIN

The Pennsylvania State University Press
University Park, Pennsylvania

Library of Congress Cataloging-in-Publication Data

Names: Eber, Irene, 1929–2019, author. | Hellerstein, Kathryn, editor, writer of introduction.
Title: Jews in China : cultural conversations, changing perceptions / Irene Eber ; edited with an introduction by Kathryn Hellerstein.
Other titles: Dimyonot (University Park, Pa.)
Description: University Park, Pennsylvania : The Pennsylvania State University Press, [2020] | Series: Dimyonot: Jews and the cultural imagination | Includes bibliographical references and index.
Summary: "A collection of essays delineating the centuries-long dialogue of Jews and Jewish culture with China, all under the overarching theme of cultural translation"—Provided by publisher.
Identifiers: LCCN 2019038712 | ISBN 9780271084961 (cloth)
Subjects: LCSH: Jews—China—History. | Jewish literature—Translations into Chinese—History and criticism. | Translating and interpreting—China. | LCGFT: Essays.
Classification: LCC DS135.C5 E235 2020 | DDC 951/.004924—dc23
LC record available at https://lccn.loc.gov/2019038712

CONTENTS

Introduction

Kathryn Hellerstein

This volume presents a selection of articles and chapters published over the past several decades by Irene Eber, the pioneering scholar in the second half of the twentieth century in the field of Jews and China. While Eber has expanded on these themes and topics in her many publications over the past fifty years, each of the essays in this book presents a unique entrée into the subject. What makes this collection valuable is that it represents the full range of the history of Jews in dialogue with China and China in dialogue with Jewish culture.

Irene Eber, who died April 10, 2019, was the Louis Frieberg Professor of East Asian Studies, emeritus, in the Department of East Asian Studies at the Hebrew University of Jerusalem, where she taught Chinese history and culture for thirty years (1969–1999). A brief account of her life will place the scholarship of this remarkable person into context. Born in Halle, Germany, into the Geminder family in 1929, Irene and her family were deported by the Nazis to Mielec, Poland, in 1938.[1] There she attended the Bais Yaakov School for religious girls until the family was incarcerated in the Dębica ghetto. There they hid in an attic to avoid deportation to Auschwitz.[2] Irene, at age thirteen, disobeyed her father and decided to escape from the ghetto. Digging under a fence, she took a train back to Mielec, but the Polish inhabitants of her former hometown refused to help her until a Polish refugee family hid her in a chicken coop for almost two years.[3] Her father was shot in a work camp; her mother, a typist, worked in the office at Oskar Schindler's camp, where she and Irene's sister, Lore, survived the war.[4]

After the war, Irene, by then age fifteen, was reunited with her mother and sister, and the three went to Germany, where they first stayed with her mother's sister. Somewhat later, Irene left and went to several displaced persons camps in the American zone[5] until she was able to make her way to New York, where she found a job, attended night school, and learned English. In 1955, she earned her B.A. in Asian studies at Pomona College; in 1961, her MA at the State University of California, Sacramento; and in 1966, her PhD in Asian studies at Claremont Graduate University.[6] Before she arrived at Hebrew University, where she served several terms as chair of the Department for East Asian Studies, Eber taught at Whittier College. During her tenure at Hebrew University, she was periodically a visiting professor or scholar at the University of Michigan, Wesleyan University, and Harvard University.[7] The recipient of major grants, Eber had served on the editorial boards of the *Journal of Sino-Western Communications, Moreshet Israel: A Journal for the Study of Judaism,* and *Zionism and Eretz-Israel;* had been the curator and consultant to the exhibitions Jewish Communities in China (Widener Library, Harvard University) and The Jews of Kaifeng (Nahum Goldman Museum of the Jewish Diaspora, Tel Aviv); and organized and/or chaired numerous conferences and workshops, such as The Bible in Modern China and Confucianism: The Dynamics of Tradition (both at the Hebrew University).

Eber was the author or editor of some eleven books and published more than sixty-six scholarly articles and numerous book reviews and introductions, as well as her own short stories.[8] Her most recent book, *Jewish Refugees in Shanghai, 1933–1947: A Selection of Documents* (Goettingen, 2018), presents a groundbreaking documentary history of the approximately twenty thousand Jews from Central and Eastern Europe who survived World War II by finding refuge in Shanghai. This collection of almost two hundred sources—originally composed in German, English, Yiddish, Hebrew, Russian, and Chinese—attests to the efforts of these Jews, made stateless by the Nazis, to sustain their material needs as well as their community and culture in the face of poverty, displacement, and political adversity. The documents, culled from Eber's collection of some two thousand items, show how these Jews received help from Jewish aid committees in Shanghai and international aid organizations, how they were perceived by the Chinese and Japanese authorities, and the reactions of Nazi officials in Shanghai. With this documentary evidence, Eber shows the complexity of this historical moment and prepares the ground for solid, fact-based future scholarship on this fascinating period.

In *Voices from Shanghai: Jewish Exiles in Wartime China* (Chicago, 2008), Eber collects and translates a first-time selection of poetry, fiction, diaries, memoirs, and letters written and published in Yiddish, German, and Hebrew by some of the Jews who took refuge in Shanghai from the Nazis. This collection gives evidence of the creative and cultural expression of these European Jews and attests to the role that literature and culture play as modes of human survival under the direst circumstances. Eber's other books include her major study *Wartime Shanghai and Jewish Refugees from Central Europe: Survival, Co-existence, and Identity in a Multi-ethnic City* (Berlin, 2012) and *Chinese and Jews: Encounters Between Cultures*, which came out in Hebrew (Jerusalem, 2002) and in English (Valentine Mitchell, 2008).

Eber's books extend beyond the history of Jews in Shanghai and beyond the twentieth century. Her definitive biography of the translator into Chinese of the Hebrew Bible, *The Jewish Bishop and the Chinese Bible, S. I. J. Schereschewsky, 1831–1906* (Leiden, 1999), was also published in Chinese translation in Taiwan (2003), and she coedited a collection, *Bible in Modern China: The Literary and Intellectual Impact* (Nethetal, 1999), of which the Chinese edition appeared in Hong Kong (2003). She edited a volume on *Confucianism: The Dynamics of Tradition* (New York, 1986), translated from the German Richard Wilhelm's *Lectures on the I Ching: Constancy and Change* (Princeton, 1979), and wrote on modern Chinese authors in *Voices from Afar: Modern Chinese Writers on Oppressed Peoples and Their Literature* (Ann Arbor, 1980).

Martin Buber Werkausgabe, Eber's volume in German on Martin Buber's writings on Chinese philosophy and literature (Gueterslohe, 2014), was groundbreaking, as was her searing account of her life as a young girl in Poland during World War II, *The Choice* (New York, 2004), which was translated into German (Munich, 2007) and Chinese (Beijing, 2013). As her books demonstrate, this prolific, pioneering scholar achieved international distinction by introducing readers in English, Hebrew, German, and Chinese to the various intersections and cross-pollination of Jewish and Chinese cultures.

Jews in China: Cultural Conversations, Changing Perceptions stands as Irene Eber's twelfth book. It makes available to teachers, students, and scholars, as well as to general readers an overview of the range and depth of her work in the field of Jews and China and presents a sampling from Eber's extra-ordinary scholarly career. The fourteen essays published in this volume were selected from her sixty-six articles published in journals and anthologies between 1972 and 2010. Eber organized this volume according to the over-arching theme of cultural translation, which she places in a historical context.

The book's three sections move from historical context and narrative to translation of classical or traditional texts in both Judaism and Daoism to the reciprocal translation of modern literature, both Chinese and Jewish. The first section, "Overview," presents three essays that set out chronolog-ically the history of Jews in China over a period of almost a millennium. The first of the three essays in this section, "Overland and by Sea: Eight Centuries of the Jewish Presence in China," describes the diversity and distinctiveness of Jewish communities in China from the first arrival of Jews in that nation in the late eighth or early ninth century. Jewish cotton traders from Persia via India traveled the Silk Road or came by sea and established a community in the northern city of Kaifeng, where they intermarried with the native population yet maintained their Jewish religion and identity for almost nine hundred years, building a temple for worship, scribing Torah scrolls and other liturgical texts in Hebrew, and recording their communal history in Chinese on stone stelae and in genealogical books. Acknowl-edged and tolerated by the emperor and local governments, these Jewish families produced sons who either became merchants or entered the gov-ernment. In the seventeenth century, Jesuit missionaries discovered the Kaifeng Jews and recorded their presence in words, drawings, and rubbings. In the nineteenth century, the community experienced a decline through their Sinification, the destruction of their temple by floods, the death of the last rabbi, and the lack of continued knowledge of Hebrew. A Protestant bishop purchased the stone stelae, inscribed with the community's history in 1489 and in 1663, and preserved them. While previous scholars have doc-umented this moment as the end of the Kaifeng Jewish community, Eber argues more subtly that Sinification was not a destructive erasure of Judaism in this population. Rather, the Jews' adaptation to Chinese culture by taking on Chinese names and not, it seems, establishing charitable societies, as was conventional among Jewish communities elsewhere in the world, was a case of true intercultural intermingling and transformation. These Jews became Chinese Jews through their lineage in a "family-centered identity" (p. 243) and in the correspondences or similarities between Chinese philosophies and folk practices and Judaism. Integrated into Chinese society, these Jews nonetheless remained Jews, albeit living a new kind of Judaism—a truly Chinese Judaism.

With equal nuance, Eber examines the "mosaic" of Jewish communities in the international city of Shanghai, focusing on the Baghdadi Jewish community, whose members flourished as merchants of opium, as bankers, and as real estate moguls in Shanghai from the mid-nineteenth century through 1949. She also discusses the larger Russian Jewish community in Shanghai, who arrived in 1904 and in 1917, following, respectively, the Russo-Japanese War and the Russian October Revolution, many of them having come south from Harbin. She then focuses on the German and Austrian Jews who fled Hitler and found a haven in Shanghai starting in 1938 and on the Polish Yiddish-speaking Jews, both secular and religious, who arrived in Shanghai from Lithuania and Japan. In this brief essay, Eber shows the complexity of the interaction between the various groups of Jews in Shanghai, their religious lives, their communal organizations, their secular entertainment and publishing, and the range of ways they survived economically under the Japanese military rule of Shanghai during the Pacific War in World War II.

"Chinese Jews and Jews in China: Kaifeng–Shanghai," the second essay, develops in more detail Eber's ideas about how the centrality in Chinese culture of family identity, rather than communal identity, influenced the Kaifeng Jews and transformed their Judaism into a Chinese Judaism. This essay, first published in 2015, brings the questions of the identity of these Chinese Jews into the twenty-first century and examines the relationship between current Kaifeng residents of Jewish lineage and Jews of the United States and Israel. Similarly, Eber revisits the topic of the Shanghai Jewish communities and their organizations, institutions, and cultural manifestations to expand in greater detail the broad strokes of her earlier essay. She also considers Judaism in China today, in Hong Kong and Shanghai.

The third essay in the "Overview" section, "Flight to Shanghai: 1938–1939 and Its Larger Context," places the initial arrival of the Jewish refugees from the Nazis into the context of Shanghai and its recent history. The essay focuses on Jewish immigration to Shanghai before 1938, on the German interests in East Asia from 1935 to 1939, on the "Shanghai scene" into which the refugee

Jews from Germany and Austria arrived in 1938–1939, and on the ambivalent responses by the Japanese, the Chinese, and the British to the arrival of some twenty thousand stateless Jews. This first section, "Overview," moves from a large-scale outline of the historical picture of Jews in different regions of China over almost a millennium to a focused analysis of two crucial years before the start of World War II.

Section 2, "Translating the Ancestors," contains three essays on textual and literary translation of classical texts of Chinese literature and the Hebrew Bible. The first of these, "A Critical Survey of Classical Chinese Literary Works in Hebrew," reviews the century of translations of Chinese literature into modern Hebrew since the revival and development of modern Hebrew starting in the nineteenth century. Eber notes that many of the earlier translations came into Hebrew through intermediary languages, such as Russian, English, or German, but that a number of more recent translations have been made directly from the Chinese by "a small and dedicated group of Hebrew speakers and native-born Israelis" who learned Chinese at universities in Israel, Europe, and China (p. 302). The popularity of translations into Hebrew of Chinese writings grew after China and Israel established diplomatic relations in 1991, tourism ensued, and media images of China expanded through television and, more recently, the internet. Eber notes two of the many problems of translating from Chinese into Hebrew—how the convention of omitting diacritical vowels from modern Hebrew leads to mispronunciation of Chinese names and concepts and how and whether Hebrew translators have transliterated Chinese names and concepts according to the now obsolete Wade-Giles system or according to the current standard of pinyin. The essay then discusses the limited number of sources available in Hebrew on China, from the first history of China in Hebrew by S. M. Perlmann, *The Chinese* (1911), through the authoritative but now dated 1974 *Hebrew Encyclopedia*. Eber contrasts this paucity of historical sources with the plethora of translations made in the 1960s and 1970s from Russian and English of Mao Zedong's writings, works about the Chinese Communist revolution and the Cultural Revolution, and a biography of Mao. Eber attributes this Israeli fascination with China's then contemporary history to an interest in societal transformation that corresponded to the development in Israel of secularism and of the labor movement's "socialist economic ethos," as well as the success of the kibbutz movement. In subsequent decades, as

Israeli society changed, so too changed the interests of Hebrew readers of Chinese texts in translation.

Eber traces translations of classical Chinese philosophy into Hebrew back to 1937, with A. E. Aescoly's partial rendition from the German of the *Daode jing*, and Martin Buber's translation of another eight chapters, from either German or English, in 1942. Donald Leslie translated seventeen chapters directly from Chinese (1964), and Yuri Grause translated the complete text from Chinese into Hebrew in 1973. Eber compares Grause's 1971 translation with a more scholarly and literary translation by Daor and Ariel in 1981, as well as with a "mystically inclined" rendition by Ben-Mordekhai in 1996 and a comic book version by Saragusti in 1995. Turning to translations of the *Zhuangzi*, Eber comments on a selective translation of only the stories by Israeli novelist Yoel Hoffman (1977) and a more complete selection of entire chapters by Donald Leslie (1964). Her evaluation of the *Liezi* rates the annotated version by Dan Daor very highly. But she considers Leslie's 1969 scholarly translation of the Confucian text, the *Lunyu*, clumsy in style and questions his rendering of key Chinese terms, which distorts the concepts. These problems raise the question of how a translator can render "culture-specific philosophical concepts" without sacrificing the flexibility of meaning in the original language and imposing "Western philosophical assumptions." Eber praises Andrew Plaks's translation of the *Daxue* for its facing-page format of the Chinese with the Hebrew, its numbered sentences, and its interpretive notes. Eber is critical of the two translations into Hebrew of the *Yijing*—by Visman in 1983 and by Yuri Grause in 1993—because both fail to place the work into its centuries-long scholarly and philosophical context.

When Eber turns to Hebrew translations of Chinese fiction and poetry, she emphasizes the rather arbitrary selections of Chinese authors and the mixed success of translations. In the 1940s and 1950s, many works by a single author, Lin Yutang, were translated into Hebrew from the English as well as an autobiography of a woman soldier, Xie Bingying. After 1983, fiction by the eighteenth-century writer Shen Fu was translated directly from the Chinese into Hebrew by Dan Daor as well as a collection of short stories by famous May Fourth writers. Eber lauds these works as well as the renditions by Amira Katz, who translated some of these stories and other collections of short fiction by Lu Xun, Shen Congwen, and Feng Menglong. Both Daor and Katz translated classical and modern fiction, depending on publishers' demands, and both translators evince sensitivity and effectiveness in transforming Chinese into readable idiomatic Hebrew. Eber is critical of the uneven quality of Hebrew translations of Chinese poetry, mostly from intermediary languages. Dov Sadan (Dov Stock), a founding scholar of Yiddish studies in Israel, translated the eighth-century classic poet Li Bai into Hebrew in 1930 with questionable results. Perhaps Stock translated Li Bai from the Yiddish translations by Meyer Shtiker (New York, 1926).[9] In 1960, the Israeli poet Aharon Shabtai translated thirty-two Chinese poems, ranging from Li Bai and the ninth-century poet Du Mu to the eighteenth-century Manchu poet Nalan Shengde, alongside translations from the Japanese. Neither Stock nor Shabtai indicates what their source texts were—in other words, what intermediary translations of these poems they used for their Hebrew translations. More substantial selections of Chinese poems appeared in Hebrew translations by Ben-Zakai (1970) and Garin (1990), but Eber questions the choices and results of these works too. In contrast, verse translations of classical poetry of the Tang dynasty (618–907 C.E.) directly from the Chinese by Yuri Grause (1977) and Dan Daor (2001) merit Eber's praise for their selection, poetic form, and sensitive choice of diction and phrasing in Hebrew that reflects the Chinese original. In Eber's judgment, the most significant translation into Hebrew is *Dream of the Red Chamber* by Plaks and Katz.

Eber concludes this essay by noting the three types of Hebrew translation that were under way at the writing of this essay in 2003: (1) reliable translations directly from the Chinese, (2) translations catering to fashionable notions of "the East," and (3) informative translations of contemporary Chinese fiction. Although the "perfect translation" is impossible, Eber values the translations that she deems successful by those who know Chinese culture and, better yet, the language and who are able to bring Chinese philosophy, fiction, and poetry across into Hebrew in a sensitive and interpretive way.

In the other two essays in section 2, Eber turns our gaze to the first translation of the Hebrew Bible into Chinese by Samuel Isaac Joseph (S. I. J.) Schereschewsky, a Lithuanian Jew who converted to Christianity and became a Protestant missionary bishop in Shanghai. These two essays expand on previously unexamined aspects of the biography that Eber wrote about Schereschewsky, *The Jewish Bishop and the Chinese Bible: S. I. J. Schereschewsky, 1831–1906.*[10] In "The Peking Translating Committee and S. I. J. Schereschewsky's Old Testament" (1998) Eber examines the complexities of Protestant missionary Bible translations into Chinese and examines the mid-nineteenth-century Peking Translating Committee's rendering of the New Testament from the Greek into Mandarin, the spoken language of northern China, and Schereschewsky's Mandarin translation of the Old Testament from the Hebrew. As the first translations from the Bible's original languages into spoken Chinese, these versions greatly expanded the readership of the Bible in China. The Translating Committee, which began its work in Peking in 1864, consisted of four missionaries (two British and two American) who were proficient in Chinese from having lived in China for years as well as a number of Chinese scholars who set the appropriate style and characters to keep the text appropriately accessible and understandable and who taught the missionaries about Chinese culture and language. The committee members worked harmoniously on drafting, criticizing, and revising the translation as it progressed. Because Schereschewsky was, by birth, a Jew from Lithuania who had achieved an advanced rabbinic education before he converted to Christianity in 1855, his colleagues on the committee assigned him the translation of the Old Testament. Supported by the British and Foreign Bible Society and the American Bible Society, the committee took some ten years to complete the translation. The New Testament was published in 1872; the Old Testament appeared in 1874 and 1875. The Mandarin Bible was the most widely used in China for forty-five years. Eber examines the strategies and principles by which Schereschewsky translated the Hebrew text into an idiomatic and culturally accessible Chinese. He eschewed an incomprehensible literal translation for a translation that relied on Chinese idiom and included explanatory phrasing or explicitness where the Hebrew text was suggestive or implicit. Schereschewsky chose to transliterate the sound rather than transmit the meaning of proper names, but finding the right word for God in Chinese was problematic both theologically and pragmatically. Depending on the context, Schereschewsky varied the terms he used for the deity. Eber brilliantly argues that this interpretive mode of translation developed from Schereschewsky's knowledge of German biblical criticism as well as his yeshiva study of the great eleventh-century commentator on the Pentateuch, Rashi. That Rashi's interpretations, rendered into Chinese by a former Jew, would shape the translation of the Old Testament that would help convert Chinese people to Christianity is an astounding discovery.

Equally amazing is Eber's discussion of the controversy of how to translate the term *God* into Chinese, an argument that caused theological and political rifts among the Protestant missionaries in China. Eber brings to life the unsuccessful peace-making efforts of the Peking Translating Committee to establish an acceptable choice. Schereschewsky's challenge was more difficult, though, because the Hebrew Bible uses different names for God in different parts of the text. He managed to retain these differences, although not without causing controversy, because he had the final word on the Old Testament translation.

In "Translating the Ancestors: S. I. J. Schereschewsky's 1875 Chinese Version of Genesis" (1993), Eber examines more closely how Schereschewsky's Jewish background shaped his translation enterprise. A detailed biographical sketch shows how the orphaned boy's traditional Jewish education was set off by the Haskalah, or Jewish Enlightenment, which introduced Western education and culture to eastern European Jews, and by the government-sponsored rabbinical seminaries under the reign of Tsar Nicholas I, which taught secular alongside traditional subjects. In such a seminary in Zhitomir in Ukraine, Eber reasons, Schereschewsky likely read a Yiddish or Hebrew translation of the New Testament. In Breslau, he was influenced by a Jewish convert to Christianity, one Dr. Neumann, who may have introduced him to modern biblical criticism. In 1854, now in America, he converted, was ordained a deacon, and left for China in 1859. His involvement with the Peking Translating Committee began in 1864 and ended in 1875, after which Schereschewsky raised funds for and helped found St. John's University in Shanghai. He was elected as missionary bishop of Shanghai but became paralyzed in 1881 and spent his last twenty-one years revising his translation of the Bible and producing a new translation of the Bible into classical literary Chinese.

The essay continues by analyzing the relationship between vernacular Bible translation and the missionary's work and points out the special problems the translators into Chinese faced: the daunting literary heritage of China, the many vernacular languages within China, the divide between written and spoken Chinese, and the lower-class implications of the northern vernacular. Eber also examines more closely the invaluable role played in the Peking Translating Committee's translation project by the anonymous Chinese informants. Returning to her discussion of the term question, Eber focuses on the role of Schereschewsky's translation choices and his interpretive notes on the translation and presents close readings of his renditions of the creation story in Genesis 1 as well as problems he encountered when translating God's covenant with Abraham that required circumcision (Genesis 17:10–11). The most vexed of the problems of translation, though, was that of the concept of the promised land in Genesis 12—that is, the biblical ideas of nation and peoplehood; in his translation, Schereschewsky avoided such political diction. Eber explains that Schereschewsky's notes "do not attempt to present theological interpretations, and they are not a vehicle for the Christian message in the OT. Rather, they exemplify the translator's concept of a Chinese Christianity 'trained on the soil and for the soil.'"[11] At the same time, Eber shows how the translator based his notes on the medieval Jewish commentary tradition of Rashi. Schereschewsky glossed details in the text and supplied the meanings of the Hebrew proper names that he chose to transliterate. These notes, Eber argues, bring the biblical text to life for the Chinese reader, anchoring it in concrete terms and imparting a distinctly Jewish scholarship into the beginnings of Chinese Protestant Christianity. Even more intriguing is Eber's statement that the translator's profound respect for Chinese civilization led to his belief that "becoming Christian did not mean becoming Westernized, that a genuinely Chinese Christianity was both possible and desirable."[12]

Section 3 of the collection, "Modern Literature in Mutual Translation," gathers eight essays that highlight the theme of cultural reciprocity between modern Jewish and Chinese cultures through the act of translation. In a book full of surprises, this section presents some of the most unexpected examples of cultural exchanges. Two essays here examine Yiddish poems written by Jews in China in the 1930s and 1940s: "Bridge Across Cultures: China in Yiddish Poetry" (2001) and "Meylekh Ravitch in China: A Travelogue of 1935" (2004). In "Bridge Across Cultures," Eber presents poems written by four Polish Yiddish poets during their sojourns in China in the 1930s and 1940s. Meylekh Ravitch (the pen name of Zekharia Khone Bergner, 1893–1976) traveled across China for six months in 1935 as an emissary for a Jewish organization that supported vocational training for Jews and as a representative of the Yiddish PEN Club of Warsaw, which he had helped found. He kept an extensive travel journal and wrote poems describing the suffering and poverty that he observed and heard about among Chinese people during this turbulent time. In contrast, six years later, E. Simkhoni (Simkha Elberg), Ya'akov Fishman, and Yosl Mlotek arrived in Shanghai from Poland via Lithuania and then Kobe, Japan, in 1941 as stateless refugees from Hitler. Despite their own displacement, poverty, and immense losses, each of these poets wrote with compassion of the enormous suffering they observed among the Chinese in Shanghai— "coolies," young prostitutes, street vendors, and beggars. Eber develops a more extended discussion of Meylekh Ravitch's travelogue and poems in her 2004 essay "Meylekh Ravitch in China," where she places his poems on the Trans-Siberian Railway journey and on Harbin, Peking, Shanghai, and Canton into the context of his daily journals.

Two essays in section 3 focus on the translation of Yiddish literature into Chinese. In "Sholem Aleichem in Chinese?" (2010), Eber presents her personal account of why she translates Chinese and Yiddish. A casual remark by her long-ago professor Chen Shouyi that Yiddish fiction had been translated into Chinese awoke Eber's curiosity, which prompted her to read the Chinese translations of short stories by classic Yiddish writers Sholem Aleichem, I. L. Peretz, and others alongside the Yiddish originals. These bilingual readings led her to realize that the Chinese translators had themselves used translations into English or Esperanto in order to make the Yiddish stories accessible to their Chinese readers and to understand what drew the Chinese translators to Yiddish in the 1920s. Juxtaposing Martin Buber's translation of Chinese philosophy into German in 1910 and 1911 and into Hebrew after 1938 with Schereschewsky's 1974 translation of the Hebrew Bible into Chinese, Eber asserts the importance of translations and translating to the imagination and understanding of all the peoples in the world.

In "Translation Literature in Modern China: The Yiddish Author and His Tale" (1972), her first published scholarly article, Eber presents a full-scale study of Chinese translations of Yiddish literature as if in answer to her professor's question. With a historian's eye, Eber catalogs the Chinese translators and analyzes the works they translated from the Yiddish within the political and social contexts in which they published their translations, between 1923 and 1959. Eber's startling discovery in her essay is the connection between the Chinese literary and intellectual revolution of the May Fourth Movement in 1919 and the secular Yiddish literature written in Poland and Russia starting in the 1890s. Who would have imagined that Chinese writers of the rising nationalism in the 1920s engaged in the project of creating a "new and 'human' literature . . . concerned with the universal experiences of men and women" (294) written in the vernacular rather than literary register of Chinese would find kinship with the Jews of eastern Europe, who were "without a land and without national cohesion" (295)? As Eber puts it, the attraction of Yiddish literature to these Chinese writers was "the portrayal of an oppressed society, oppressed by its own tradition and a hostile environment . . . and of a society faced with the necessity for change and modernization in order to survive" (295).

A third pair of essays deals with the translation of the great German-language Jewish writer Franz Kafka into Chinese ("The Critique of Western Judaism in *The Castle* and Its Transposition in Two Chinese Translations" [1996]) and of classical Chinese philosophy into German by the German Jewish philosopher Martin Buber ("Martin Buber and Chinese Thought" [2007]).

The final two essays in the book address the ways that Chinese and Jews have perceived each other from the nineteenth century until the present and how those perceptions continue changing to create bridges between the Chinese and Jewish cultures. In "Chinese and Jews: Mutual Perceptions in Literary and Related Sources" (2000), Eber compares the perpetually changing views expressed in Chinese writings about Jews and the equally mutable Jewish perceptions of China and the Chinese people in Yiddish literature. The concluding essay in the book opens the door from the present into the future. "Learning the Other: Chinese Studies in Israel and Jewish Studies in China" (2010) brings the discussion of mutual cultural perceptions from the page into the university; reports on the establishment of Chinese and East Asian studies departments at the Hebrew University of Jerusalem, Tel Aviv University, and Haifa University; and surveys the rise of Jewish studies institutes and centers in China at Beijing University, Nanjing University, the Shanghai Academy of Social Sciences, Shandong University, Henan University, and Sichuan University. This final essay provides both practical guidance for a reader who wants to pursue formal studies and evidence of the rich and continuing dialogue in the exchanges between Jewish and Chinese cultures, histories, scholars, teachers, and students.

NOTES

1. Renee Levine Melammed, "The Long Road to China: Irene Eber's Path," *Jerusalem Post*, July 18, 2013, https://www.jpost.com/Jewish-World/Jewish-Features/The-long-road-to-China-Irene-Ebers-path-320323, accessed February 4, 2019; Irene Eber, "Holocaust Education and Displaced Persons (DP) Camps," *Contemporary Review of the Middle East* 3, no. 3 (2016): 231–236, https://journals.sagepub.com/doi/pdf/10.1177/2347798916651173, accessed February 4, 2019. For the most eloquent account of her life from 1939 to 1945, see Irene Eber, *The Choice: Poland 1939–1945* (New York: Schocken, 2004).

2. Melammed, "Long Road."

3. Ibid.

4. Ibid.

5. Eber, "Holocaust Education," 234.

6. Irene Eber, "Curriculum Vitae," 1–2. Courtesy of Irene Eber.

7. Ibid.

8. See Irene Eber, "'Bright Moon Rises over Heavenly Mountain': Love and Torah Scrolls in Kaifeng," *Kerem* 14 (2014): 123–140.

9. See Kathryn Hellerstein, "China in Two Yiddish Translations: Ethnographic and Modernist Appropriations," in *Un/Translatables: New Maps for Germanic Literatures*, ed. Catriona MacLeod and Bethany Wiggin (Evanston, IL: Northwestern University Press, 2016), 145–156.

10. Irene Eber, *The Jewish Bishop and the Chinese Bible: S. I. J. Schereschewsky, 1831–1906* (Leiden: Brill, 1999). A Chinese translation of this article was published in 2013.

11. Irene Eber, "Translating the Ancestors, S. I. J. Schereschewsky's 1875 Chinese Version of Genesis," *Bulletin of the School of Oriental and African Studies* 56, Part 2 (1993): 231.

12. Ibid., 233.

SECTION 1
Overview

CHAPTER 1

Overland and by Sea

Eight Centuries of the Jewish Presence in China

INTRODUCTION

When speaking of Jews in China, we must remind ourselves that various kinds of Jews arrived at different times in the empire and later in the Republic of China. There were Sephardim and Ashkenazim, religious and secular Jews, Orthodox and Reform Jews. They came as early as the twelfth century, if not before, and again in the nineteenth and twentieth centuries. Yet our knowledge about all these groups is fragmentary, and reliable accounts of how they lived, their livelihoods, and their religious practices are few.

We, furthermore, know nothing about the several ancient Jewish communities that existed in Ningbo and Yangzhou on China's southeastern coast and in Ningxia in the far northwest. They had disappeared already by the seventeenth century, and the only community that will be discussed in these pages is that of Kaifeng. In the modern period, there were also Jewish communities in Harbin and Tianjin. However, space does not permit discussion of those communities, and I will confine myself here to the Shanghai communities.

A number of questions will be raised in the course of this essay. The most important among these concerns the problem of the identity of the Kaifeng Jews. How was it possible that despite intermarriage with Chinese women, loss of contact with other Jewish communities in Asia and the West, and loss of traditions that some Kaifeng Jews retained their identity until the twentieth century? Another concerns the Central European refugees who arrived in

Shanghai after Hitler came to power in 1933. How was it possible for nearly twenty thousand Jews to reach China's shores when most other countries closed their gates to the hapless refugees?

THE CHINESE JEWS OF KAIFENG: HISTORY

Jewish traders first came to China probably in the late eighth or early ninth century. Having arrived by sea, Jews as well as Arabs traded together in the south at Canton (Guangzhou) and, no doubt, also in the north in the Chinese capital of Chang'an, where they arrived overland from Central Asia and Persia. By the ninth century, the capital was a cosmopolitan city with two large markets—one of these set aside for international merchants.[1] Traders of many kinds and performing artists flocked to Chang'an over land. There were Persians and others from farther west as well as Jews. Although there is no evidence that they established a permanent community or that they arrived in sufficient numbers to do so, two pieces of evidence point to the presence of Jews at this time. One of these is a Selikhot prayer written on paper, which was recovered at Dunhuang, one of the traditional gateways to China and an important center for the caravan trade in the Tang dynasty.[2] As paper was then widely used only in China, the prayer must have been written in the great empire rather than elsewhere. The other is a clay figurine produced for necrological purposes that depicts a person who is quite likely Jewish. Despite facial features reminiscent of other such figures usually identified as Persian or Semitic, his attire—a short coat, high boots, a round head covering, and a sack slung over his shoulder—indicate a more Western origin.[3]

Tantalizing as these two pieces of evidence are, concrete testimony of a Jewish presence comes to us, however, only centuries later, from the city of Kaifeng. The history of the Jews there has been preserved on five stelae inscriptions dating from 1489, 1512, 1663a and 1663b (one on each side of the stele), and 1679.[4] But *history* may be too decisive a term, for the inscriptions contain very little historical data. They are more useful for supplying names of leading Jewish families and for indicating how they understood their Judaism, as well as how they wanted their Judaism to be regarded by others.

What then can we learn from the inscriptions about their arrival in Kaifeng? According to the 1489 inscription, they came from India as cotton merchants.[5] This seems quite likely, for cotton was only beginning to be cultivated in the twelfth century in the Yangzi delta and was not widely available. Imported cotton might, therefore, have been a lucrative item. Arriving by sea at one of China's southeastern coast ports, the merchants with their fairly bulky goods had to make their way overland to Kaifeng, the capital of the Northern Song dynasty (906–1126), in what is today Henan province, and their arrival can be dated to around 1120. By 1123, northern China was on the verge of being invaded by her inner Asian neighbors, the Jurchen, and it is highly unlikely that merchants would have risked an overland journey under the threat of hostilities. Moreover, according to the 1489 inscription, the synagogue was built in 1163.[6] How to construct a synagogue, even if the actual work was carried out by Chinese workmen, had to be in the memory of those who arrived in Kaifeng. Yet it would seem that a sufficient number of Jews had to be present to warrant the construction of a synagogue, and if these traded together with other merchants (Indian, Arab, etc.), any one group could not have been very large. Hence one must assume that several groups of Jews arrived in Kaifeng, some of these also overland from Central Asia and Persia.

But why come to Kaifeng? The city was, to be sure, the royal capital of the Song dynasty, where the emperor and the royal court had their seat. But it was much more than that, with its over one million inhabitants and its flourishing commercial and entertainment establishments. Situated at the hub of an extensive transportation network, Kaifeng was an "open" city,[7] in which a group of foreign merchants would have had no difficulty finding their place. Neither then nor later, when the city also had a sizable Muslim minority, can one detect signs of anti-Semitism. Although after January 1127 Kaifeng was no longer the royal capital, having come under the domination of the Jurchen invaders who established the Jin dynasty (1115–1234) and causing the Chinese court to flee to Hangzhou in the south, trading relations between north and south continued to be favorable. What may have been considered a temporary residence at first became a permanent home for the Jews, even after Kaifeng became an insignificant backwater and other Chinese cities grew in importance.

Despite the lack of evidence, it must be assumed that relations with other Jewish communities in Ningbo or Yangzhou were maintained under Jin rule and especially during the subsequent Yuan dynasty (1269–1368). In this, the Mongol period, caravan and sea trade flourished, and Jews from other parts of the vast bicontinental empire may have come to settle in

Kaifeng, as they did in other Chinese cities. Jews are probably mentioned in the *Yuan shi* (the official history of the Yuan), various terms are used for them, and they were perhaps also alluded to by Western travelers to China.[8] However, it is the materials from Kaifeng that furnish evidence, and it is to the inscription from 1512, written during the Ming dynasty (1368–1664) and the subsequent 1663a inscription on the eve of the Ming demise, that we turn next.

According to the former, the teaching of Israel (*Yiciluoye jiao*)[9] entered and was established in China in the Han dynasty.[10] According to the latter, the teaching was handed down in China (*zhongzhou*) even earlier, during the time of the Zhou dynasty.[11] Two significant aspects should be noted. One is the later the inscription, the earlier the origin of the Jewish teaching in China. The earliest 1489 inscription dates the Jewish arrival to sometime in the Song dynasty, whereas the later 1663a inscription would have them arrive one thousand or two thousand years earlier. The second aspect is related to the question of Sinification in distinction from "Confucianization" or "assimilation." By Sinification, I refer to the adopting of Chinese patterns selectively, leading to an accommodation to the society in which they found themselves. As these stelae were displayed outside, written in Chinese, and meant to be read by the Chinese, the time of their arrival would obviously best be stated in familiar terms—those of Chinese history.

Not only time but place also underwent a process of Sinification.[12] India was not unknown, even if not many Chinese traveled there,[13] and the 1663a inscription states that the origin of the teaching is India. According to the 1512 inscription, however, it was Adam who came from India,[14] though it was not he with whom the Jewish teaching began, but with Moses, who transmitted the scriptures. Establishing the succession of transmitters of the teaching is another feature of the Sinification process. On this, the 1489 inscription is most explicit, specifying Abraham as the founder of the teaching. Significantly, he was of the nineteenth generation of Pan Gu-Adam, thus joining the Chinese and Jewish men who were present at the beginning of the world.[15] From Abraham, the teaching was transmitted to Moses, and from him to Ezra.[16] The 1663a inscription considers the transmission from Adam to Noah and then to Abraham, as does also the 1679 inscription.[17] However, the 1512 inscription emphasizes the transmission of the scriptures that were handed down from Adam to Noah and to Abraham, Isaac, and Jacob, who passed them on to the twelve tribes. They, in turn, passed them on to Moses, who handed them down to Aaron, and from him they were passed on to Joshua and then to Ezra.[18]

Which Chinese terms to use for specific concepts of Judaism must have presented considerable difficulties. But here, we must be careful. Although by the time these inscriptions were written, the Kaifeng Jews were Chinese speakers, we do not know whether in everyday speech the same terms would have been used as in writing. Nor must we forget that the stones were in public view and were meant to be read by Jews and non-Jews alike. Thus the term for "scripture" is *jing*—that was and continues to be used in the Chinese classics. The meaning is not "holy writ" but writing revered since antiquity and containing the wisdom of the sages.[19] When the construction of the synagogue is referred to, the term *si*—a general term for shrines—is used.[20] But there was not, nor is there today, one Chinese term by which Chinese refer to a monotheistic God.[21] In the 1489 inscription, the term most frequently used and that most likely refers to God is *Dao*, often literally translated as "the Way." Depending on the context, *Dao* also has transcendental connotations. Sometimes *Tian* (heaven) occurs or *Tian Dao* (the way of heaven).[22] The term *Di* is used once in the 1663a inscription in connection with Moses[23] and, in Chinese, comes closest to the meaning of God.

It is not otherwise surprising that the Chinese Jews did not introduce a new name for God but instead used terms that a Chinese reader would be familiar with, avoiding, however, the use of all Chinese terms that might in some way identify their beliefs with Chinese religious beliefs. The stelae and their inscriptions were not a means for setting them apart; rather, as will be further discussed below, they were proof of the extent to which they were part of Kaifeng society without sacrificing their identity. Unfortunately, the inscriptions tell us almost nothing about observances, rituals, and the like. To gain a better understanding of Jewish practices in the seventeenth and eighteenth centuries, the writings of the various visitors who came to Kaifeng must be consulted.

CATHOLIC AND PROTESTANT VISITORS

At the very beginning of contact between the Chinese Jews of Kaifeng and Westerners was the momentous meeting of the Jew Ai Tian and the Jesuit father Matteo Ricci (1551–1610) in Beijing in 1605. As described by Ricci,

Ai Tian thought Ricci was Jewish, and Ricci thought that the Chinese man facing him was Christian. They eventually sorted out their respective identities, and Ricci learned some facts about Jewish Kaifeng life—namely, that they practiced circumcision, did not eat pork, and had a great synagogue. Ai Tian knew Old Testament stories, such as those about the twelve tribes, Moses, and Haman and Mordekhai.[24]

Following this encounter, a number of Jesuits visited Kaifeng, as described in the excellent account by Michael Pollak,[25] but it was not until one hundred years later, in 1704, that more information was gathered by Father Jean-Paul Gozani (1647–1732). He confirmed that the Jews had a synagogue, they had a religious leader (*zhang jiao*), they observed Passover, and they practiced Kashrut butchering and therefore were called by the Chinese "the sect that extracts the sinews" (*tiaojin jiao*).[26] Gozani also saw in the synagogue the thirteen Torah scrolls, twelve of which, it was explained to him, were dedicated to the twelve tribes and the oldest of which, the thirteenth, was dedicated to the memory of Moses.[27] The memoir of Gabriel Brotier, written about 1770 and based on letters written by several Jesuit visitors, supplies some additional information. The synagogue was oriented to the West (Jerusalem), and the Jews observe Shabbat and other festivals. They had prayer books and four books of the Mishnah and could read Hebrew.[28] According to Jean Domenge (1666–1735), during his visit in 1722, he noted the celebration of Simhat Torah, but most significantly, he prepared several drawings of the synagogue, including those of the interior and exterior.[29]

After 1724, the Jesuits were confined to Beijing and Guangzhou and were eventually expelled from China. The Kaifeng Jews were not visited again until China was opened to Western penetration and the arrival of the Protestant missionaries. The first visitors were two Chinese Protestant converts, Qiu Tianshang and Jiang Rongji, who were dispatched in November 1850 from Shanghai by the Reverend George Smith, bishop of Victoria. They were equipped with a letter written in Hebrew introducing the two men to the Chinese Jews, but although they recognized the Hebrew writing, none in Kaifeng could read it any longer. Upon their return in 1851, Qiu Tianshang and Jiang Rongji each wrote a report that told much about their journey. About Kaifeng, they wrote that the synagogue was in a dire state of disrepair and that some extremely poor Jewish families were living in shacks on synagogue grounds, but services were still apparently conducted in the synagogue. Like the Jesuits before them, the Chinese informants stated that there was neither intermarriage nor polygamy (both assertions are most likely wrong, as will be discussed below). Shabbat observance and abstinence from pork continued, but Hebrew had fallen into complete disuse with the death of their last rabbi some fifty years earlier.[30]

When, fifteen years later, in 1866, the Protestant missionary W. A. P. Martin came to Kaifeng, the synagogue was no longer standing. It had been dismantled, the remnants sold, and only the 1489 stele remained in a puddle of mud.[31] Martin's visit of no more than three days produced no further concrete information about the condition of the Jews, but it led to S. I. J. Schereschewsky's decision the following year to undertake the journey. A Jew from Lithuania, Schereschewsky had converted to Episcopalianism, was engaged in translating the *Tanakh* from Hebrew into Chinese, and had established the Episcopal mission in Beijing. However, his visit, like that of Martin before, even if it lasted longer, also failed to achieve anything, and after being beset by a mob, Schereschewsky hurriedly departed the city.[32] Other visitors came at greater or shorter intervals,[33] among them also Jews. None of these added substantially to the record laid out here.

At this point, at least two questions must be raised. What prompted these Christians' curiosity about the Chinese Jews? Was it that they hoped to convert the Jews, or were there some other reasons? From the Jesuit accounts, it is clear that they conducted long conversations with various Jews, but it seems that the purpose was to obtain information rather than to persuade them to accept Christianity. One fact of special importance was the nature of the *Tanakh* in Kaifeng. Might the Chinese Jews have, so the reasoning went, a more authentic version that would contain the prediction of the messianic dream? Thus Jesuit curiosity about the Kaifeng Jews was more about their scriptures, the Torah scrolls, than it was about their rituals and lives as Jews. For this reason, the Jesuits attempted, always unsuccessfully, to buy the scriptures from the Jews.[34] The Protestants, some one-hundred-odd years later, were more successful in obtaining the coveted writings. Indeed, the major purpose of the two men sent by George Smith was to acquire whatever scriptures they could. Whereas they did not succeed during the first 1850 visit, a second one in 1851 was crowned with success: in July 1851, the two returned to Shanghai with six scrolls of the Torah and many other manuscripts. They were accompanied by two brothers from the Zhao family, who were to study Hebrew. The scrolls as well as the books were legally purchased, although later, some Kaifeng Jews claimed that they were cheated of their writings.[35]

The loss of Hebrew and the synagogue, the demise of the last rabbi, intermarriage, and the abandonment of most rituals and observances nonetheless did not lead to total assimilation and loss of identity. As late as 1932, visitor David A. Brown from the United States noted the eagerness of those assembled to be identified as Jews.[36] We must ask, therefore, why centuries of Sinification did not lead to the disappearance of the Chinese Jews.

SINIFICATION AS THE AFFIRMATION OF IDENTITY

Sinification was discussed above as significant in the inscriptions. I now want to turn to a similar phenomenon in social and religious life. As a continuous process, Sinification suggests not assimilation, but how, by combining Chinese social and religious characteristics with Jewish ones, Chinese Jews were able to preserve their identity. One major factor in this story is the acquisition of Chinese surnames. It is impossible to say precisely when this took place, though it probably occurred early in the fifteenth century. The Chinese family organization into lineages was probably adopted at about the same time, if not earlier. The transition was not a major step, since as Sephardi Jews, clan organization was a familiar feature. But Chinese lineages differ in several ways from what is understood by *clan*. A lineage generally consists of a number of families, is domiciled in one locality, and holds properties, including a burial ground, in common. The stelae inscriptions provide evidence for the assumption of lineage organization. According to the 1663a inscription, "seven surnames" (*qixing*) indicates that lineages are referred to.[37] A more obvious example is the 1679 inscription that speaks of more than five hundred families (*jia*).[38] These would be families of perhaps three generations that belong to a lineage.

The fact that none of the inscriptions mentions charitable organizations connected with the synagogue further substantiates lineage organization, for charitable works were generally a function of the lineages. Thus borrowing money, aid for widows and orphans, and the like would be supplied by the lineage, and there was no need for other organizations.

The third example of a lineage organization is furnished by cemeteries. If a Jewish cemetery ever existed in Kaifeng, it has long disappeared, and lineage cemeteries came into use. It is uncertain when this custom was adopted. It may have been after the disastrous 1642 flood, or earlier, but certainly after the lineage family organization had become prevalent. Wang Yisha refers to the Jin and Li cemeteries, each of which had a "foremost" grave marked "Old Ancestor's Grave."[39] Graves thus marked were meant to indicate symbolically agnatic affiliation and the original ancestor of the lineage.

What does this transformation into lineages indicate? It shows, I suggest, that identification with a larger Jewish community beyond China's borders became less important than identification with the lineage and the agnatic group. Kaifeng Jewish identity became a family-centered identity as long as the family remained domiciled in the Kaifeng locality and identified with the lineage. Moreover, individual Jewish men were unlikely to abandon their Jewishness as long as they were members of families.

A family-centered Jewish identity was, furthermore, reinforced by how they and, no doubt, their Chinese neighbors regarded Jewish practices. In many parts of China, including the North China Plain, where Kaifeng is located, popular and syncretic sectarianism flourished. A highly fragmented and localized phenomenon, sectarianism was a mixture of Daoist, Buddhist, Confucian, and folk elements.[40] Several superficial characteristics can be taken as being not too dissimilar from those of the Jews. Sectarians had a meeting place and a leader; they had a set of sacred writings used only by the congregants; they had specific dietary practices. Like Chinese sects, the Jews were called a *jiao*, and this is how they refer to themselves in the inscriptions. By their Chinese neighbors, they were called more specifically the "sinew-extracting sect," mentioned earlier, or the "scripture-teaching sect" (*jiaojing jiao*). Finally, sect membership was not merely an association of individuals. Those who joined tended to bring in other members of their households. Therefore, sect membership was frequently family membership.[41] By this means, the connection to a foreign and universal religion was severed, and a link to native local religions was forged without, however, sacrificing their identity as Jews.[42]

The questions of intermarriage and polygamy are related to these processes of integration into Chinese society. That the Jews were polygamous was mentioned earlier. But whether they adopted the Chinese custom whereby a man who was sufficiently wealthy or who had no male offspring took a second wife and/or concubines is uncertain. Donald Leslie is cautious on the issue of polygamy[43] despite the fact that we know of its practice in Sephardi communities. His important translation and work on the *Memorial Book* reveal that some Jewish men married non-Jewish—that is, Chinese—women, identified in this book as "daughters of Adam." It is not clear, however, whether these were secondary wives. Unfortunately, the *Memorial Book* was closed around 1670, and therefore there is no way of knowing whether more intermarriage occurred in, say, the eighteenth century or earlier. In any event, by the nineteenth century, W. A. P. Martin and others remarked on the Chinese physiognomy of the Jews.

Another related question concerns the size of the Jewish population—a subject on which there is much uncertainty. Clearly, the Jewish population would not have remained stable over the centuries. Depending on their fortunes, prosperity or decline, families would have moved to other cities or provinces to assimilate with the local Chinese population there. The flood of 1642, which destroyed the synagogue and most of Kaifeng, also took its toll. Presumably, there were seven lineages (Ai, Zhang, Zhao, Jin, Gao, Li, and Shi), but how many families at any one time belonged to them and their size are impossible to estimate.[44] The more recent account, which gives five thousand Jews for the Ming dynasty (1368–1644), is most certainly exaggerated.[45] Without a doubt, there were always several hundred Jews in Kaifeng, and at its peak, there may have been more than one thousand, but they never represented a significant percentage of Kaifeng's Chinese population. Thus to estimate accurately Kaifeng's Jewish population is as difficult as it will be to estimate Shanghai's Jewish inhabitants, as we shall see below.

SHANGHAI'S JEWISH COMMUNITY: HISTORY

The Shanghai story is entirely different from that of Kaifeng. This is not because Shanghai's Jewish communities are closer to us in time—their presence cannot be dated earlier than the nineteenth century—and that we therefore know more about them. Actually, their history too can be told only in fragments. The difference is mainly due to the setting: Shanghai was a vastly different place. There were foreigners who, after emerging victorious in the 1842 Opium War, opened five cities to foreign trade.[46] These were the so-called treaty ports, where land was acquired by treaty and where foreigners resided.

Let us look briefly at Shanghai to understand a little about it, the kind of town it was, and the city that it became, where Jews found a welcome home. In 1842, Shanghai was a walled town and a county seat with the religious and administrative institutions such towns contained. Far from a mere fishing village, walled Shanghai in the nineteenth century was prosperous, with well-off Chinese inhabitants whose wealth derived mainly from extensive cotton trade. Junks from many parts of China made port in Shanghai, and the presence of merchants from various areas imbued the city with the "cosmopolitan" character it had even then. The town's hinterland was no less impressive—like "one vast beautiful garden," according to one account, with large quantities of green vegetable crops, wheat, barley, rice, and cotton.[47]

Shanghai grew rapidly due to the influx of population and trade.[48] Not only foreigners but also Chinese from many provinces flocked to the town. Merchants and workers came in search of a better livelihood, and rebellions in the countryside, especially the disastrous Taiping Rebellion (1850–1864), caused thousands of refugees to seek safety among the foreign Westerners.

The foreigners who came did not live in the walled town but gradually built their homes in the northern suburbs outside the city walls. This area later became the International Settlement, with its favorable location on the Huangpu River. Eventually, the International Settlement, with Hongkou across the Suzhou Creek, came to be governed by the Shanghai Municipal Council (SMC), composed of British, American, Chinese, and Japanese officials. The SMC was, however, never sovereign; it was responsible to the consular body, and its function was purely administrative. Adjacent to the International Settlement was the French Concession, which was governed by the French consul-general, who, in distinction from the SMC, held considerably more power. The third governing body in Shanghai was the Chinese Municipal Administration, which was responsible for the Chinese areas that developed outside the walled Chinese city.[49] The Chinese Municipal Administration did not fully function until the Nationalist (Guomindang) government came to power in 1927 and established its capital in Nanjing.

Shanghai, as described above, developed as a mosaic of people—a city of immigrants, Chinese and foreign, all of whom came from different parts. Nor did the city develop as a unified urban complex; it was fragmented into several interlocking and interrelated areas with their own administrations and police forces. Shanghai was, furthermore, not a colony in the sense in which we tend to think about colonies established by the Western powers in Asia. The treaty port did not become the means for extracting profit from Shanghai or for providing jobs only for Western officials. Rather, the growth and development of Shanghai served Chinese interests as well. The treaty system, it has been argued, "unleashed entrepreneurial energy, and drew in to itself individuals and groups . . . who sought to maximize their own ability to take advantage of the system."[50] In time, Shanghai became a modern city, where a Chinese middle class and a Chinese capitalist class emerged. Within this metropolis of more than 3,500,000 people, Western-ers, moreover, were always a minority. Although consisting of more than sixty nationalities, Shanghai in 1937 had only 58,688 foreigners.[51]

Within this diverse setting, where none of the power holders wielded absolute power—even, in fact, the Japanese when they occupied the entire city between 1942 and 1945—the Jewish communities and the various groupings within them could gain a foothold. Among the earliest British and American newcomers in the second half of the nineteenth century were the Sephardi, or Baghdadi, Jews. They came mostly via Bombay, where they had prosperous business firms, and their aim was to establish branches in the newly opened treaty ports.[52] In this, the Sassoon family was preemi-nently successful with two firms: D. Sassoon and Co. and E. D. Sassoon and Co., the latter established by Elias David Sassoon (1820–1880) in 1867.[53] Although the Baghdadi community was small, never numbering more than one thousand persons at its height, many families had considerable wealth. As merchants and brokers, the companies of such families as Toeg, Abra-ham, or Ezra were well known. Despite boasting more wealthy families than any other Jewish community in Shanghai, there were also the less well-off and poor Baghdadi Jews. These tended to find employment in the firms of the affluent families. Thus the creation of charitable institutions for desti-tute members was not part of the early history of the Baghdadi community.

Cotton and opium were initially the two major products of the India-China trade,[54] and the Sassoons, though latecomers, were vigorous competitors. But they soon branched out into other commodities and busi-ness ventures. One of these was banking, and even if an account of their far-flung business interests is still lacking, a large loan of £238,000 sterling was made in 1935 to the Nationalist government's Huai River Commission.[55] The Sassoons were also making large real-estate purchases in and around Shanghai. Rumor had it that much of Hongkou property was owned by the Sassoons.[56]

By far the largest real-estate owner in Shanghai, however, was probably Silas Aaron Hardoon (1851–1931), one of Shanghai's most unique and colorful personalities. He arrived penniless in Shanghai in 1874 and was employed by David Sassoon and Co. as a rent collector and watchman. Less than thirty years later, Hardoon was on his way to becoming one of Shanghai's major landowners, and by 1916, according to Chiara Betta's account, he owned most of the properties along Nanking Road, which was to become Shanghai's most fashionable commercial street. At the time of his death, he may have been the richest foreigner in East Asia.[57] Silas Hardoon was not only known for his fabulous wealth. He and his wife, Luo Jialing (also known as Liza, 1864–1941),[58] contributed to many Chinese causes and institutions. The couple legally adopted eleven children of Eurasian and Russian Jewish parentage who were mostly raised by Luo Jialing. She was an exacting mother, whereas Silas Hardoon seems to be remembered chiefly by one of his adopted children for being an absent father.[59]

Unlike the other Jewish communities in Shanghai, the Baghdadis showed an interest in the fate of the Kaifeng Jews. In 1900, they organized the Society for the Rescue of the Chinese Jews, its purpose being not only to study their history but also "to preserve their sites and monuments."[60] Letters were dispatched back and forth, and a number of Jews arrived in Shanghai from Kaifeng. Most returned, and some remained, were circumcised, and received a Jewish education in the homes of affluent Baghdadis. However, despite their good intentions to rebuild the synagogue or establish a school, nothing came of these plans, interest waned, and as Meyer observes, "Ironically, the Orphan Colony appeared to be receiving more relief from the Christian missionaries than from their coreligionists."[61] Arthur Sopher's hopeful prediction, written in 1926, that "the miracle . . . may yet be accomplished and these sons of Abraham and of Moses rescued from the very jaws of total annihilation"[62] was not to happen.

The Baghdadis were English speakers (aside from the older generation), and as the years went by, they increasingly identified with British interests and tastes. The affluent members of the community built their fashionable residences in the International Settlement, where the home and "garden" of Silas Hardoon occupied a whole city block on Bubbling Well Road. Known as the Marble Palace, the Kadoorie family home also was widely admired for its grand style.

The Russian Jewish community, in contrast, while not exactly poor, was certainly not as affluent. Russian Jews arrived late in Shanghai; the earliest arrivals may have come after the Russo-Japanese War (1904–1905), but the majority, including Polish Jews, came only after the Russian October Revolution of 1917. Eventually, they formed a larger community than the Baghdadis, numbering between six thousand and eight thousand persons by the 1930s. Among them were well-to-do businessmen, store owners of often fashionable shops, and men engaged in export-import. But the great majority had been refugees and had arrived with little capital. They had come via the overland route on the Trans-Siberian Railway, with their first stop in Harbin, and from there, they made their way south, with a sizable community remaining in Tianjin.

The Russian Jews were culturally and linguistically different, and their community developed separately from that of the Baghdadis. Most of them settled in the French Concession, where they were in close—though far from amicable—proximity to the White Russian community, most of whom also were refugees. Like the Jews, they had arrived in part after the revolution and partly after the civil war (1918–1923) in Russia's Far East; among the latter were many military personnel. By 1939, their numbers had grown to twenty-five thousand, outnumbering both Jewish communities.

Many among the poorer Russian Jews went to live in Hongkou and other outlying Chinese areas, where rents were cheaper. Unlike their more affluent compatriots, these were craftsmen, small shopkeepers, and boardinghouse owners who suffered great losses during the Sino-Japanese hostilities in 1932 and again in 1937, when war broke out between China and Japan. The newly founded Shanghai Jewish Communal Association, which had held its first general meeting in June 1931,[63] was not equal to the task of helping the destitute families. Nor was the Jewish Russian community able to support the refugees who fled to the more secure areas in the French Concession.[64] While certainly not all Baghdadis were wealthy, many among the Russian Jews remained poverty stricken.

Yet not all was bleak. A goodly number of young men found employment in the Shanghai Volunteer Corps (SVC), and the community took considerable pride in their large participation. First formed in 1853, the SVC eventually included volunteers and units from twenty-seven countries, including a Chinese and Jewish company. The latter dated from 1932 and 1933 and consisted of 120 former scouts and Betar members. A Star of David worn on their uniform collars identified the members of the Jewish company. The poet Meylekh Ravitch (Zekharia Khone Bergner, 1893–1976) visited Shanghai in 1935 and marveled at the fact, as he put it, that Shanghai was the only place where Jewish soldiers with guns and the Star of David could be seen.[65] Regretfully, these sparse materials will have to suffice, for a systematic history of this important community is still lacking and perhaps cannot be written due to a lack of materials.

The last group to arrive and settle in Shanghai were the German Jews, who were joined by Austrian Jews after the annexation of Austria by Germany in March 1938. An initial group of twenty-six families, mostly men who had been active in the medical profession, arrived already in the fall of 1933.[66] By 1934, eighty physicians, surgeons, and dentists had come to Shanghai,[67] all of whom had lost their positions in the German medical establishment after Hitler had come to power in January 1933. Not all remained in Shanghai; some went to Qingdao, which, as a former German possession, still had a German-speaking community. But this initial trickle slowed down for the next two-odd years until the fateful year of 1938, when Austria was annexed, Polish Jews were expelled from Germany in October, and "Kristallnacht" (the night of broken glass) took place in both Germany and Austria in November. To this list must also be added the Évian Conference of July 1938 that amply demonstrated the closing of doors to Jewish emigration of all but a few countries.[68] Since the avowed policy of the Nazi regime had been the emigration of Jews and since the exodus was far too slow in its view, a new policy of forced emigration gradually took shape.

Shanghai as a destination for Jews had been mentioned as early as September 1936,[69] but this suggestion was not taken up until two years later. By then, Adolf Eichmann had gained considerable experience in forcing Jews to emigrate from Austria—an experience that was considered also useful for Germany. In Austria, this had consisted of the arrest of Jews, their confinement to a concentration camp, and their release upon showing evidence of speedy emigration. This technique was now also applied in Germany. Eichmann, however, went even further and, enlisting the services of Heinrich Schlie,[70] head of the Hanseatic travel offices in Vienna and Berlin, arranged to charter ships for refugee travel to Shanghai. One ship, the *Usaramo*, was indeed thus engaged, arriving in Shanghai with 459 passengers on June 29, 1939.[71]

Jews leaving by ship from German and Italian ports, though they may have traveled on luxury liners, arrived in Shanghai nearly penniless and with few possessions. By the time Germany invaded Poland in September 1939, nearly twenty thousand German-speaking refugees had arrived. Some came before Italy entered the war in the summer of 1940, but thereafter, the sea route via the Atlantic as well as the Pacific was no longer open to ocean traffic.

The majority of the German and Austrian refugees settled in Hongkou, large portions of which had been reduced to rubble in the 1937 hostilities, but where rents were far cheaper than in the International Settlement (across Suzhou Creek) and the French Concession. Hongkou, by then, had been settled by Japanese civilians and military personnel, although it never became a formal Japanese possession. This need not further concern us. Important for our purposes is the fact that the English-speaking Baghdadis and the Russian-speaking community were, by the autumn of 1939, outnumbered by German-speaking Jews, who were, in addition, also culturally different from both.[72]

The fourth and final group of Jews to arrive in Shanghai were Polish and, for the most part, Yiddish-speaking Jews. They had fled to Lithuania after the German invasion of Poland and consisted of secular Jews—among them performers, journalists, and writers, as well as members of Yeshivoth, including the entire Mir Yeshiva.[73] While still in Kovno, they were able to obtain visas to Curacao (a Dutch possession) from the consul Jan Zwartendijk and transit visas via Soviet Russia to Japan. Perhaps two thousand Jews made their way overland, using the Trans-Siberian Railway, to Vladivostok and from there by ship to Kobe. No doubt they had hoped to weather the calamity of war in Japan, but it was not to be. In 1941, the Japanese authorities shipped these religious and secular Polish Jews to Shanghai, where they remained for the duration of the war.

Clearly, Shanghai was a mosaic not only of areas—Chinese, Japanese, the International Settlement, the French Concession—but also of peoples. The Chinese population was by far the largest, continuing to grow as refugees poured into the metropolis in 1937. There were, in addition, the White Russians, Japanese, Germans, French, Americans, and British, and among these foreigners were the culturally and linguistically different Jews from various parts of the world. They were, to be sure, a minority among the foreign minority, yet in the near absence of anti-Semitism, even among foreigners, each group was able to build and develop its institutional life. To this topic we turn next.

SYNAGOGUES, RABBIS, OBSERVANCES, AND COMMUNAL ORGANIZATION

No political authority able or empowered to enforce uniformity and conformity existed in the treaty port, and thus variations and differences among the religious groups could be maintained and perpetuated. The three Jewish groups—Baghdadi, Russian, and Central European—maintained separate synagogues. Beth El, the synagogue of the Sephardim, was established in 1887, and its splinter group, Shearith Israel, in 1900. Two splendid structures eventually replaced the temporary prayer houses: Ohel Rachel in 1920 and Beth Aharon in 1927. The first was financed by Sir Jacob Elias Sassoon, the second by Silas Hardoon. The Russian Jews at first used the premises of the Shearith Israel congregation, calling their congregation Oihel Moishe (Ohel Moshe), but in 1927, the congregation moved into its own building. Finally, in 1941, the New Synagogue was completed in the French Concession, and the congregation moved there. Due to their diversity and their sojourner status, the Central European refugees did not build a synagogue of their own. The several congregations—Orthodox, Liberal, and Reform—used existing premises on festivals and high holidays, while the ultra-Orthodox rabbis and their students made do with Beth Aharon.[74]

For the Sephardi and Russian communities, finding rabbis familiar with both their respective liturgies and their languages was often difficult. Obviously, the rabbi would have to come from abroad, where he received his rabbinical training. Whereas the Baghdadis never really solved their problem of rabbinic leadership,[75] the Russian Jews were luckier. In 1926, they managed to recruit Rabbi Meir Ashkenazi, who, after serving in Vladivostok, remained the Russian congregation's leader for twenty-one years.[76] The German and Austrian communities had no lack of rabbis, and neither did the ultra-Orthodox Yeshivot, which were established in Shanghai with their own rabbis.

Except for the staunchest of secularists, Jews celebrated major festivals and observed the high holidays. Simhat Torah, for example, was celebrated as joyously by the members of the Mir Yeshiva as if they had never left home.[77] A constant irritant to the Orthodox community, however, was that much of the Jewish population did not continue to maintain strict Shabbat observance. Sephardi businessmen had been observant at one time but had grown lax by the 1930s. Russian merchants did not close for the Shabbat, and the Central European refugees did not desist from trying to make a living. Kashrut was maintained longest by the Sephardim, yet both Russians and Central Europeans were less strict. In the shelters (Heime), where many of the destitute refugees lived upon arrival, kosher kitchen facilities existed, and the organizations responsible for refugee welfare made every effort to adhere to dietary laws.[78]

Communal organizations emerged slowly and relatively late as a response to felt needs. The Sephardi burial society was, of course, the earliest and was established in 1862, probably at about the same time as the founding of its first cemetery. The Russian community organized its burial society in 1922, and the refugees added theirs in 1940. Eventually, all three communities acquired land for their separate cemeteries.[79] Unfortunately, the Chinese authorities moved the cemeteries between 1957 and 1959, and they have since disappeared.[80]

The Sephardi Shanghai Jewish Community Association began functioning only in 1909, and the Ashkenazi community association, mentioned earlier, was established in 1931. Both communities also maintained Zionist organizations, and Russian Jews especially emphasized physical training and sports in their Betar and Kadimah organizations. The organizations that came into being to provide aid to the refugees when the large influx began in 1939 were of singular importance. Such men from the Sephardi community as Michel Speelman, Sir Victor Sassoon, and Ellis Hayim, who took the lead in the Committee for the Assistance of Central European Jews in Shanghai and procured Jewish Joint Distribution Committee (JDC) on a continuing basis, must take much credit for helping the refugees in Shanghai. Between April 26, 1939, and September 18, 1939, alone, more than seven thousand refugees arrived on German, French, Italian, and Japanese liners.[81] Had it not been for the building of dormitory facilities and the opening of soup kitchens, these mostly penniless unfortunates would have found themselves hungry and without shelter. More might have been done, perhaps even more efficiently, yet it must be remembered that aid was organized by businessmen, not by trained social workers, and funds were circumscribed.

ENTERTAINMENT AND PUBLISHING

While thousands continued to languish in the dormitories, others—luckier perhaps or earlier arrivals who still came with funds—created a lively coffeehouse, concert, and theater scene in Hongkou. Among the Central

European refugees, there was a lack of neither initiative nor talent. Those fortunate enough to have found jobs had apparently some spending money for a meal or just coffee in one of the roof gardens,[82] to take in one of the latest American movies shown in theaters in the French Concession and Hongkou,[83] or go to a German-language play,[84] not to mention plays written in Shanghai about Shanghai life.[85] The restaurant and entertainment scene was, of course, part of Chinese middle-class life. Affluent Chinese Shanghainese frequented nightclubs, bars, and movie houses. Shanghai's flourishing movie industry was one of the best in the 1930s. In this cosmopolitan city, the European coffeehouse was not an anomaly.

Similarly, publishing in various languages became part of Shanghai life; indeed, since the 1920s, Shanghai was a major publishing center in Chinese and English. To this was now added the press for the refugee community in German and Yiddish. One of the oldest papers was the English-language monthly *Israel's Messenger*, which almost exclusively served the Sephardi community and was the official organ of the Shanghai Zionist Association. The *Gelbe Post*, for the more intellectually inclined reader, commenced publication as early as October 1939,[86] and the *Shanghai Jewish Chronicle* started even earlier, in January 1939. Whereas a number of papers appeared and disappeared or merged with other papers, the *Shanghai Jewish Chronicle* survived longest, until the end of the Second World War, because its publisher, Ossi Lewin, apparently cooperated with Japanese censorship. Agudat Yisrael published two Yiddish papers: *Di Yiddishe Shtime fun vaytn Mizrakh* (The Jewish voice from the Far East) and *Dos Vort* (The word). For Russian readers, there was *Nasha Zhizn* (Our life), which included a Yiddish page, later replaced by an English page,[87] no doubt due to the Japanese censorship.

The newspapers featured news and cultural events, as well as advertisements. They were important, however, for still another reason: they provided writers and poets with an opportunity to publish articles, fiction, and poetry in their own languages. Yiddish poets such as Yosl Mlotek or Ya'akov Fishman found an outlet in *Unzer Lebn*: the Yiddish supplement of *Nasha Zhizn*. German poets such as Egon Varro published their poetry in the *Shanghai Woche*.

Not only newspapers but books too were published. Although the topic of publishing still needs more investigation, in November 1941, the first Yiddish book by J. Rappaport appeared about the social function of poetry.[88] Books of the Talmud, prayer books, and Bibles soon fell apart from heavy use, and furthermore, not enough were available. The Mir Yeshiva rabbis soon found a Chinese printer who was able to reproduce many books by lithography—an accomplishment that was hailed a "historic event" in the Yiddish press.[89]

THE PACIFIC WAR AND ITS AFTERMATH

For China, hostilities and war actually began already in 1931, when Japanese forces invaded China's three northeastern provinces (generally called Manchuria in the West) in March of that year. The gradual expansion of the Japanese also led to hostilities in the Shanghai area, which laid waste to portions of Chinese-inhabited Shanghai. Then, in July 1937, open warfare broke out between the two powers; as a result of which, the Nationalist government retreated from its capital in Nanjing to China's interior. There it remained for the duration of the Pacific War, until 1945. Following the 1937 clashes, the Japanese now occupied the Chinese portions of Shanghai. These partially destroyed parts, under Japanese control, did not include the International Settlement and the French Concession. Hongkou, south of the International Settlement across Suzhou Creek, came to be more firmly Japanese controlled without, however, becoming an outright Japanese concession. Between November 1937 and the outbreak of the Pacific War in December 1941, Shanghai thus was in a semioccupied condition—a period of time often referred to as *gudao* (lonely island), when the foreign areas were neutral and increasingly besieged enclaves and when Chinese puppet governments succeeded one another in the Chinese parts.

Coming in 1938 and 1939, the Central European refugees would have been little aware of China's precarious political situation, though they could not help but be influenced by the pervasive Japanese presence. The Baghdadis, on the other hand—the community's businessmen, financiers, and brokers—were keenly aware of the ever tighter noose created by the encroachment of Japanese business interests. The Russian Jewish community was perhaps less affected, but all three felt the growing inflation and the instability of Shanghai life. Increasingly, frequent anti-Semitic articles in the Japanese-controlled Chinese press,[90] together with White Russian agitation, added an element of insecurity.

The Pacific War brought a complete change to the lives of the Jews. Many, if not most, of the Baghdadis were British nationals with British passports and were interned as the 1940s wore on (several, like Ellis Hayim, managed to leave Shanghai as part of a prisoner exchange). Those fortunate enough to have passports other than enemy nationals (such as Portuguese, for example) did not face internment. The Russian community, some of whose members had Soviet passports, were not touched; Japan and Soviet Russia were not at war. German and Austrian refugees who were stateless when their passports were no longer renewed by the German consulate were most affected by the war. In February 1943, the refugee community was dealt a severe blow when the Japanese authorities ordered all stateless refugees to relocate in Hongkou by May within a "designated area."[91] Moreover, money from the Joint Distribution Committee (JDC) had ceased to arrive to feed the destitute, and until new ways were found to transmit funds, the situation in the shelters reached dire proportions.

Those who had managed to establish businesses in the foreign areas once more lost their livelihood. In the overcrowded conditions of the ghetto, as it came to be called, both hunger and disease were rampant. To leave the ghetto, a pass had to be obtained from the Japanese authorities. A kind of unarmed police force (foreign *Baojia*) was organized under Japanese supervision, and starting October 1942, all males between the ages of twenty and forty-five were required to serve. One of its duties was also control of passes.[92] Existing organizations aiding refugees ceased functioning, especially the Baghdadi-led Committee for the Assistance of Central European Jews in Shanghai, and in its place, the Jewish Russian-led Shanghai Ashkenazi Collaborating Relief Association (SACRA), under Japanese control, came into being. At the end of the war, the latter was not remembered very fondly.[93]

Whether there was active cooperation with the Japanese occupiers must await further investigation. Was it, as Bernard Wasserstein remarks, that "the Jews preserved an attitude of studied neutrality toward the Far Eastern war"? Were the Japanese influenced by Shanghai's Nazis to take stronger measures against the Jews?[94] And were there instances of active resistance, as recounted by A. I. Zunterstein?[95]

CONCLUSIONS

An era ended during the Pacific War and Japan's occupation of Shanghai. The treaty port days were clearly over, and Shanghai would never be the same after the war ended. Undoubtedly, many Russians, as well as Baghdadis, might have considered remaining in or returning to Shanghai at the end of war, but the civil war between the Nationalist and Communist forces and the eventual victory of Mao Zedong's armies precluded such a possibility. Shanghai had changed and would continue to change, and they would never be able to lead the kind of Jewish lives that they and their forebears had created in the treaty port. For the Baghdadis, the Sephardi-Shanghai past was transformed into a time remembered wherever they would make their new homes.

Some of the Central European refugees returned to their countries of origin, but most opted for America or Israel, as did the majority of the Jewish Russian community, while others found new homes in Australia. Wherever they went, they became part of Jewish communities and congregations, similarly observant or secular. Shanghai seems to have been no more than a passing episode of hardship in the lives of the ultra-Orthodox and yeshivoth, and they continued an existence of study and prayer in their new environment, whether in Israel or the diaspora.

The erstwhile Shanghai-landers, as some like to refer to themselves, remember their China days with great fondness. Forgotten, or turned into an adventurous postscript, is the final horror of the rain of American bombs on Hongkou on July 17, 1945, that resulted in many Chinese and Jewish casualties.[96] In the last two decades, reunions have taken place and tours travel to Shanghai to revisit the homes where they once lived, where they were children or teenagers. Memories are kept alive, as well as undergoing change, in documentaries about them—particularly about the refugees—and in memoirs about the Jewish Shanghai past.[97]

I now want to return to one of the questions posed at the beginning of this essay—namely, how it was possible for nearly twenty thousand Jews to reach China at a time when most countries closed their doors to Jewish immigration. The answer is, to some extent, contained above, but let me summarize. A confluence of two events provided the opportunity. One was the Nazi policy of forced emigration that preceded the final solution. The other was the Sino-Japanese War, as a result of which passport control at the port of entry ceased. Between July 1937 and the end of 1941, passports were no longer examined by officials of the Nationalist government or, for that matter, by anyone else for their validity or for containing valid visas.[98] This does not mean that no visas were required, as it is generally stated. It means that visa requirements were arbitrarily enforced when purchasing passage or by official agencies. Some refugees arrived with visas, others without. There was, furthermore, no difficulty obtaining a visa at one or another of the European Chinese consulates. It should be noted that as He Fangshan, consul-general in Vienna in 1938, wrote in his memoir, China (that is, the Nationalist government) did not have a uniform policy toward issuing visas to Jews.[99] There was, in short, no discrimination.

But one further consideration must be mentioned—namely, why only twenty thousand refugees reached China. Why not thirty thousand? Or even fifty thousand? The answer here is largely one of a tragically missed opportunity, because the Jewish leadership in Europe and America did not seem to grasp the significance of the Shanghai option. In Europe, the attitude toward the Shanghai destination was generally negative. In America, priorities other than Shanghai were set.[100] Had there been more support for the Shanghai alternative, foreign currency to charter ships would have had to be sent to Germany, for the Nazi regime was quite unlikely to use its still scarce foreign currency reserves for that purpose.[101] Thus the Shanghai option was largely ignored when saving lives should have been the overriding priority. By autumn 1941, it was already too late. On October 23, the Nazis prohibited Jewish emigration.

The other question that was raised concerns the Kaifeng Jews and their retention of identity. An answer to this question must remain tentative—even ambiguous, perhaps—for the time being. Sinification—that is, the combination of Chinese characteristics with Jewish customs rather than assimilation—explains much of the processes in the course of centuries. Memory, assisted by oral tradition, can also explain why the Jewish background was not forgotten, despite intermarriage, the lack of Hebrew, and the loss of written scriptures. That there was a dispersion of Jewish families from Kaifeng in the twentieth century due to war and revolution must also be assumed. After 1949 and the establishment of a Communist local and national government, religious expression of any kind was unacceptable. A new generation would come of age after the demise of Mao Zedong in 1976 and the economic liberalization of the past two-odd decades. To what extent this liberalization includes freedoms of worship and belief, except for a number of officially recognized groups, remains to be seen.

To be sure, Jewish and Israeli visitors today travel freely to Kaifeng. In 1998, even a documentary, *Minyan in Kaifeng*, was produced, and Len Hew, a descendant of the Zhao family, wants to revive the community.[102] Professor Xu Xin of Nanjing University conducts seminars for Kaifeng Jews, trying to reintroduce them to a Judaism he has learned about in the West.[103] How valid these efforts are and whether they will lead to a revitalization of Kaifeng Judaism also remain to be seen. But what kind of Judaism is to be revived in Kaifeng? Or, if it is to be Jewish culture that is to be revived, as some maintain, then what is meant by "Jewish culture"? And where should the line between culture and observance of religious commandments (mitzvoth) be drawn when culture includes belief, worship, and observance?

NOTES

I thank the Truman Research Institute and the Louis Frieberg Research Fund for their partial support of this research. A Hebrew version of this article appeared in *Moreshet Yistael*, Vol. I (November 2004).

1. For an account of the Chang'an markets at the height of the Tang dynasty (618–906), see Edward Schafer, *The Golden Peaches of Samarkand: A Study of T'ang Exotica* (Berkeley and Los Angeles, 1963), 20–21.

2. William C. White, *Chinese Jews: A Compilation of Matters Relating to the Jews of Kaifeng Fu*, 2nd ed. (Toronto: University of Toronto Press, 1966), Part I, 140; and P. Berger and M. Schwab, "Le plus ancien manuscrit hébreu," *Journal Asiatique*, 2nd Ser. II (1913): 139–175.

3. The figurine was probably glazed or painted at one time. Its provenance is unknown. It is today in the Wilfrid Israel Museum in Kibbutz Hazoreah.

4. White, *Chinese Jews*, Part II, 35–39, 51–54, 80–85, 94–95, 104–107, contains the texts in Chinese and in English translation. Only two inscriptions are preserved today, those on the 1489 stele with its obverse inscription from 1512, which is in the Kaifeng museum. The stone with the two 1663 inscriptions disappeared in the nineteenth century. The 1679 stele was built into the wall of a house and is presumably still in Kaifeng. This inscription is badly damaged and is partly reconstructed by White in ibid., 104–107. The stelae were erected to commemorate special occasions in communal life, such as the rebuilding of the synagogue after a fire or flood or the erection of an archway. For a Hebrew translation of the 1489 inscription, see the appendix by Andrew Plaks, *The Memorial Stone at the Renovation of the Synagogue "Truth and Purity" in Kaifeng (1489)*, Pe'amim 4 (1989): 83–87. A German translation of the 1512 inscription is by Willy Tonn, "Eine judische Inschrift der Synagoge in K'aifeng Fu aus dem Jahre 1512," *Gemeindeblatt der judische Gemeinde zu Berlin* 20, no. 8 (August 1930): 360–364.

5. White, *Chinese Jews*, Part II, 37. White's Chinese text for the inscriptions is used throughout.

6. Ibid.

7. Heng Chye Kiang, *Cities of Aristocrats and Bureaucrats: The Development of Medieval Chinese Cityscapes* (Honolulu: University of Hawai'i Press and Singapore University Press, 1999).

8. Donald D. Leslie, *The Survival of the Chinese Jews: The Jewish Community of Kaifeng* (Leiden: E. J. Brill, 1972), 11–16.

9. I translate *jiao* throughout as "teaching" and not as "religion." The term *religion* is of modern usage in Chinese and did not exist at the time the inscriptions were written. Depending on context, *jiao* can be translated as "teaching" or "sect." In the latter sense, it has, of course, religious connotations.

10. White, *Chinese Jews*, Part II, 52. The Han dynasty ruled China from 206 B.C.E. to 220 B.C.E.

11. Ibid., 82. The Zhou dynasty is traditionally dated from 1122 B.C.E. to 221 B.C.E.

12. I am grateful to Professor Max Deeg, who has helped me pinpoint the two aspects of time and space by noting a similar process in the spread of Buddhism in China.

13. The most famous traveler to India was the Buddhist monk Xuan Zang (596–664), about whose travels the widely known popular novel *Xiyou ji* (Journey to the West) was published in the sixteenth century. The complete novel was translated and edited by Anthony Yu, *The Journey to the West*, 4 vols. (Chicago: University of Chicago Press, 1977–1983). The abridged Hebrew rendition, prepared from Arthur Waley's translation, is of extremely poor quality.

14. White, *Chinese Jews*, Part II, 82, 52.

15. The inscription here attempts apparently to connect the beginning of heaven and earth (*kaibi*, "opening" or "separating") with Chinese creation myths. According to one of these, Pan Gu was a giant from whose body the world was created.

16. White, *Chinese Jews*, Part II, 35.

17. Ibid., 80, 104.

18. Ibid., 53.

19. For a discussion of the *jing* in Chinese culture, see the introductory essay by I. Eber, "What Are the Chinese Classics?," in *Da Xue* (Great learning), trans. Andrew Plaks (Jerusalem: Bialik Institute, 1997), 7–18.

20. For example, White, *Chinese Jews*, Part II, 104.

21. For the difficulty this problem of nomenclature created for the later Protestant missionaries, see I. Eber, "The Interminable Term Question," in *Bible in Modern China: The Literary and Intellectual Impact*, ed. Eber, Wan, Waif, and Malek, 135–161 (Sankt Augustin: Institut Monumenta Serica, 1999).

22. White, *Chinese Jews*, Part II, 36.

23. Ibid., 80.

24. Ricci's letter is cited in Leslie, *The Survival of the Chinese Jews*, 31–32.

25. Michael Poliak, *Mandarins, Jews, and Missionaries: The Jewish Experience in the Chinese Empire* (Philadelphia: Jewish Publication Society of America, 1980), 15–38.

26. Leslie, *The Survival of the Chinese Jews*, 48–49.

27. Poliak, *Mandarins, Jews, and Missionaries*, 86. For the later history and dispersion of the scrolls, see Michael Poliak, *The Torah Scrolls of the Chinese Jews: The History, Significance and Present Whereabouts of the Sifrei Torah of the Defunct Jewish Community of Kaifeng* (Dallas: Bridwell Library Southern Methodist University, 1975).

28. White, *Chinese Jews*, Part I, 49–63.

29. The model of the Kaifeng synagogue as based on Domenge's drawings (and improved by J. Brucker) is as of this writing on display in Beth Hatefutsot, Tel Aviv.

30. SOAS Library, Council for World Missions (1795–1940), *Pam* 30, no. 7; "The Jews at K'ae-fung-foo: Being a Narrative of a Mission of Inquiry, to the *Jewish Synagogue at K'ae-fung-foo*, on Behalf of the London Society for Promoting Christianity Among the Jews" (Shanghai, 1851), 47, 29.

31. W. A. P. Martin, "Affairs in China," *New York Times*, August 29, 1866, 2.

32. I. Eber, *The Jewish Bishop and the Chinese Bible: S. I. J. Schereschewsky (1831–1906)* (Leiden: E. J. Brill, 1999), 97–102.

33. Although hardly a visitor, mention must be made among them of Bishop William Charles White (1873–1960), who established the Anglican mission in Kaifeng in 1898 (?), where he served as bishop until 1933. His splendid compilation *Chinese Jews* was first published in 1942.

34. See Poliak, *Mandarins, Jews, and Missionaries*, 100–105, who describes several misfired attempts by Domenge.

35. Ibid., 157–163. Poliak wonders whether the purchase was indeed legal.

36. Ibid., 230–234.

37. White, *Chinese Jews*, Part II, 94.

38. Ibid., 105.

39. Wang Yisha, "The Descendants of the Kaifeng Jews," in *Jews in Old China: Studies by Chinese Scholars*, trans. Sidney Shapiro (New York: Hippocrene Books, 1984), 183–184.

40. See the highly informative account on syncretic sectarianism by Daniel L. Overmyer, *Folk Buddhist Religion: Dissenting Sects in Late Traditional China* (Cambridge: Harvard University Press, 1976).

41. Susan Naquin, *Millenarian Rebellion in China: The Eight Trigrams Uprising in 1813* (New

Haven: Yale University Press, 1976), 223 and 100, n. 101.

42. For a more detailed account of this process, see I. Eber, "K'aifeng Revisited: Sinification as Affirmation of Identity," *Monumenta Serica* 41 (1993): 231–247.

43. Donald D. Leslie, *The Chinese-Hebrew Memorial Book of the Jewish Community of K'aifeng* (Belconnen, ACT: Canberra College of Advanced Education, 1984), 177.

44. Wang Yisha, *Zhongguo Youtai chunqiu* (Spring and Autumn of Chinese Jews) (Beijing–Haiyang, 1992), 197, mentions a lineage register (*jiapu*) for the Shi and Zhao families. Unfortunately, he does not give further particulars about them, though the registers are invaluable for at least roughly calculating population size.

45. Michael Freund, "How Wen-Jing Became 'Shalva,'" *Jerusalem Post*, June 22, 2004.

46. It is important to differentiate between the five treaty ports and Hong Kong, which was ceded to Great Britain and was a British Crown colony until it was returned to China in 1997.

47. Robert Fortune, *Three Years' Wanderings in the Northern Provinces of China, Including a Visit to the Tea, Silk, and Cotton Countries; with an Account of the Agriculture and Horticulture of the Chinese, New Plants, Etc.* (London: John Murray, 1847), 125–126.

48. Hanchao Lu, *Beyond the Neon Lights: Everyday Shanghai in the Early Twentieth Century* (Berkeley: University of California Press, 1999), 27. According to Lu, in 1844, 44 foreign ships entered Shanghai harbor. Twenty years later, 3,400 foreign ships arrived.

49. According to Betty Peh-ti Wei, *Shanghai: Crucible of Modern China* (Hong Kong: Oxford University Press, 1987), 84, the wall around the Chinese city was only razed between 1912 and early 1914.

50. Robert Bickers and Christian Henriot, introduction to *New Frontiers: Imperialism's New Communities in East Asia, 1842–1953*, ed. Bickers and Henriot (Manchester: Manchester University Press, 2000), 5.

51. *Newspaper Directory of China (including Hong Kong) and Advertising Manual* (Shanghai: Carl Crow, n.d.), 121.

52. According to the "List of Commercial Houses, Agents, Etc.," *Chinese Repository* 15, no. 1 (January 1846): 7, Eliaoo (Elias) D. Sassoon established a firm in Guangzhou with Moses Dahood and A. d'Miranda.

53. Chiara Betta, "Marginal Westerners in Shanghai: The Baghdadi Jewish Community, 1845–1931," in *New Frontiers*, 50, 41.

54. Opium was used in China perhaps as early as the ninth century for medicinal purposes. But in the eighteenth century, the British East India Company (established in 1600) began to export opium to China on an increasingly large scale. Successive Chinese emperors issued edicts against the sale and use of opium, but to no avail. Addiction spread and culminated in the Opium War after Lin Zixu publicly burned the imported opium. The classic account of Lin's career continues to be Hsin-pao Chang, *Commissioner Lin and the Opium War* (Cambridge: Harvard University Press, 1964).

55. Frank H. H. King, ed., *Eastern Banking: Essays in the History of the Hong Kong and Shanghai Banking Corporation* (London: Hong Kong Bank Group History Series, no. 1, 1983), 409. The Huai is a major river between the Yellow River and the Yangzi and is subject to frequent floods.

56. Ibid.; and Yad Vashem Archive (YAV), 078/21, H. (Peter) Eisfelder, "Chinese Exile: My Years in Shanghai and Nanking, 1938 to 1947" (1985), unpublished manuscript, 2nd rev. ed., 9. Eisfelder's memoir was published recently in Victoria: Makor Jewish Community Library (2003).

57. Chiara Betta, "Myth and Memory: Chinese Portrayals of Silas Aaron Hardoon, Luo Jialing and Aili Garden between 1924 and 1925," in *Jews in China, from Kaifeng . . . to Shanghai*, ed. Roman Malek (Sankt Augustin: Monumenta Serica Institute, 2000), 377. For a largely anecdotal account, see also Xu Zhucheng, *Hatong waizhuan* (Hardoon's unofficial history) (Hong Kong: Wuxing jishu baoshe, 1982).

58. A brief biography of Liza Hardoon is Ephraim Selmanson, "Liza Hardoon: Die Geschichte der reichsten Erbin Asiens," *Shanghai Morgenpost*, November 16, 1941, 7.

59. YVA, 078/69, I. Eber interview with Maple Doron, February 16, 1977.

60. Maisie J. Meyer, *From the Rivers of Babylon to the Whangpoo: A Century of Sephardi Jewish Life in Shanghai* (Lanham: University Press of America, 2003), 42–43.

61. Ibid., 45. For a detailed account of the society's efforts and failing (?), see 39–51.

62. Arthur Sopher, *Chinese Jews, Shanghai* (1926), pamphlet.

63. *Constitution and By-Laws of the Jewish Communal Association (Ashkenaz)* (Shanghai: Nashe Zarya, 1931). In its by-laws, the association declared that it was "the official representative of the Ashkenazi Jewish population in dealing with Municipal and Government institutions."

64. Jewish Joint Distribution Committee (JDC), file 456, Rabbi M. Ashkenazi to Mr. Alkow, August 23, 1937. Ashkenazi was asking the JDC for financial support. See also JDC, file 456, excerpts from a letter by Joe Hollzer, Shanghai to Judge H. A. Hollzer, Los Angeles, December 25, 1937, who mentions Russian Jewish immigrants whose poverty reduced them "almost to savagery."

65. Jewish National and University Library, Ravitch Collection, file 2:374, 138–139. This is Ravitch's unpublished travelogue, which he wrote in Yiddish.

66. Shanghai Municipal Police (SMP), reel 18, D5422 (c), police report dated November 7, 1933.

67. *China Press*, November 26, 1938, 3.

68. For an extensive summary of the conference and the negotiations that followed, see Henry L. Feingold, *The Politics of Rescue: The Roosevelt Administration and the Holocaust, 1938–1945* (New Brunswick, NJ: Rutgers University Press, 1970), 22–68.

69. "Report by Oberscharführer Hagen on Jewish Emigration, 13 September 1936," in *The Holocaust: Selected Documents in Eighteen Volumes*, ed. John Mendelsohn (New York: Garland, 1982), 5:40–57.

70. Schlie apparently turned a tidy profit from refugee travel generally. His name appears on a list of Swiss bank account holders that was published in the *Jerusalem Post*, July 25, 1997.

71. SMP, reel 18, D5422 (c), police reports on ship arrivals, January–July 1939. The

correspondence among Schlie, Eichmann, and others is in YVA, 051/0S0/41, dated variously February 17, 1939; March 5, 1939; May 31, 1939; and June 2, 1939. For more details on this topic, see A. Altman and I. Eber, "Flight to Shanghai, 1938–1940: The Larger Setting," *Yad Vashem Studies* 28 (2000): 51–86.

72. For more details on how German and Austrian refugees reached Shanghai, see I. Eber, *Chinese and Jews: Encounters Between Cultures* (Jerusalem: Bialik, 2002), 62–91.

73. For a history of *die yeshiva* in Kobe, Japan, and Shanghai, see Yosef Hertsman, *Mirer Yeshiva in Goles* (Mirer Yeshiva in exile) (Reprint of 1950, Amherst: National Yiddish Book Center, 1999).

74. For details on the religious life of the Shanghai Jewish community, see I. Eber, "Chinese Jews and Jews in China: Kaifeng–Shanghai," chapter 2 in this volume.

75. The complex question of Sephardi rabbis is discussed in Meyer, *From the River of Babylon*, 100–108.

76. David Kranzler, *Japanese, Nazis and Jews: The Refugee Community of Shanghai, 1938–1945* (New York: Yeshiva University Press, 1976), 60, 79–80.

77. Hertsman, *Mirer Yeshiva in Goles*, 27.

78. Kranzler, *Japanese, Nazis and Jews*, 410.

79. The high mortality rate among the refugees required adding a fourth cemetery in 1941. I thank Ralph B. Hirsch for making available the list of Central European Refugees Who Died in Shanghai, 1940–1945. The list consists of 1,433 names. I thank Itamar Livny for his preliminary examination of the list, which shows that infant mortality was comparatively higher than that of older children.

80. JDC, RG 33-44, file 487, letter from P. Udelevich to Igud Yotsei Sin, October 27, 1958; and P. I. Yudalevich to Henri Elfenbein, AJDC, Geneva, January 6, 1960.

81. SMP, reel 18, D5422 (c), police reports on ship arrivals.

82. For example, advertisements of roof-garden cafés in *Jüdisches Nachrichtenblatt*, August 2, 1940; August 16, 1940; and August 22, 1941.

83. For example, *Gelbe Post* 1, no. 4 (June 16, 1939); and *Shanghai Jewish Chronicle* 2, no. 119 (May 2, 1940): 6. The Eastern Theater was

showing *The Sign of the Cross*, with Charles Laughton and Claudette Colbert; the Broadway Theatre was showing *The Wedding Night*, with Gary Cooper.

84. The *Shanghai Herald, German Language Supplement*, April 1946, 14–15, lists the titles of plays, performers, dancers, and technicians in a lengthy article.

85. *Jüdisches Nachrichtenblatt* 3, no. 3 (January 30, 1942): 5, lists a comedy performed by the Collective Shanghai Stage Artists.

86. For more about the paper and its editor, see Françoise Kreissler, "Ein Journalist im Exil in Shanghai: Adolph J. Storfer und die Gelbe Post," in *Jews in China*, ed. R. P. Malek, 511–524.

87. An unpublished chart of forty-six Jewish papers in all of China is in the YIVO Archive and was prepared by Asher Rozenboim, *Di Yiddishe presse in Chine, 1937–1947* (The Jewish press in China, 1937–1947). A good summary of the German Jewish press is provided by LaFrance, "Die Presse der Emigration," *Shanghai Herald, German Language Supplement*, April 1946, 11.

88. *Kultur Kronik* (Culture chronicle), *Zamelheft, In Weg* (November 1941). A review of J. Rappaport, *Der mahut fun dikhtung un ir soziale funkzye* (Essential poetry and its social function).

89. *Nidpas beShanghai* (Printed in Shanghai), *Unzer Lebn* 54 (May 15, 1942). See also Ernest G. Heppner, *Shanghai Refuge: A Memoir of the World War II Jewish Ghetto* (Lincoln: University of Nebraska Press, 1993), 66, who mentions the lithographic process.

90. A number of these appeared in *Xin Shenbao*, successor to the widely circulated *Shenbao*. The British and the Shanghai Municipal Council also were uneasy about the growing anti-Semitism, as expressed in several of their communications. See, for example, YVA, 078/85, Shanghai Municipal Archive, unsigned to Sir Herbert Phillips, December 28, 1938.

91. Proclamation Concerning Restrictions of Residence and Business of Stateless Refugees. Copy of document obtained from YIVO.

92. Foreign Pao Chia, *Jüdisches Nachrichtenblatt* 5, no. 26 (July 31–August 2, 1944).

93. Die Herren von der "S.A.C.R.A.," Eindruecke eines Opfers, *Shanghai Herald, German Language Supplement*, April 1946, 27.

94. Bernard Wasserstein, "Ambiguities of Occupation: Foreign Resisters and Collaborators in Wartime Shanghai," in *Wartime Shanghai*, ed. Wen-hsin Yeh (London: Routledge, 1998), 26.

95. YVA, 078/70, A. I. Zunterstein, Shanghai: 1938–1949, A. I. Zunterstein tape, 16.

96. Ernst Pollak, "Der Herr hat gegeben, der Herr hat genommen . . . ," *Jüdisches Nachrichtenblatt* 6, no. 29 (July 27, 1945): 1–2; and Heppner, *Shanghai Refuge*, 123–127.

97. One recent highly recommended documentary is *Shanghai Ghetto*, produced by Dana and Amir Mann. Memoirs about Shanghai have proliferated in recent years. I thank Iramar Livny for reminding me that a critical review article about this literature is much overdue.

98. Altman and Eber, "Flight to Shanghai," 62–63.

99. He Fangshan, *Waijiao shengya sishi nian* (My forty-year diplomatic career) (Hong Kong: Chinese University Press, 1990), 75.

100. Altman and Eber, "Flight to Shanghai," 53–54.

101. YVA, 05 l/0S0/41, signature illegible, Vermerk II 1 12, July 14, 1939, and Schlie to Hagen, July 7, 1939. Foreign ships could not be chartered for Reichsmark, and German ships used fuel oil that was imported and had to be paid for with foreign currency.

102. Len Hew, "Len Hew's Story," *Points East* 17, no. 3 (November 2002): 1, 6–9.

103. Xu Xin, "Kaifeng Jewish Descendants Learn About Jewish Heritage at Nanjing Seminar," ibid., 1, 5–6.

CHAPTER 2

Chinese Jews and Jews in China

Kaifeng–Shanghai

In both imperial and modern China, Jews were a small minority in comparison to the larger Muslim and Christian minorities. At most, there may have been several thousand Jews in past ages and possibly around thirty thousand by the mid-twentieth century. Yet these small communities have invited considerable scholarly attention over the years, and their histories of remoter periods and more recent times have raised a number of questions. One of these, and the one to be taken up in this essay, is how the Jews in Kaifeng and Shanghai, each at a different time and a different place, accommodated themselves to the Chinese environment. By Chinese Jews, I mean primarily those who settled in Kaifeng in the twelfth century, with the initial group probably being augmented by newcomers over the next two hundred years. By Jews in China, I have in mind the disparate groups who arrived in Shanghai after the Opium War (1839–1842) that consisted initially of mostly Sephardi Jews,[1] then Russian, and later Central European Jews.

Although we speak of Kaifeng Jews, it must be remembered that at least until the seventeenth century, Jewish communities existed in Ningbo, Yangzhou, and Ningxia. The more recent Shanghai communities were similarly not the only ones. There were also organized communities in Harbin and Tianjin, although they were smaller. In this essay, I will discuss the Kaifeng Jews, and not the other early Jewish populations, about which we lack data, and the Shanghai Jewish communities.

BEGINNINGS OF THE KAIFENG JEWISH COMMUNITY

Jewish merchants, having come overland, probably traded on the Chang'an market during the Tang dynasty.[2] They might also have reached China by sea, sailing together with Arab merchants to Guangzhou (Canton), but there is little or no evidence to support this conclusively. Nor is there evidence for the presence of an actual Jewish community during the Tang dynasty. The existence of a later Jewish community in Kaifeng is, however, amply documented on five stelae inscriptions dating from 1489, 1512, two from 1663, and 1679, although the information on these is fragmentary.[3] According to the 1489 stele, the first synagogue was built in Kaifeng in 1163, which indicates that by then a sufficient number of Jews had arrived to warrant a house of prayer. It can be assumed that they were merchants who came in small groups over a period of time together with other merchants headed for the capital of the empire. The 1489 inscription states that they were cotton merchants from India (Tianzhu). This seems plausible, as cotton began to be cultivated only during the Northern Song dynasty in the Yangzi (Changjiang) delta and was not yet widely available throughout the empire. Where precisely they came from in India is not known, nor can we be certain that they were Indian Jews.[4] Quite likely they arrived in Kaifeng before the Jurchen (Ruzhen) army laid siege to the city in the winter of 1126, capturing the capital in January 1127. It is doubtful that traders would have ventured into a war zone, which would have endangered their merchandise, either during the hostilities or even shortly thereafter. It is nevertheless clear that they built their synagogue when Kaifeng was under foreign rule and when it was no longer the capital.

The attraction for merchants to Song Kaifeng was the city's flourishing commerce. With more than one million inhabitants within the city walls and its suburbs, Kaifeng was an "open" city, with none of the constraints that had characterized earlier Chinese cities. As argued persuasively by Heng Chye Kiang, Kaifeng boasted a flowering urban culture with commerce and consumerism as a part of urban life.[5] In this new kind of city with its unrestrained commercial and entertainment establishments, a group of foreign merchants would have had no difficulty finding their place. What may have been considered a temporary residence at first became, however, a permanent home due to the unsettled conditions—a peace treaty was signed only in 1141—but also because trading relations between the Jin dynasty (1115–1234) and the Southern Song (1127–1279) were maintained.[6] The fact that they built a synagogue after Kaifeng had come under Jin control (together with the rest of North China) may very well indicate that trading conditions continued to be favorable and that they had settled permanently in Kaifeng.

No doubt, relations with other Jewish communities were maintained in the Jin period and especially during the subsequent Yuan dynasty. As a result of the flourishing caravan and sea trade in the Mongol period, Jews from other parts of the vast Mongol Empire may have settled in Kaifeng and other cities. However, we know nothing about them, how they perpetuated their Judaism, how precisely they made their living, or how they were accepted by their Chinese hosts. Further information does not appear until three centuries later, during the Ming dynasty. Even then, the data that can be gleaned from the 1489 and 1512 inscriptions are very fragmentary. The information from these that is useful to this topic can be summarized as follows. The Jews had assumed, or were permitted to assume, Chinese surnames in the early years of the Ming dynasty. Jews from other communities contributed to the reconstruction of the synagogue devastated by flood in 1461, indicative both of the prosperity of communities other than Kaifeng and of contacts between communities. Two scrolls of the Torah were provided by Ningbo Jews, which furthermore supports the assumption that it too must have been a flourishing community at the time.[7]

FROM COMMUNAL TO FAMILY IDENTITY

The Jesuits have provided more concrete information about the Kaifeng Jews in the seventeenth and early eighteenth centuries. A famous meeting took place in 1605 between the Jew Ai Tian, who had come to Beijing in search of an official appointment, and Matteo Ricci (1551–1610). This episode—in which Ricci assumed Ai Tian was Christian and Ai Tian thought Ricci was Jewish—is well known and needs no further comment. More importantly, in the wake of this meeting, a number of Jesuit fathers visited Kaifeng until the year 1723, when they were confined to Beijing and Guangzhou by order of the Yongzheng emperor (r. 1723–1735). The Jesuit letters, together with the 1663 and the 1679 inscriptions, reveal a picture of a prosperous and successful community. Its members led rich Jewish lives in addition to being active in Chinese society, with a number of families reaching elite status when their sons received official appointments in the imperial bureaucracy. A drawing of the synagogue, based on sketches prepared by Jean Domenge in 1722, shows a Chinese-style building of imposing size.[8] Unfortunately, nothing is known of the fate of the Jews between the last Jesuit visitor in 1723 and the first Protestant visitor, W. A. P. Martin, in 1866, whose dramatic description of the visit still makes for enjoyable reading.[9]

Clearly, however, by the mid-nineteenth century, the Jewish community had been declining for quite some time. There was no longer a head (*zhang-jiao*) of the community, the last one having died in 1810. Circumcision was also no longer practiced, and knowledge of Hebrew had ceased. Abstinence from pork was apparently still practiced, possibly under Muslim influence. The synagogue had, however, disappeared. It had been severely damaged by floods in 1849 and was dismantled some time thereafter.

This brief outline raises a number of questions. How had the Jews maintained their Jewish identity for seven centuries with minimal or no contacts with coreligionists outside of China? Considering that their numbers were not augmented from outside of China for something like three centuries, how were they able to maintain a numerically adequate population? Why were they not rapidly assimilated by Chinese society, which had erected no barriers against them and apparently did not discriminate against Jews? Should we seek answers concerning the maintenance of Jewish identity in the strength of Jewish practices or rather in those aspects of Chinese culture and society that were conducive to their continuing identification as Jews? In the following, I argue that it was a unique combination of both.

The acquisition of Chinese surnames, mentioned earlier, may be considered a major step in Jewish integration into Chinese society. This occurred at more or less the same time that the Chinese family organization into lineages was adopted. Such a transition was not a major step for these Jews, since most or all were undoubtedly Sephardi, whose custom it was to organize into clans. Moreover, Sephardi Jews practiced polygamy, which, depending on their means, they continued to practice in Kaifeng. Their memorial or genealogy book of some centuries later lists the first wife as Jewish and other wives as Chinese.[10] Possibly they took Chinese wives due to the scarcity of Jewish women. Be that as it may, it suggests, more importantly, a more rapid population growth than if they had been monogamous.

But Chinese lineages differ in several ways from what is normally understood by the term *clan*. A lineage generally traces its origin to one ancestor, goes by one surname, is domiciled in one locality, and holds some property, including a burial ground, in common. Evidence for the assumption of such a lineage organization by the Kaifeng Jews comes from two sources: inscriptions on the stelae and cemeteries. The 1663a inscription mentions "seven surnames" (*qixing*), clearly referring to lineages. The 1679 inscription states that seventy-three names consist of five hundred families (*jia*).[11] Second, family cemeteries came into use. Indeed, even if a Jewish cemetery had ever existed in Kaifeng, it has long disappeared. And precisely when this custom was adopted is uncertain. It may have been after the 1642 flood, but in any event, it occurred well after the lineage family organization was prevalent. Wang Yisha refers to several family cemeteries in Kaifeng's suburbs and adjoining hamlets, among which the Jin and Li cemeteries each have a "foremost" grave, marked "Old Ancestor's Grave."[12] Graves thus marked are meant to indicate symbolically agnatic affiliation and the original ancestor of the lineage.[13]

The transformation into lineages has significant implications for the question of identity. As a result of this transformation, identification with a larger and more amorphous Jewish community beyond China's borders became less important than identification with the lineage and agnatic group. As long as lineages remained Jewish, individual Jews were unlikely to abandon their Jewish identity. Although Jewishness could be abandoned and forgotten by an entire family, especially if that family left Kaifeng, Jewishness continued within the lineage as long as a family remained intact and was domiciled in the same locality. There is, furthermore, no evidence that the Jews ever were a community in the sense in which we know other Jewish communities, with institutions and their designated functions. Indeed, these were not needed, as the lineage performed such functions on behalf of its families. Therefore, instead of identifying with a Jewish people, Kaifeng Jewish identity became a family-centered identity.

This transformation was accompanied and reinforced by how they (or perhaps even more so, their Chinese neighbors) came to regard their Jewish practices—namely, as similar to those of a religious sect. Like Chinese sects, the Jews were called a *jiao*, which may be variously translated as "religion," "religious sect," or "teaching," and this is how they referred to themselves in the inscriptions. When the word Israel (*Yiciluoye*) occurs in the inscriptions, it is not used as the name of a people but refers to the founding or establishment of the teaching.[14] The inscriptions, furthermore, refer to the Jews as "followers of the teaching"—that is, as a sect.[15] But their Chinese neighbors apparently used more specific names: *Tiaojin-jiao* (sinew-extracting sect), *Jiaojing-jiao* (scripture-teaching sect), and *lanmao huihui* (blue-cap Muslims). None of these names appear on the stelae, and Jean-Paul Gozani's observation of 1704 that the name "sinew-extracting sect" was bestowed on the Jews by the "idolaters"[16] would confirm that these names were not of their own invention.

As admirably described by Daniel Overmyer, popular sectarianism—specifically syncretic sectarianism, consisting of mixtures of Buddhist, Daoist, Confucian, and folk elements—flourished in various parts of the Chinese Empire, including the North China Plain.[17] It was a localized and highly fragmented phenomenon, and the sects were known by a variety of names. Part of the rural as well as the urban scene, sectarians shared a number of characteristics that were not too dissimilar from those of the Jews. Sectarians had a meeting place, a set of sacred writings used only by those who participated in sectarian worship, a leader who kept the scriptures, and practices specific to the sect, such as dietary customs.

Which practices the Jews kept can be learned from the inscriptions, the various Jesuit reports, and the few manuscripts that have been recovered from Kaifeng. The Jews observed the major festivals, including Rosh Hodesh (the first moon), Purim, and the Ninth of Av, which commemorates the destruction of the Temple. They prayed three times a day with a minyan (ten men), read the weekly Torah portion, and on special occasions as required, read the haphtarah (prophetic portion). They kept the Sabbath, lighting no fires and doing no work. Kosher slaughter was practiced (as reflected in the name the Chinese had given the Jews), although a shokhet (butcher) is not specifically mentioned. Circumcision was also practiced, but again a mohel (expert in circumcision) is not mentioned. According to Donald Leslie, it is doubtful that they managed to keep the Jewish calendar in order, as periodic adjustments have to be made. It is therefore also doubtful that they observed the festivals at their proper times.[18] They had, of course, prayer books and scrolls of the Torah, but whether they had books of the Talmud is uncertain.[19] They followed rabbinic practices while praying, and one might conjecture that they had some Talmudic books in the early days that were later lost. Jewish practices were in some instances (Passover in spring, Tabernacles in autumn) linked to Chinese practices and observances, reinforcing the sectarian identity. Gradually, the connection to a foreign and universal religion was severed, and ties were established to native and local religions. Therefore, not only in appearance but also in their lifestyle, the Jews were neither strangers nor outsiders in Chinese society. The Sinification of Judaism allowed Kaifeng Jews to retain a Jewish identity, and it allowed them to practice a kind of Judaism that assumed specifically Chinese features.

It is obviously easier to say something about the practices that continued to be in use for close to eight hundred years than it is to discuss matters of belief. The inscriptions do not yield sufficient evidence for describing the beliefs these Jews held. A book by Zhao Yingdou—a Kaifeng Jew actively involved in community affairs—of ten chapters with the suggestive title *Mingdao xu* (Preface to the illustrious way) might have furnished some clues, but it is unfortunately no longer extant.[20] However, the inscriptions indicate that the basis of their belief continued to be monotheism. There is no mention of Chinese deities in the inscriptions, and *Shangdi* occurs only when quotations from the Chinese classics are used, in particular on the horizontal and vertical tablets.[21] Heaven (*Tian*) is used generally when God is referred to, although *Di* does occur occasionally, as in the 1663b inscription.[22] Yet there is also ample evidence in the inscriptions that monotheism was combined with Chinese moral precepts, such as the cardinal virtues of filial piety (*xiao*), loyalty (*zhong*), benevolence (*ren*), and righteousness (*yi*).[23]

Aside from questions of belief, attempts to establish succession and transmission as well as to provide Kaifeng Jewish history with a Chinese context are especially noteworthy. The succession always begins with Adam, moves on to Abraham as the founder, and continues from Abraham to Moses. The 1663a inscription adds Noah after Adam,[24] and the 1489 inscription ends the succession with Ezra.[25] In the earliest inscription, Adam is referred to as Adam-Pan Gu[26]—that is, as one person—and Abraham is said to be of the nineteenth generation after Adam. The 1512 inscription adds that Adam came originally from India (Tianzhu).[27] The 1489 inscription places Abraham's establishment of the "true teaching" in the 146th year of the Zhou dynasty, or 977/976 B.C.E. Moses is said to have lived in the 613th year of the Zhou, or 510/509 B.C.E. These dates do not seem to have any special significance in the Chinese calendar, and one wonders why they were chosen. For Ezra, no dates are supplied. Both the 1512 and 1679 inscriptions date the arrival of the teaching to the Han dynasty.[28]

Time and space (even the mythic time of Pan Gu) are the significant ingredients that have helped move Jewish history into a Chinese historical context. The important personages now have dates that coincide with the early Chinese history of the Zhou dynasty. Adam, moreover, though he is a progenitor and not a founder, is given a recognizable origin in India instead of an unfamiliar place. Therefore, Abraham, as his descendant, can also be placed in a known geographical area. Finally, the arrival of the religion in the Han dynasty provides the necessary starting point for Jewish development in China. Were there other writings that developed these ideas more concretely, ideas that are stated only briefly in the inscriptions? Perhaps, but all that can be safely stated on the basis of the stelae is that the creation of a Jewish-Chinese history contributed to and was part of the process of Sinification.[29]

After Martin's 1866 visit, a number of other visitors went to Kaifeng, leaving accounts that Michael Pollak has appropriately called in a chapter heading "Outright Lies, Tall Tales, and a Few Truths."[30] But no matter what the shortcomings of these visitors' stories were, whether they spoke to few or many, those with whom they spoke continued to think of themselves as Jews. Since the 1970s, their memories of having been Jewish have been revived through outside contacts. Jewish visitors to Kaifeng have imported knowledge about Jewish practices onto which some members of erstwhile Jewish families (especially the Shi, Jin, and Zhao families) have grafted half-remembered, half-imagined recollections in an attempt to reinvent Judaism.[31] "Descendant of Jews" (youtai houyi) is recorded on some registration cards.[32] But according to the legal (halakhic) Jewish definition, being a descendant does not necessarily establish the Jewishness of the person, as descent is determined by the status of the mother.[33] But as Pollak points out, it is unlikely that non-Jewish women who married Jewish men were converted after the last rabbi died around 1810.[34] Thus present-day Kaifeng individuals who identify themselves as Jews could be accepted as halakhically Jewish if they were to formally convert, although it goes without saying that the halakhic definition has been challenged time and again, both in Israel and in the diaspora.

It is possible, however, that some might be considering conversion. In recent years, a few young Kaifeng men have been mentioned as studying at Jerusalem's religious schools (yeshivoth), although whether their studies are for the purpose of conversion and/or returning to Kaifeng as teachers is not clear. During the 2001–2002 academic year, Shi Lei studied Hebrew and Jewish subjects at Bar-Ilan University.[35] An Institute of Jewish Studies has been established at He'nan University. Presumably it will attract Kaifeng descendants who would like to study their heritage as an academic subject. It is difficult to say how widespread, how long lasting, or how genuine this interest in Judaism will be. Can it lead to an actual revival of Kaifeng Judaism, and what characteristics might such a revival have? Historically, being Jewish in Chinese Kaifeng meant asserting particularity within a society consisting of particular groups. It did not mean religious separateness. In present-day Kaifeng, the formal assumption of Judaism would have different implications and could have different consequences.

THE SHANGHAI JEWISH COMMUNITIES

Whereas the Kaifeng Jews were not truly a community, their Judaism being family centered and sectarian, the case of Shanghai is different. From the mid-nineteenth century, three distinct communities developed in Shanghai, communities that, except for the fact that they were Jewish, had little else in common. Sephardi Jews (or Baghdadis) came to Shanghai in the 1840s together with the British. They came for the most part from Iraq via India, were English speakers, and established their homes and business enterprises in the International Settlement. Russian Jews came next, some by way of Harbin in the early 1900s and the bulk after the Bolshevik Revolution of 1917. They settled in the French Concession, while the poorer among them went to live in Hongkou, which was part of the International Settlement north of Suzhou Creek. The Central European refugees—mostly German and Austrian but also some Poles, Czechs, and others—came after 1933, the greater part arriving between November 1938 and September 1939. Most of the Central Europeans settled in Hongkou, although some took up residence in the International Settlement. A fourth and distinctly different group arrived in 1941. It consisted of a number of secular Polish-Jewish writers and intellectuals, a number of Polish and Lithuanian rabbis, and several religious students together with their rabbinic teachers.[36] This group of mostly ultra-Orthodox men (not many had brought wives and families) carved out a Shanghai existence for themselves vastly different from that of other refugees. Thus in 1941, there were English-, Russian-, and German-speaking Jews in Shanghai—aside from a small group of Yiddish speakers—each group culturally as well as religiously different from the other. Numerically, the Sephardi group remained the smallest, with something over one thousand people. The Russian group was larger, numbering between five and six thousand persons. But by the end of 1941, by far the largest group was the Central Europeans, with around twenty thousand Jews. In the treaty port of Shanghai, the culturally and linguistically different groups of Jews found a congenial environment conducive to the maintenance of their differences.

Shanghai was a mosaic of districts, consisting of the Chinese areas, the International Settlement, and the French Concession. The International Settlement was similarly a mosaic of populations made up of many different kinds of Europeans, Asians, and Chinese. The Chinese population was by far the largest and continued to grow as refugees poured into the metropolis in 1937. The number of foreigners was, in comparison, insignificant: there were White Russians, Japanese, Indians, Germans, French, Italians, and others, each forming a kind of enclave in the unique treaty port setting. But these were not, as Robert Bickers and Christian Henriot write, colonialist communities. The foreigners were rather a large collection of various kinds of people pursuing their "interests in the interstices of empire, adroitly operating on the margins of treaty legality, using extra-territoriality, and the grey areas offered by colonial citizenship and settler autonomy, to further their own end." The treaty system, the authors argue, enabled nationals to develop new identities,[37] allowing them at the same time to preserve earlier identities, such as linguistic and religious. Foreigners, writes Betty Wei, and Chinese remained separate, even while working together and competing with one another.[38] The millions of Chinese were far from a homogenous population, whether they lived in the International Settlement or in the Chinese-administered city. Shanghai's Chinese population was largely made up of people who had left their native towns and villages in search of work and livelihood in the metropolis. Together with the masses of destitute refugees who arrived after the outbreak of hostilities in 1937, the Chinese population too was composed of disparate ethnic groups.[39]

Communication within each group, Chinese and foreign, was maintained by means of newspapers and radio broadcasts. In addition to Chinese newspapers, English dailies and an array of weeklies in Russian, Polish, German, and Yiddish were available. Among the Jewish papers, some weeklies served the non-Jewish population; others specifically addressed religious or secular Jews. The subject of publishing will be discussed in greater detail below.

SYNAGOGUES, RABBIS, AND OBSERVANCES

The Shanghai Jewish communities were not only culturally diverse, but religious differences created additional fragmentation, especially within the Ashkenazi community, into secular, observant, and ultrareligious. This fragmentation duplicated, of course, the European Jewish religious scene (with the exception of the small, though highly influential Baghdadi presence). Together with the absence of a pronounced anti-Semitism (except among the White Russians), there was in the treaty port no political authority able or empowered to enforce uniformity and conformity, and thus variations and differences could be maintained and perpetuated.

The three Jewish groups—Baghdadi, Russian, and Central European—maintained separate synagogues. The earliest were those of the Sephardi Jews; Beth El was established in 1887, and its splinter group, Shearith Israel, was established in 1900. Their initially temporary prayer houses were later replaced by two splendid structures: Ohel Rachel in 1920, financed by Sir Jacob Elias Sassoon (1843–1916), and Beth Aharon in 1927, financed by Silas Aaron Hardoon.[40] By the early years of the twentieth century, enough Russian Jews had arrived in Shanghai to feel a need for a congregation of their own. They did not build a synagogue but used the premises of the Sephardi Shearith Israel synagogue. Ohel Moshe (Oihel Moishe), as it was called, moved to its own building in 1927, and in 1941, the New Synagogue was constructed in the French Concession.[41] The approximately twenty thousand Central European refugees fully reflected the complexity of modern Judaism, now transplanted into the treaty port context. Aside from the Central European and Polish secularists, the refugees represented the entire spectrum of Reform, Liberal, and ultra-Orthodox Jewry. Due to their diversity and their sojourner status, building a synagogue was out of the question; for services on festivals and the high holy days, they used various premises, while for the ultra-Orthodox rabbis and their students, Beth Aharon was made available.

During the nearly one hundred years of Jewish populations in Shanghai, rabbis, who were responsible for the communities' spiritual and everyday lives, were often hard to find. Obviously, they would have to speak the language of their congregants, and they would have had to come from abroad in order to have received rabbinic training. For the Baghdadis, finding a rabbi presented special problems because, in addition to familiarity with Sephardi liturgy and customs, he had to be an English speaker in order to represent the status-conscious community in the International Settlement.[42] The Baghdadis eventually compromised on the first requirement in preference for the English-language requirement. The Russian community was more fortunate. Rabbi Meir Ashkenazi (1891–1954), after serving in Vladivostok, came to Shanghai in 1926, remaining the Russian congregation's leader for the next twenty-one years.[43] More research is needed to better understand the religious diversity of the Central European refugees. Rabbis were certainly among them, but customs often differed within what may be broadly described as Reform Judaism,[44] and splinter groups tended to develop.

Except for the staunchest of secularists, the Jews celebrated the major festivals and observed the high holy days. Practices varied depending on cultural background and religious fervor. Simhat Torah, for example, the conclusion of the yearly cycle of Torah reading, was celebrated as joyously with song and dance by the Hasidim of the Mir Yeshiva as if they had never left their homes.[45] Whereas the ultra-Orthodox continued to maintain strict Sabbath observance, most of the Jewish population did not, which was a constant irritant to the Orthodox community. Many of the Sephardi businessmen, who had been strictly observant at one time, had grown lax by the 1930s. Russians, most of whom were merchants and storekeepers, did not close for the Sabbath. Neither did the Central European refugees desist from trying to make a living.

Kashrut (regulations concerning dietary laws) was maintained longest by the Sephardi Jews, even after other observances had been abandoned. This included ritual slaughter, abstaining from forbidden foods like shellfish or pork, and keeping meat and milk strictly separate. Both the Russian and the Central European communities were more lax. Yet in the shelters (Heime), where many of the destitute refugees lived upon arrival, kosher kitchen facilities were maintained, and the organizations responsible for refugee welfare made every effort to adhere to dietary laws.[46] It is not clear how the problem of matzoth (unleavened bread) during the Passover week was handled, especially during the three years of war, when wheat shortages developed. The ultra-Orthodox group would have been especially affected, as rituals concerning the grinding of the flour in addition to the manner of preparing the dough and baking had to be strictly observed.

COMMUNITY ORGANIZATIONS

Prior to the large number of refugees arriving in 1938, both the Baghdadi and Russian communities had each established institutions and organizational structures dealing with financial support, welfare, charity, burial, and other communal matters. These were, however, not sufficient to manage the massive aid effort required to help settle the refugees. Some form of cooperation between the two established communities was necessary, and both rose to the challenge, with the Sephardi community taking the lead, perhaps because they felt the pressure of the British more keenly than did the Russians. Even before ever-larger shiploads of refugees landed in Shanghai, the Shanghai Municipal Council had indicated that it could not be responsible for the Jews' maintenance; the burden would have to be shouldered by local Jewry.[47] As a result, several new organizations for relief purposes were established. Here I will discuss one community organization and two aid organizations only: burial societies, because of their importance in communal life, and two organizations responsible for refugee aid, the Committee for the Assistance of European Jewish Refugees (CAEJR) in Shanghai and HICEM.[48]

The ritual preparation of the corpse and burial have an important place in Jewish observances, and burial societies occupy a central position in all Jewish communities. In Shanghai, the Sephardi burial society (Hevra Kadisha) was established in 1862, probably at about the same time as the founding of its first cemetery on Mohawk Road (now Huangpu Road). The Russian community organized its burial society in 1922, having interred its dead in the Sephardi cemetery in a separate section until they acquired their own cemetery on Baikal Road (now Weiming Road). The refugees initially used both the Ashkenazi burial society and cemetery until finally they too organized their own burial society in 1940 and acquired land for their cemetery on Columbia Road. Due to the high mortality rate among the refugees, a fourth cemetery (on Point Road) was added in 1941.[49] In life as well as in death, the three communities maintained their separateness. Unfortunately, the four cemeteries were moved between 1957 and 1959 to Qingpu County in the environs of Shanghai and have since disappeared.[50]

The Committee for the Assistance of European Jewish Refugees was established in the fall of 1938 as an amalgamation of previous relief committees and brought together Baghdadis, Russians, and refugees.[51] Prominent businessmen active in Shanghai commerce assumed a major role, raising funds both locally and abroad. It is to the credit of men like Michel Speelman (ca. 1877–?) and Ellis Hayim (1894–1977), who without experience in social welfare nonetheless saw to it that the refugees were given shelter and were fed. The standing of these men in the business community enabled them, furthermore, to maintain contacts with the Shanghai Municipal Council and the Japanese authorities on behalf of the refugees.[52] The committee ceased to function after the start of the Pacific War, when British passport holders, such as Ellis Hayim, were interned by the Japanese. Thus in February 1943, when the Japanese authorities ordered the relocation of stateless refugees to the "designated area," or ghetto, in Hongkou, they also ordered the Russian communal association to assume the care of the refugees. The new committee was known as the Shanghai Ashkenazi Collaborating Relief Association, or SACRA.[53]

The HICEM office, under the direction of Meyer Birman (1891–1955), engaged in an unprecedented rescue operation that was just short of heroic. First in Harbin and then in Shanghai from September 1939 until December 1941, when the office was closed by the Japanese, Birman disseminated information about China and helped move refugees in and out of Shanghai. He wrote thousands of letters to relief agencies throughout the world, trying to help locate and relocate refugees. Despite limited funds, his office paid fees for border crossings and for documents required by the Shanghai Municipal Police, ship passage for visa holders, and the like. Birman tirelessly explored every avenue and followed every lead, both of how to bring Jews to the safe haven of Shanghai and, as the clouds of war gathered, of how to find other countries of refuge once routes from Shanghai increasingly closed down.[54]

EDUCATIONAL INSTITUTIONS AND PUBLISHING

Schools for the young developed, but slowly and in accordance with the needs and growth of the three communities. In the early years of the Baghdadi community, Jewish education for boys was taken care of at home. They were instructed in prayers and Bible by their fathers or the community's teacher (melamed), essentially a private tutor who taught the boys in their homes. But by 1902, a Hebrew school (Talmud Torah) for boys was established on the premises of the Shearith Israel synagogue. In time, this religious school developed into the Shanghai Jewish School with a British-based curriculum and instruction in English. Those who could afford it preferred, however, to send their children to British public schools, so only pupils from less-affluent Baghdadi families attended the Shanghai Jewish School.[55] Some Russian parents, particularly those who wanted their children educated in the British style, also sent their children to this school. Whereas socially the parents of Ashkenazi and Sephardi Jews remained distant, some of the younger generation interacted, at least during school hours.

Despite the fact that few of the Central European refugees brought families with school-age children and large families were quite the exception,[56] more school facilities were nevertheless required due to the influx. Sir Horace Kadoorie (1902–1995), well known for having endowed a number of educational institutions in China, Asia, and the Middle East, established in 1937 the Shanghai Jewish Youth Association (better known as the Kadoorie School). Instruction was also in English, and the curriculum included Hebrew, Bible studies, and Chinese. The nominal fee charged attracted children from less-well-off families.[57] As in the Shanghai Jewish School, the younger generation here too had an opportunity to interact.

The Organization for Rehabilitation through Training (ORT) vocational school fulfilled a vital function for older teenagers and adults from 1941 on by providing training in various skills and trades. Significantly, Russians cooperated with Sephardi Jews to make this vocational school a success.[58] William Deman, a refugee from Vienna, established on his own initiative a business school that offered training in office skills and languages. The Gregg School of Business (later Gregg College) also operated from 1941 on.[59] Finally, the Asia Seminar also should be mentioned. Creatively organized by W. Y. Tonn, who had pursued Chinese studies in Berlin, the seminar offered instruction in languages as diverse as Hebrew, Urdu, Sanskrit, Chinese, and Japanese from 1943 on. Its lecture series on Chinese thought and art added an intellectual dimension to the otherwise drab Hongkou existence.[60]

The rabbis and their students were part of the refugee community, yet they lived their lives separately from the others, as indeed they had done earlier in Kobe, where they had first landed after leaving Lithuania, and still earlier, in Poland. Once they were settled, the yeshiva students, under the guidance of their rabbis, resumed rigorous study schedules. The distance that separated their way of life from that of the secular Jews did not prevent, however, a number of refugee teenage boys from joining them, and in the Mir Yeshiva, they were apparently accepted by both teachers and students. It may have been the strictly regulated life of prayer and study that attracted the youngsters, or perhaps it was the better-quality food available among the ultra-Orthodox.[61] There is no denying, however, that the yeshiva students' unflagging devotion to study as well as their maintenance of ritual purity in daily life were exemplary.

Study in the yeshiva is the study of texts. Concerned about the scarcity of Talmudic books for their students, the rabbis decided to reproduce the books they had by lithography. They succeeded in finding a Chinese printer, and over time most of the titles of the Talmud were reprinted,[62] an accomplishment that was hailed as a "historic event" in the Yiddish press.[63]

Aside from this undertaking, a considerable number of Jewish newspapers and journals flourished in Shanghai, printing in German, Yiddish, and Russian. Although some of the weeklies or monthlies were short lived, publishing only a few issues before they folded, as a communication effort within each community, this publishing activity was a remarkable feat. Here I will mention only some of the papers. The *Jüdisches Nachrichtenblatt* and *Gemeindeblatt der jüdischen Gemeinde* addressed the religiously observant German refugee population. For secular German speakers, there was the *Shanghai Jewish Chronicle*, which had the longest run among the various publications; *Die Gelbe Post* was intended for the more intellectually inclined reader.[64] Russian readers read *Nasha Zhizn* (Our Life), which included a Yiddish page, later replaced by an English page. The religious party Agudat Yisrael published two Yiddish papers, *Di Yiddishe Shtime fun vaytn Mizrakh* (The Jewish voice from the Far East) and *Dos Vort* (The word). Last but not least was the English-language monthly *Israel's Messenger*, which served almost exclusively the Sephardi community and was the official organ of the Shanghai Zionist Association. More research is necessary to do full justice to this impressive publishing activity, of which the above is only the barest outline.[65] Nevertheless, from it we can safely conclude that the intellectual level of the three Jewish communities was remarkably high, not only consisting of readers, but also boasting a considerable number of writers whose contributions were featured in the papers.

The exodus from China after World War II was gradual, lasting well into the 1950s. A few Baghdadis, like members of the Kadoorie family, who had been pillars of the Shanghai community, resettled in Hong Kong, eventually finding their last resting place in the Hong Kong Jewish cemetery.[66] Undoubtedly, many Baghdadis might have considered remaining in Shanghai after the end of the war, yet the treaty port days were clearly over, and Shanghai would never be the same. Nor would they ever again be able to lead the kind of Jewish lives that they and their forebears had created in the treaty port. The Sephardi-Shanghai past was transformed into a time and place remembered.

Some of the Central European refugees returned to their countries of origin, but most opted for America or Israel, as did the majority of the Russian community, while others made their homes in Australia. The Judaism they had brought with them from Germany, Austria, or Russia had not essentially changed in Shanghai. Wherever they went thereafter, they would again be part of Jewish communities and congregations similarly observant or secular. Shanghai seems to have been no more than a passing episode of hardship in the lives of the ultra-Orthodox and yeshivoth, and they continued a life of study and prayer in their new environment, whether in Israel or the diaspora.

The erstwhile Shanghai-landers, as some like to refer to themselves, remember their China days with great fondness. If some had felt regrets over years lost,[67] such feelings vanished in time and are not perpetuated by the younger generation. In the last two decades, reunions have taken place and tours undertaken to Shanghai to revisit the homes where they once lived and where they were children or teenagers. Memories are kept alive (or undergo change) in documentaries about Shanghai-landers—in particular, the refugees among them—and in memoirs about their Jewish-Shanghai past.

JUDAISM IN CHINA TODAY

Except for Hong Kong and an incipient Shanghai community, today there are no organized Jewish communities with synagogues and Jewish institutions in China. Those individuals who identify themselves as Jewish in Kaifeng today are not Jewish in accordance with halakha. They are the descendants of Jews. Can we say that by following the reintroduced religious practices that they are now "Jewish"?[68] But perhaps whether Kaifeng Jews are, or are not, halakhically Jews does not matter to those who are interested in the revitalization of Kaifeng Judaism. Anson Laytner, for example, speaks of "reviving Jewish culture," and Len Hew, a descendant of the Zhao family, wants to revive the community. I would question the term *revival*, however, for it is surely not Qing dynasty Kaifeng Judaism that they wish to see revived. Nor is it obvious what is meant by "Jewish culture" and where to draw the line between culture and observing religious commandments (mitzvoth). Well meaning, no doubt, as these efforts at revival are, they raise a number of questions, including those of faith and belief.

Today Jews from Western countries and Israel work in China—150 are said to reside in Beijing—as transient businessmen and professionals. The largest number is in Shanghai, estimated at three hundred, and in 2002 the Shanghai Jewish Community Center was inaugurated.[69] But these Jews are only temporarily in China, remaining there for longer or shorter periods of time. They do not have synagogues, although services take place in Beijing and at several locations in Shanghai. The Ohel Rachel synagogue is not used for daily prayer.

Matters are different in Hong Kong. A small but vital Jewish community was reconstituted after World War II that has flourished ever since and has, in fact, grown larger than it was between the wars. Consisting of Ashkenazi and Sephardi Jews, this community represents the entire spectrum of Judaism, from Orthodox observance of the Habad movement to Reform Judaism. The Jewish Club, donated by Sir Eli Kadoorie (1867–1944) in 1909 to the community, is now the Jewish Community Center, and Ohel Leah, the synagogue built by Sir Jacob Sassoon in 1902, is still in use. Even though a large number of Hong Kong's Jews live there only temporarily, its nearly three thousand Jews are an interesting mix of descendants of old Sephardi families, Australians, South Africans, Americans, Israelis, and British, and their common language is English. Thus in this tiny corner of China, Judaism continues to flourish, not of Chinese Jews, but of Jews in China, many of whom, nonetheless, consider China their home.

REFERENCES

Abraham, Wendy. 2001. "History in the Making: First Chinese Descendant from Kaifeng Set to Study in Israel." *Points East* 16, no. 2: 1, 6.

Alboim, Avishai. 1999–2000. "D'fusei Shanhai v' 'She'erith haplita'" (Shanghai publishing and "Israel's remnant"). *Ma'ayan*, 74–86.

Altman, Avraham, and Irene Eber. 2000. "Flight to Shanghai, 1938–1940: The Larger Setting." *Yad Vashem Studies* 28:51–86.

Bar-Gal, Dvir. 2002. "Shanghai Agrees to Stop Jewish Gravestone Sale." *Jewish Chronicle* (2000).

Berger, P., and M. Schwab. 1913. "Le plus ancien manuscrit hébreu." *Journal Asiatique* 2 Ser. II: 139–175.

Bickers, Robert, and Christian Henriot. 2000. "Introduction." In *New Frontiers: Imperialism's New Communities in East Asia, 1842–1953*, 4–5. Manchester: Manchester University Press.

BIYS. 2002. *Bulletin Igud Yotsei Sin* 372:1.

Central Archive for the History of the Jewish People (CAHJP). 1941a. "DAL 101. Birman Letter to Polish Relief Committee." Melbourne, November 6, 1941, and November 13, 1941.

———. 1941b. "DAL 101. Birman Letter to JDC." December 2, 1941.

Cohen, Myron L. 1990. "Lineage Organization in North China." *Journal of Asian Studies* 49, no. 3: 509–534.

Deeg, Max, and Bernhard Scheid, eds. 2015. *Religion in China: Major Concepts and Minority Positions*, 65–89. Vienna: Verlag der österreichischen Akademie der Wissenschaften.

Eber, Irene. 1999. "The Interminable Term Question." In *Bible in Modern China: The Literary and Intellectual Impact*, edited by I. Eber, S. K. Wan, and K. Walf, with R. Malek, 135–161. Sankt Augustin: Monumenta Serica.

Eber, Irene, and Adrian Hsia. 2003. "A Focus for Remembering: The Jewish Cemetery in Hong Kong." *Pe'amim* 98–99:333–350 (in Hebrew).

EJ. 1971. *Encyclopedia Judaica.* Vol. 10. Jerusalem: Keter.

Fein, Yoni. 1945. "A lid vegn Shanghaier ghetto" (A song about Shanghai ghetto). *Unzer Vort, Zamelheft,* 27–30.

Ghosh, Amitav. 1992. *In an Antique Land.* Delhi: Ravi Dayal.

Heng, Chye Kiang. 1999. *Cities of Aristocrats and Bureaucrats: The Development of Medieval Chinese Cityscapes.* Honolulu: University of Hawai'i Press and Singapore University Press.

Hertsman, Yosef. 1999. *Mirer Yeshiva in Goles* (Mir Yeshiva in exile). Amherst: National Yiddish Book Center. (Reprint of 1950.)

Honig, Emily. 1992. *Creating Chinese Ethnicity: Subei People in Shanghai, 1850–1980.* New Haven: Yale University Press.

Joint Distribution Committee (JDC). 1958/1960. "RG 33-44, file 487." Letter from P. Udelevich, President, American Far Eastern Society, Inc., N.Y., to Igud Yotsei Sin, Tel Aviv, October 27, 1958, and P. I. Yudalevich, Chairman, Council of the Jewish Community, Shanghai, to Henri Elfenbein, AJDC, Geneva, January 6, 1960.

Kontras. 1960–1961. "D'fusei Shanghai (Shanghai printing)." *Kontras Hasefer Hatorani* (Pamphlets on scriptural literature), no. 9: 52–53.

Kranzler, David. 1976. *Japanese, Nazis and Jews: The Jewish Refugee Community of Shanghai, 1938–1945.* New York: Yeshiva University Press.

Kreissler, Françoise. 2000. "Ein Journalist im Exil in Shanghai: Adolph J. Storfer und die Gelbe Post." In Malek 2000, 511–524.

Laytner, Anson. 1982. "Rediscovering Remnants of Jews in China." *Heritage* 16.

Leslie, Donald D. 1972. *The Survival of the Chinese Jews: The Jewish Community of Kaifeng.* Leiden: E. J. Brill.

———. 1984. *The Chinese-Hebrew Memorial Book of the Jewish Community of K'aifeng.* Belconnen: Canberra College of Advanced Education.

Malek, Roman, ed. 2000. *Jews in China: From Kaifeng . . . to Shanghai.* Sankt Augustin: Monumenta Serica Institute.

Martin, W. A. P. 1866. "Affairs in China." *New York Times,* August 29, 1866, p. 2.

Meyer, Maisie. 2000. "The Sephardi Jewish Community in Shanghai and the Question of Identity." In Malek 2000, 345–373.

———. 2003. *From the Rivers of Babylon to the Whangpoo: A Century of Sephardi Jewish Life in Shanghai.* New York: University Press of America.

Neusner, Jacob, trans. 1984. *The Talmud of the Land of Israel: A Preliminary Translation and Explanation.* Vol. 26: *Qidushin.* Chicago: University of Chicago Press.

Overmyer, Daniel. 1976. *Folk Buddhist Religions: Dissenting Sects in Late Traditional China.* Cambridge: Harvard University Press.

Pollak, Michael. 1980. *Mandarins, Jews, and Missionaries.* Philadelphia: Jewish Publication Society of America.

Public Record Office (PRO). 1940. "Fo/371/24684, dispatch no. 567." Letter from A. H. George, Consul General, to Foreign Office, September 5, 1940.

Rabinowitz, Louis I., and Philip Grossman, trans. 1965. *The Code of Maimonides Book Five: The Book of Holiness.* New Haven: Yale University Press.

Shiba, Yoshinobu. 1983. "Sung Foreign Trade: Its Scope and Organization." In *China Among Equals: The Middle Kingdom and Its Neighbors, 10th to 14th Centuries,* edited by Morris Rossabi, 89–115. Berkeley: University of California Press.

Tobias, Sigmund. 1999. *Strange Haven: A Jewish Childhood in Wartime Shanghai.* Urbana: University of Illinois Press.

UL. 1942. "Nidpas beShanghai" (Printed in Shanghai), *Unzer Lebn* 54 (May 15,

1942). (*Unzer Lebn* was the Yiddish page in the Russian weekly *Nasha Zhizn.*)

Wang, Yisha. 1984. "The Descendants of the Kaifeng Jews." In *Jews in Old China: Studies by Chinese Scholars,* translated and edited by Sidney Shapiro, 167–187. New York: Hyppocrene Books.

Wei, Betty Peh-T'i. 1990. *Shanghai, Crucible of Modern China.* Oxford: Oxford University Press.

Werblowsky, R. J. Zvi. 1994. "A Note on the Jewish Community in Kaifeng: A Liturgical Perspective." In *Gnosisforschung und Religionsgeschichte—Festschrift für Kurt Rudolph zum 65. Geburtstag,* edited by H. Preissler and H. Seiwert, 587–595. Marburg.

White, William C. 1966. *White, Chinese Jews: A Compilation of Matters Relating to the Jews of K'aifeng Fu.* Part II. Toronto: University of Toronto Press.

Wren, Christopher. 1982. "Ancient Jews of China: The Last Trace Is Fading." *New York Times,* May 18, 1982.

Xu, Zhucheng. 1983. *Hatong Waizhuan* (Unofficial biography of Hardoon). Shanghai: Wuxing ji chuben.

Yad Vashem Archives (YVA). 1938/1939. Yad Vashem Archives, 078/85, "Shanghai Municipal Archives," cable from Philips, Secretary [Shanghai Municipal] Council to German Jewish Aid Committee, HIAS-ICA, Emigration Association, AJDC, December 23, 1938, and letter from the Shanghai Municipal Council to members of Council, April 12, 1939.

———. 1988. Yad Vashem Archives, 078/56B, "William Deman, Tagebuchblätter eines Heimatvertriebenen, ein verlorenes Jahrzehnt." Shanghai, 1939–1949.

NOTES

I thank Professor A. Altman for his careful comments on this essay and the Truman Research Institute of the Hebrew University of Jerusalem for its partial support of this research.

Sephardi communities were widespread throughout the Mediterranean countries, North Africa, and the Balkans but also in portions of Western and Central Europe. Sephardim have distinctive rituals and differences in liturgy and some traditions that differ from those of the Ashkenazim. Most of the Sephardim who came to Shanghai hailed originally from Iraq and are often also referred to as Baghdadis.

1. Deeg and Scheid 2005, 65–89.

2. A *selikhot*, or penitential prayer, written on paper and dating from the Tang dynasty was found in Dunhuang. As paper was not in general use in Europe at that time, it must be assumed that it was written in China by someone who left by the overland route (Berger and Schwab 1913, 139–175). Figurines of Persians and so-called Semitic merchants and musicians are well known. Among them are figurines in distinctive, non-Persian garb that could be of Jews from farther west or even from Franco-German lands.

3. The stelae were inscribed and erected to commemorate special events in communal life. The 1489 inscription commemorates the reconstruction of the synagogue buildings after the disastrous flood of 1461, and that of 1512, on the reverse side, provides supplementary information. The stone with the two 1663 inscriptions (now lost) was erected after the 1642 flood. The occasion for the 1679 inscription was the erection of the Zhao family archway. The Chinese texts can be found in White 1966, II, 35–39, 51–54, 80–85, 94–95, and 104–107.

4. Merchants from different places tended to band together for sea voyages, constituting a polyglot society that traded far and wide (Ghosh 1992). There is apparently a Kaifeng connection to both Persia and Yemen in the later liturgy of the Kaifeng Jews (Werblowsky 1994, 587–595).

5. Heng 1999.

6. Shiba 1983, 102–103.

7. Leslie 1972, 27–30.

8. The drawing is of the synagogue that was rebuilt in 1663 after it had been destroyed by a flood in 1642 caused by Li Zicheng (ca. 1605–1645) rebels cutting the Yellow River dikes in the waning days of the Ming dynasty.

9. Martin 1866, 2.

10. Leslie 1984. The memorial book was closed ca. 1670. It is now held at the Library of the Hebrew Union College in Cincinnati, Ohio.

11. White 1966, II, 94. For the Chinese texts of the inscriptions, I have used those reproduced in White.

12. Wang 1984, 183–184.

13. Cohen 1990, 513. Cohen points out that the Old Ancestor's grave was at the apex of a triangular arrangement of graves.

14. White 1966, II, 35, 52, 80.

15. White 1966, II, 83, 94, 104.

16. Leslie 1972, 108.

17. Overmyer 1976.

18. Leslie 1972, 86–90.

19. Leslie 1972, 154. Leslie doubts that they had Talmudic books but writes that they were definitely rabbinates.

20. White 1966, II, 66, 123–124; Leslie 1972, 47.

21. White 1966, II, 121–154.

22. White 1966, II, 80. Apparently the men who composed the inscriptions were not troubled, as would be later Protestant missionaries, by whether the term *Tian* truly reflected the monotheist concept. See Eber 1999.

23. White 1966, II, 81.

24. White 1966, I, 80.

25. White 1966, II, 35.

26. According to one of the Chinese creation myths, Pan Gu is the giant from whose body the world was created.

27. White 1966, II, 52.

28. White 1966, II, 52, 104.

29. I am grateful to Max Deeg, who, in his excellent conference lecture and essay (see Deeg and Scheid 2015), has helped me pinpoint the two aspects of time and space.

30. Pollak 1980, 235.

31. Shi Zhongyu, for example, remembered that during the spring festival, his father wrote Chinese characters with chicken blood on the door frame of his house "to guard against the devil." With minor variations, this story is repeated by others. Some remember Japanese soldiers searching for Jews in Kaifeng (Wren 1982; Laytner 1982).

32. A photocopy of a Shi family member's registration card is in the author's possession.

33. *EJ* 1971, 23. The *Mishnah* tractate *Qidushin* (3:12) of the Talmud states succinctly that the offspring of a gentile woman (married to a Jewish man) receive her status, to which Maimonides (Moses Ben Maimon; 1135–1204) added that the status of the father is not considered in this case (Neusner 1984, 201–202; Rabinowitz and Grossman 1965, 98). The Talmudic injunction is based on the biblical pronouncement (Ex. 19:6 and Lev. 20:26).

34. Pollak 1980, 235.

35. Abraham 2001, 1, 6.

36. Most of them had fled Poland for Lithuania before August 1940. They were able to obtain Curacao visas that, in turn, enabled them to procure Russian and Japanese transit visas. They arrived in Kobe and remained there until the Japanese shipped them to Shanghai.

37. Bickers and Henriot 2000, 4–5.

38. Wei 1990, 104.

39. Honig 1992 describes one such ethnic group, the much-maligned Subei people, who hailed originally from Jiangsu province, north of the Yangzi.

40. Silas Hardoon (1851–1931) was a colorful Shanghai personality who, perhaps influenced by his Eurasian wife, played a considerable role in Chinese affairs. For an anecdotal biography, see Xu 1983.

41. Kranzler 1976, 60–61.

42. Meyer 2000, 363. Meyer discusses this and other questions in greater detail elsewhere (Meyer 2003).

43. Kranzler 1976, 60, 79–80.

44. Reform congregations, for example, might or might not have separate seating for men and women, head coverings for men, a choir, an organ, and the like. The general term *reform* does not adequately describe these differences.

45. Hertsman 1999, 27.

46. Kranzler 1976, 410.

47. YVA 1938/1939.

48. HICEM stands for HIAS ICA-Emigdirect. The organization was supported by the American Jewish Joint Distribution Committee (JDC), the Hebrew Sheltering and Immigrant Aid Society (HIAS), and the London-based Jewish Colonization Association (ICA). The HICEM bureau was located in Harbin until September 1939, when it moved to Shanghai. The CAEJR was supported by the JDC and by funds raised in Shanghai.

49. Kranzler 1976, 425. I thank Ralph B. Hirsch for making available to me a list of "Central European Jewish Refugees Who Died in Shanghai, 1940–1945." The list—first published in the New York *Aufbau*, April 12, 19, and 26 and May 3, 1946—consists of 1,433 names. I thank Itamar Livny for his preliminary examination of the list, which shows that nearly twice as many men died than women in Shanghai and that infant mortality was comparatively higher than that of older children. The higher male mortality reflects, no doubt, the larger number of Jewish men in Shanghai. A more detailed analysis of the list should reveal further useful data.

50. JDC 1958/1960. In July 1958, the Jewish community was notified by the Chinese authorities that four thousand graves were to be moved. By January 6, 1960, three cemeteries had been moved. About current efforts to recover some of the gravestones, see Bar-Gal 2002.

51. Kranzler 1976, 93–96.

52. This sometimes backfired. For example, in 1940, Inuzuka Koreshige (1890–1965) demanded that Ellis Hayim write a letter stating how grateful the Jews were for the way the Japanese treated them. Hayim refused (PRO 1940).

53. Kranzler 1976, 521–522.

54. Altman and Eber 2000, 51–86. Birman's letters often reveal the desperation that must have been felt in Shanghai as war seemed inevitable. For example, on November 6, 1941, Birman wrote that Shanghai was cut off from most countries and, one week later, on November 13, 1941, that "the situation is growing steadily worse, Shanghai is now also cut off

from Central and South America" (CAHJP 1941a).

55. Meyer 2000, 365–366.

56. Large intact families were mostly found among the ultra-Orthodox from Poland. For example, according to Birman, in a group of ten rabbis, only three were without families. The others had four or five children each (CAHJP 1941b).

57. Meyer 2000, 369; Kranzler 1976, 390–391.

58. Kranzler 1976, 395–396.

59. YVA 1988, 124–126.

60. YVA 1988, 154–155.

61. Tobias 1999, 79.

62. Kranzler 1976, 434. According to Kranzler, nearly 100 titles were reprinted. Another list mentions 104 titles (Alboim 1999–2000, 74–86). *Kontras* (*Kontras* 1960–1961) states that between 1941 and 1942, the Mir Yeshiva published 56 or 58 titles of 100–150 copies each. The titles included prayer books and complete Bibles with commentaries (*Mikra'ot gedolot*).

63. *UL* 1942.

64. For more about the paper and its editor, see Kreissler 2000, 511–524.

65. The unpublished "Di Yiddishe Presse in Chine, 1937–1947," prepared by Asher Rozenboim and held by the Institute for Jewish Research Archive (YIVO/Yidisher Vissenshaftlikher Institut), lists forty-six Jewish publications in all of China. Unfortunately, only single issues of most of these papers are available. Some have disappeared altogether.

66. This is an unusually beautiful and interesting cemetery with its many styles of gravestones and varieties of inscriptions representing the different cultural backgrounds of Hong Kong Jewry. See Eber and Hsia 2003 (in Hebrew).

67. Fein 1945, 27–30.

68. This and other problems are also raised in a 1998 documentary *Minyan in Kaifeng*, in which a group of young Western Jews questions the many complex aspects of Jewish identity.

69. *BIYS* 2002, 1.

CHAPTER 3

Flight to Shanghai

1938–1939 and Its Larger Context

On November 24, 1938, the *Conte Verde* luxury liner docked at 2 P.M. alongside the Shanghai and Hongkou Wharf on the Shanghai side. Among the ship's 350 passengers were 187 German and Austrian refugees who were greeted by representatives of the International Committee for Granting Relief to European Refugees.[1] This was the first large contingent of refugees, and probably only some among the leaders in Shanghai's international community suspected that the trickle since August 1938 would in the next eight months turn into a flood. The refugees arrived mainly on German, Italian, and Japanese ships and to a lesser extent also on French liners. Between July 3 and 31, 1939, alone, eight ships (four Japanese, one Italian, three German), for the most part luxury liners, docked in Shanghai, with 1,315 refugees on board.[2] As late as September 18, 1939, after the start of World War II in Europe, the *Hakusan Maru* still brought seventy-nine more refugees.[3] Meanwhile, small numbers of refugees also reached Shanghai overland via Manchukuo (the Japanese puppet state) and from there by ship from Dairen. Toward the end of 1941, around twenty thousand refugees from Central Europe had found a haven in Shanghai.

Both the *Anschluß* in March 1938 and the *Kristallnacht* of November that year were, of course, major triggers for the Jewish exodus to Shanghai and elsewhere. Although in recent years a growing number of works, including memoirs, have dealt with the journey to and the years in Shanghai, these generally do not account for the context within which the flight took place.

It may be useful, therefore, to briefly examine other events and circumstances that made possible this sudden and unexpectedly large emigration of no more than eight months. Did Germany's economic interests in China and her diplomatic relations with Japan play a role? What function can be assigned to German-Japanese and German-Chinese relations concerning the Jewish exodus? And what was Shanghai like in 1938–1939, the crucial years of Jewish flight? How were these Central European Jews, deprived of their property and possessions, viewed by Shanghai's foreign powers?

In this essay, I will propose that Jews fleeing to Shanghai to avoid Nazi persecution were able to do so because by mid-1938 the larger context had taken shape. This context consisted of finding a solution to Germany's foreign currency problems, setting a new course in relations with Japan, and tightening Nazi control over Jewish emigration. Part of these three was the Gestapo's mobilization of the means for shipping Jews to Shanghai.

JEWISH IMMIGRATION TO SHANGHAI PRIOR TO 1938

After their assumption of power in March 1933, the Nazi regime's solution to the "Jewish problem" in Germany was to urge voluntary emigration. This was to be accomplished by restricting Jewish activities and segregating Jews from German society. As early as April 1933, Jews were by law excluded from holding public office.[4] A year after the infamous Nuremberg Laws of November 1935 were enacted, Herbert Hagen, head of the Security Service of the SS (*Sicherheitsdienst des Reichsführers-SS*),[5] described the steps necessary in the eventual *Entjudung* of Germany in a September 1936 proposal: (1) eliminate Jews from the economy; (2) bring greater political and legal pressure on Jews, forcing their departure; and (3) increase the technical possibilities for emigration. In this proposal, Hagen also mentioned China, saying only that, according to him, a number of Jews had immigrated there since 1934.[6] Actually, a group of twenty-six families, among them at least five well-known physicians, had reached Shanghai already at the beginning of November 1933.[7] At that time, and despite what could have been no more than a handful, German diplomatic circles at once noted the Jewish arrivals. They did not look kindly on this new phenomenon, and the German consulate in Beijing sent a telegram in December 1933 warning of the influx of Jewish physicians.[8] Even earlier, in August, the German Foreign Office received a warning from other quarters that Jewish professors who were dismissed from their universities were negotiating employment in China. It seemed doubtful, stated the informant, that such men were friendly toward us and should represent the new Germany.[9]

Some of these professionals went on to North China, like the physician Wolf Dubinski and the dentist Rosemarie Pfeil, who came to Shanghai in 1934 and, not finding anything suitable, traveled north to Qingdao, where both obtained permission to practice.[10] Others went to Nanjing, like the dentist Leo Karfunkel, who sought and obtained Chinese citizenship in January 1936 in order to open a practice.[11] But most seem to have remained in Shanghai. Aside from those who had settled elsewhere, by spring 1934, presumably eighty refugee physicians, surgeons, and dentists had arrived in Shanghai.[12] Nonetheless, conditions for acting on Hagen's tentative suggestion to consider China a destination for the Reich's Jews were not yet ripe, and it was not taken up in 1936. Not until two years later, after German East Asian diplomacy had undergone significant changes after Hitler had reshuffled his government and Nazi Party men were in full control of the Foreign Office, would the Gestapo give serious consideration to China and Shanghai as a destination for Jews.

GERMAN INTERESTS IN EAST ASIA, 1935–1939

Germany's Asian diplomacy was closely related to economic considerations and especially to the regime's shortage of foreign currency needed for imports. Her trade with China, which collapsed after Germany's defeat in World War I, had begun to revive after the mid-thirties. Germany exported machinery, metals, railroad construction materials, chemicals, fertilizers, pharmaceuticals, and dyes, and as time went on, increasingly armaments. Between 1935 and 1936, German exports to China increased appreciably,[13] and in 1937, this trade brought in close to eighty-three million *Reichsmark* in much-needed foreign currency. Moreover, 37 percent of Germany's total armament exports went to China.[14] The commercial relationships between the two governments were further extended in 1934 and 1935, when General Hans von Seeckt visited China. Subsequently, a German military mission was dispatched to Chiang Kai-shek, and increased Chinese weapons and heavy industry purchases were negotiated.[15]

However, it has also been pointed out that armaments constituted only 1 percent of Germany's total exports and that even a more aggressive export policy could not have solved her foreign currency crisis. Although it is claimed that weapon exports earned Germany little foreign currency,[16] they were direly needed for such imports as food—especially soybeans—raw materials for her industrial recovery, and after 1936, to help finance Göring's Four-Year Plan of rearmament.[17] Just how crucial the foreign currency question was emerges clearly from various sources, among them a German Foreign Office report of August 1938 sent to the Qingdao consulate, which stressed that Jewish capital transfers abroad must be forbidden "from economic considerations of our foreign currency interests."[18] Thus exports, even if other than arms, to Chiang Kai-shek's China were important in bringing in some foreign currency and, furthermore, gave the German Armed Forces Ministry access to much-needed tungsten imports from China.[19]

Together with her China trade, German diplomats also held commercial talks with Manchukuo, which resulted in the July 1938 trade accord. Although Manchukuo figured in her export interests, Germany rather wanted to obtain larger soybean imports, which she needed for scarce oils and animal fodder.[20] The accord was useful but did not solve the foreign currency problem.[21]

Supported by industrialists eager for export markets, the German Foreign Office under Constantin Freiherr von Neurath pursued a pro–Chiang Kai-shek policy. Meanwhile, Joachim von Ribbentrop, with his eyes on the Foreign Office, laid the groundwork for a pro-Japan policy, being well aware that the Japanese government was not happy with the Nazi regime's pro-Chiang stand. Ribbentrop's rise to power had begun already in 1933, when Hitler set him up in an advisory office on foreign policy. In the five years until he became foreign minister, Ribbentrop, together with Oshima Hiroshi,[22] developed a pro-Japan policy outside of Foreign Office channels, which was cemented by the Anti-Comintern Pact of November 1936, although meanwhile, the Foreign Office continued its pro-Chiang policy. A candid remark in an otherwise bland memoir by Herbert von Dirksen, German ambassador to Japan, describes the relationship between Ribbentrop's Bureau and the foreign ministry as a "state of war" in the course of which the latter was never informed about the former's talks and negotiations.[23] The foreign ministry was furthermore opposed to massive Jewish emigration to China, considering the Jewish presence detrimental to German commercial aims. Even Ribbentrop, after assuming power in 1938, could not entirely dismiss the Jews-or-trade problem; massive Jewish emigration to Shanghai, it was still feared, would jeopardize German commerce with China.[24]

Nonetheless, when in July 1937 Japanese and Chinese troops clashed in the so-called Lugouqiao (Marco Polo Bridge) Incident, the "undeclared war" that followed made it imperative to resolve the pro-Japan or pro-China policy issue. This occurred at last when Hitler announced Germany's recognition of Manchukuo in his Reichstag speech of February 1938 (the agreement was signed later in May), thus signaling the end of Germany's pro-China policy. The Japanese were well satisfied when, in April 1938, Göring also ordered the cessation of weapon exports to Chiang Kai-shek[25] and when, in May, the military advisers were recalled even though Germany continued to recognize Chiang Kai-shek's government until July 1941.[26]

The move from a pro-China to a pro-Japan foreign policy in East Asia took place within the context of Hitler's major reshuffling of his government. In February 1938, Hjalmar Schacht, minister of the economy, was replaced, and Ribbentrop replaced von Neurath as foreign minister; Trautmann, ambassador to China, went on indefinite leave, and von Dirksen was reassigned.[27] German commercial circles may not have been aware, however, that as a result of these developments in early 1938, Hitler's expansionist plans (even if he thereby acquired more Jews to be gotten rid of) were beginning to take precedence over export markets.[28] Within the changed context of 1938, the possibility of forcing the departure of German and Austrian Jews to China (and confiscating their foreign currency assets), mentioned by Hagen in 1936, was raised again.

One other event is significant and no doubt had a role in the Gestapo's decision to explore China and Shanghai as a destination for forced Jewish emigration. This was the conference in Évian-les-Bains, which met July 6–15, 1938, to discuss the refugee question. Proposed by President Franklin D. Roosevelt for the purpose of mobilizing international support in solving what was becoming a major crisis, the conference was attended by thirty-two countries. The results of the conference were vastly disappointing. An increase in the U.S. quota was not forthcoming, nor were the participating nations willing to open their doors to immigration.[29] A report on Évian circulated by the German Foreign Office stated clearly, "Nearly all countries characterized Jewish immigration as a burden and rejected raising their quotas."[30]

Finally, the revamping of the Reich Representation of German Jews (*Reichsvertretung der deutschen Juden*) into the Reich Association of Jews in Germany (*Reichsvereinigung der Juden in Deutschland*), completed in February 1939, was also important.[31] Controlled by the Ministry of the Interior, the association was in effect closely supervised by the Reich Security Main Office (RSHA, *Reichssicherheitshauptamt*) under Reinhard Heydrich. Section IV of the Main Office was the Gestapo, and IV B4, under Adolf Eichmann,[32] was responsible for Jews.[33] Jewish emigration, a major function of the association, thus was directly supervised by Eichmann and his cohorts. The pressure that was exerted to force emigration is reflected in the following communication from the *Hilfsverein*: "Please trust us when we tell you that we are unable to diminish emigration from Germany, and the only possibility to prevent our people from going to such places as Shanghai ... [consists in finding other places]." Colonization schemes under consideration by the Jewish organizations, pleaded the letter, "might come too late for a very great part of German Jewry."[34]

On orders from Eichmann, Heinrich Schlie of the Vienna Hanseatic Travel Office was dispatched sometime in early February 1939 to the Japanese and Chinese consulates to ascertain their attitudes toward sending large numbers of Jews to China.[35] The Japanese were not enthusiastic.[36] But Japanese policy was, as we shall see, not to antagonize the Germans, who were, after all, allies and who, as was well known in Japanese circles, wanted to rid themselves of the Jews. The Chinese, on the other hand, were amenable to Schlie's proposal, even offering pro-forma visas for illegal entry to Palestine, with fees and bribes to be settled later. Nor were they opposed to special refugee ships equipped to carry large numbers of people at any time.[37] Despite the lukewarm Japanese response, Schlie and the Gestapo nevertheless began to explore possibilities of using chartered ships for voyages to Asia.[38] One chartered vessel, the *Usaramo*, did, in fact, land in Shanghai on June 29, 1939, with 459 refugees on board.[39]

THE SHANGHAI SCENE, 1938–1939

Beneath the glittering facade of an international metropolis, there persisted a profound sense of unease ever since August 1937, when hostilities broke out between Chinese and Japanese armed forces in and around Shanghai. In 1938, Shanghai consisted of three distinct areas: the International

Settlement, with its extraterritorial rights, together with Hongkou across the Suzhou Creek; the French Concession; and the Chinese districts and neighborhoods that had developed around the foreign enclaves. The Chinese were, however, not confined to these, and a considerable Chinese population also resided in the foreign areas. Japanese merchants, who began to arrive toward the end of the nineteenth century, settled in ever-increasing numbers in the Hongkou district. Although they outnumbered the British already by 1915, they did not then or later attempt to establish a concession along the lines of the European model.[40] By the summer of 1938, the Japanese population was nearing forty thousand.[41]

Shanghai was a mosaic of discrete districts; it was also a mosaic of different kinds of people, of no less than forty-seven different nationalities.[42] According to the 1935 census, 1,120,860 Chinese and 28,583 foreigners were in the International Settlement; 479,294 Chinese and 18,899 foreigners (not including the White Russians) were in the French Concession; and in the Chinese municipality were 2,089,007 Chinese and 10,125 foreigners.[43] The more than three million Chinese vastly outnumbered the foreigners, especially after the 1937 clashes in the vicinity of Shanghai, when refugees poured into the city.[44]

Among the foreign community in the International Settlement, there were no more than one thousand Baghdadi Jews, most of whom had come via India and were closely identified with British interests. The Russian Jewish community, consisting largely of people who had fled the Bolshevik Revolution and were partly domiciled in the French Concession, was larger, with approximately six thousand souls.[45] But both communities were obviously a small minority within Shanghai's population generally. Unobtrusive at first, the Jewish presence became more visible after the refugee influx.

Superimposed on Shanghai's complex society was a no-less-complex government structure. The International Settlement, governed by the Shanghai Municipal Council (SMC), was not sovereign territory and was merely empowered by the governments of the council's members to carry out decisions taken by the consular body, which represented their sovereign countries. In comparison, the consul-general in the French Concession had sole charge, and his appointed council implemented his orders.[46] Yet another system of government was that in the Chinese parts of Shanghai, where, since the autumn of 1937, when the Japanese occupied the Chinese

districts of Shanghai, a succession of Japanese-controlled puppet administrations came into being. Since the Nanjing regime (established in 1938) was
not recognized by the British or by any other treaty power—the Japanese
extended its recognition only in March 1940—Shanghai in 1938 was not
legally within any sovereign power's jurisdiction.[47] As a result of the armed
clashes in 1937, moreover, and the subsequent Japanese occupation of Chinese Shanghai, Hongkou, where most of the refugees came to live, became
for all practical purposes detached from the council's jurisdiction and was
run by the Japanese Special Landing Party.[48]

During the 1937 hostilities, shipping came to a halt, and Shanghai's ports
remained closed even after the fighting in the Chinese parts of Shanghai
had subsided. By November 1937, the Japanese had brought in nearly
250,000 armed forces, dislodging the Nationalists from their positions in
the Chinese districts and leaving much of the Chinese districts in rubble,
particularly in Hongkou, where some of the fiercest battles had taken place.
Disturbances, mainly by Chinese guerillas, did not cease even in 1938, and
sporadic gunfire continued to be heard in the foreign areas.[49] But business
activities gradually resumed in the first part of 1938, though Yangzi shipping
to the interior remained closed to all but the Japanese.[50]

Meanwhile, Chinese installations located in the International Settlement were gradually closed or taken over by the Japanese.[51] Japanese censors
were installed in the Chinese Telegraph Administration in November 1937,
in the Wireless Administration in January 1938, and in the Post Office in
March. The Chinese radio station was taken over by the Japanese, and
restrictions on Chinese newspapers took effect in spring 1938. The Japanese, furthermore, consistently refused to restore SMC jurisdiction over
its "sphere of authority" in Hongkou and Yangzipu.[52]

The general instability was further exacerbated by the struggle
between the two puppet regimes, the government in Nanjing and the Chinese municipal administration in Shanghai, each vying for domination
over Shanghai and its revenues. Assassinations and terrorist attacks were
common events. The ever-more aggressive and insolent tone adopted by
the Japanese authorities led to mounting anxiety over Shanghai's instability, which is reflected in the quarterly consular reports sent to the British
Foreign Office.[53] Thus when the *Conte Verde* landed the first large contingent of Jewish refugees in November 1938, businesses in Shanghai had
good reason to be jittery.

SOME RESPONSES TO THE REFUGEES' ARRIVAL

But we must retrace our steps to the closing weeks of 1938. Neither the SMC nor the Japanese welcomed the refugees with open arms. They could not keep them out, however, because what is usually described as no visa requirements for Shanghai was, by the time the refugees began to arrive, the absence of passport control.[54] Until the outbreak of the Sino-Japanese War, the Nationalist government had been in charge of this function, but after its office ceased to exist, no other country represented in Shanghai was empowered to exercise passport control, and the consular body was not about to ask the Japanese to take charge.[55]

The Japanese were in a quandary. Germany was Japan's ally, and since the refugees carried German passports, they could hardly press for preventing their entry. Nor could they jeopardize their relationship with the United States, where they believed Jews exercised extraordinary power. Since early December 1938, the Japanese consul-general in Shanghai had been in touch with Foreign Minister Arita in Tokyo regarding the refugees. How to handle this new situation is made abundantly clear in a secret dispatch of December 1938 between the two: "There is no question that it is necessary to make certain that the Jewish problem does not affect Japanese-German friendly relations. However, the manner in which the problem is handled immediately has [also] an effect . . . on our operations *vis-à-vis* America."[56] The SMC, on the other hand, and mainly the British were troubled by the economic situation and how thousands of destitute refugees would be housed and fed with no public funds at the SMC's disposal and at a time when the Settlement barely coped with the Chinese refugees.[57] Categorically refusing to assume responsibility for the newcomers, the secretary of the SMC sent a telegram to the London-based Council for German Jewry, the Paris HICEM, and the American Jewish Joint Distribution Committee in which he threatened, "[The] Council may be compelled to take steps to prevent further refugees landing in the International Settlement."[58] Over the next nine months, the correspondence that followed between embassies and consulates, reporting on contacts with German and Italian offices, raised two major issues: Who would pay for supporting the new arrivals, and what measures might be taken to stop the refugees from departing Europe in the first place?

The latter was the main concern. Neither for political nor for economic reasons was Germany or Italy willing to curtail the refugee traffic, which was, moreover, bringing in handsome additional earnings for the shipping lines. The British, however, feared that, unless halted, British and foreign interests would suffer, as the Japanese were liable to institute passport inspections.[59] Indeed, according to a police informant, the Japanese authorities, concerned about the presence of communist and procommunist elements among the refugees, were discussing measures for establishing a passport examination system on ships docking in Shanghai.[60]

The British were, furthermore, troubled by the specter of anti-Semitism. This was first pointed out in a confidential communication to Sir Herbert Phillips, British consul-general: "It seems to me that a large influx of Jewish refugees would have most upsetting results here, and we certainly do not want anti-Semitic problems added to our Shanghai problems."[61] Anti-Semitism was also raised by the British Foreign Office, which worried that it might be "exploited to embarrass the British authorities on the spot."[62] British fears were quite justified, for the Japanese actively supported militant fascist and pro-Japanese elements among the thirty-thousand-strong White Russian population, which was not known for its pro-Jewish sentiments. Anti-Semitic leaflets in English had appeared, which attacked "by name" influential, wealthy British and Iraqi Jewish families in Shanghai. A campaign against admitting more Jews had started in the Japanese-controlled Russian and Chinese press, labeling Jews, according to some reports, as "bearers of the Communist virus."[63]

Thus the Japanese-controlled Chinese-language *Xin Shenbao* (*New Shenbao*)[64] printed anti-Semitic views, apparently designed to raise apprehension among Shanghai's Chinese population about the newcomers. In addition to the threat of numerous communists among the refugees,[65] there was the more ominous suggestion of a Jewish capitalist takeover. The Jewish problem had become an East Asian problem, stated one article, since those Jews who came to Shanghai earlier had already established themselves in business and amassed capital. It claimed that within twenty-five years, the wealth of China's economy might very well gravitate into Jewish hands, and Jews would then be able to control China.[66]

But neither propaganda nor British diplomatic efforts and consular consultations[67] succeeded in limiting the refugee influx until early fall 1939. The near cessation of the refugee flow after only eight months was, however, again the result of a new configuration of circumstances. Scarce ship accommodations had been a problem all along,[68] and these were further reduced by the outbreak of war in Europe when German vessels no longer sailed to Shanghai. Beyond the one chartered liner, the Germans did not see their way to further invest foreign currency, and elsewhere no efforts were made to charter ships for Shanghai-bound Central European Jews.

The move to stop the refugee influx was initiated by the Japanese in August 1939, when they announced the closure of Hongkou to refugee residence.[69] The British followed suit with an even stronger measure, declaring the port itself closed to refugee traffic.[70] Thus under Japanese pressure, but with eager British consent, the Shanghai Municipal Council (partially reversing itself) evolved a formula some two months later for limiting the number of Jewish refugees in Shanghai and instituted a system of permits and "show money." With their focus on Shanghai, which had no passport control, Eichmann, Hagen, and others had miscalculated Japan's response to the Jewish presence. Nor had they sufficiently considered the tense atmosphere in the treaty port or the reaction of the Municipal Council to the refugee influx. The next chapter in the Shanghai destination—with its gates already partially closed—would be increasingly dictated by the Japanese and the interests they pursued in China.

NOTES

This essay was part of a larger research project undertaken together with my colleague Professor Avraham Altman about the Jewish communities in China under Japanese occupation. I wish to thank the J. K. Fairbank Center for East Asian Research, Harvard University, for its hospitality during my 1996–1997 sabbatical leave, when this research was carried out, and the Andover-Newton Theological School, where I was Judson Visiting Professor.

1. *The China Press*, November 26, 1938, 3. The International Committee (abbreviated as IC) was organized in August 1938, with Paul Komor as its honorary secretary and treasurer. For more on Komor, see David Kranzler, *Japanese, Nazis, and Jews: The Jewish Refugee Community of Shanghai, 1938–1945* (New York, 1976), 91–92.

2. Shanghai Municipal Police Files, 1894–1944, Records of the Central Intelligence Agency, RG 263 (henceforth SMP), D54422

(c), police reports dated July 3, July 7, July 9, July 15, July 24, and July 31, 1939.

3. Ibid., September 18, 1938.

4. Howard Margolian, "Bureaucracy and the 'Jewish Question' in Prewar Nazi Germany: The Nuremberg Legislation of 1935 as a Case Study," in *Holocaust Studies Annual 1991: General Essays*, ed. Sanford Pinsker and Jack Fischel (New York–London, 1992), 69–70.

5. English translations of German offices are according to Israel Gutman, ed., *Encyclopedia of the Holocaust*, 4 vols. (New York–London, 1990).

6. "Report by SS Oberscharführer Hagen on Jewish Emigration," September 13, 1936, in *The Holocaust: Selected Documents in Eighteen Volumes*, ed. John Mendelsohn (New York–London, 1982), 1:40–57.

7. SMP, D 5422, police report dated November 7, 1933. The five prominent doctors were Rosenthal, Löwenberg, Hess, Elchengrun, and Kleinwald.

8. The telegram, dated December 4, is mentioned in Yad Vashem Archives (henceforth YVA), JM/4857, M. Fischer, Peiping, to the Foreign Office, Berlin, March 17, 1934. A copy was sent to the German embassy.

9. YVA, JM 11701, Dr. Mohr, East Asian Organization Hamburg–Bremen, to Dr. Altenburg, East Asian Division, Foreign Office, Berlin, August 8, 1933. Mohr also mentioned that a Chinese student who had studied with a professor Kaestner advised him to go to China.

10. YVA, JM/4857, Bracklo of the German consulate in Qingdao to the Foreign Office, Berlin, April 14, 1934. According to the latter, Dubinski was not a German citizen and claimed to be a Christian, but former Russians considered him Jewish, and he moved—according to them—in Jewish circles.

11. YVA, JM 11701, M. Fischer, German Embassy, Nanjing, to German Consulate Hankou, September 17, 1937.

12. The China Press, November 26, 1938, 3.

13. See H. G. W. Woodhead, ed., The China Yearbook 1938 (Shanghai, n.d.), 44–45, 59. German exports to China rose by 46 percent between 1935 and 1936, from $105,385,294 to $150,238,093.

14. Karl Drechsler, Deutschland—China—Japan 1933–1939, das Dilemma der deutschen Fernostpolitik (Berlin, 1964), 13, 54.

15. Ibid., 17–18. See also Julius Epstein, "Seeckt und Tschiang-Kai-Schek," in Wehrwissenschaftliche Rundschau 3, no. 11 (1953): 534–543. According to Seeckt's memorandum, he recommended importing weapons plants from European firms instead of building factories, which, of course, would benefit German suppliers.

16. Willi A. Boelcke, Die deutsche Wirtschaft, 1930–1945 (Düsseldorf, 1983), 109, 100. See also, however, Herbert von Dirksen, Moskau, Tokio, London. Erinnerungen und Betrachtungen zu 20 Jahren deutscher Außenpolitik, 1919–1939 (Stuttgart, 1949), 185, who writes that a number of German firms earned considerable sums in the arms trade with China.

17. Avraham Barkai, Das Wirtschaftssystem des Nationalsozialismus. Ideologie, Theorie, Politik, 1933–1945 (Frankfurt, 1988), 211–213.

Jewish money in 1938 helped partially relieve the foreign currency crunch.

18. YVA, JM/4857, Foreign Office, Berlin, August 13, 1938, 7. This document is a long report on the Évian Conference.

19. Otto J. Seiler, Einhundert Jahre Ostasienfahrt: Der Hapag-Lloyd AG, 1886–1996 (Hapag-Lloyd, n.d.), preface 1986, 97, records ninety journeys to East Asia in 1938, of which the great majority were freighters. See also von Dirksen, Moskau, Tokio, London, 185.

20. See Kungtu C. Sun, The Economic Development of Manchuria in the First Half of the Twentieth Century (Cambridge, 1969), 58–59. Soy beans and gaoliang were Manchukuo's major agricultural products. Soy bean production was exceptionally high between 1936 and 1938 and was accompanied by high export figures.

21. According to the North China Herald, May 13, 1936, 281, the decline of German foreign currency reserves led to reduced soy bean imports in 1936. See also "German-Manchu Trade Accord Concluded," in The North China Herald, July 27, 1938, 153. The accord was essentially a barter agreement, according to which German and Manchukuo imports were to double. Nonetheless, Germany continued to import more than Manchukuo.

22. According to Michael Bloch, Ribbentrop (New York, 1992), 81, both Oshima and Ribbentrop believed that Germany and Japan were "natural allies." First appointed as a military attaché to the Berlin embassy, Oshima became Japan's ambassador in October 1938.

23. Dirksen, Moskau, Tokio, London, 168; Bloch, Ribbentrop, 96.

24. YVA, RG 051/0So/File 41, note, signature illegible, from Kurt Lischka's office II 112, with copy to the Vienna Central Office, Berlin, May 31, 1939; note, signature illegible, from Lischka's office II 112, with copy to the Vienna Central Office, Berlin, June 8, 1939; telegram from Dr. Knochen, Chief of Security Main Office (Sicherheitshauptamt) to the Central Office, Vienna (?), June 14, 1939. The telegram is the record of a discussion between Hagen and Eichmann. Lischka was the head of the Berlin Reich Centre for Jewish Emigration.

25. Ordering the end of exports was apparently easier than stopping shipments.

On November 24, 1938, *The China Press* still reported the arrival in Mandalay of a German ship carrying six thousand tons of ammunition. The ammunition was to reach the Chinese via Yunnan province.

26. Bloch, *Ribbentrop*, 344.

27. Other major changes gave Hitler control over the military when the minister of war, Werner von Blomberg, and the supreme army commander, Werner von Fritsch, were also removed.

28. Boelcke, *Die deutsche Wirtschaft*, 193.

29. See Henry L. Feingold, *The Politics of Rescue: The Roosevelt Administration and the Holocaust, 1938–1945* (New Brunswick, NJ, 1970), 22–68, for an extensive summary of the conference and the negotiations that followed. According to Feingold, Roosevelt was to blame for wanting to "conceal the largely Jewish character of the refugee crisis" (35).

30. YVA, J4 JM57, dated August 13, 1938, signature illegible.

31. The actual document of its establishment was dated July 1939. See *Documents on the Holocaust: Selected Sources on the Destruction of the Jews of Germany and Austria, Poland, and the Soviet Union*, ed. Yitzhak Arad, et al. (Oxford–New York, 1981), 139–143. Article 1, paragraph 2, states, "The purpose of the Reichsvereinigung is to further the emigration of Jews."

32. Eichmann had made a name for himself in the Vienna Central Office for Jewish Emigration (Zentralstelle für Jüdische Auswanderung), when between August and October 1938, he presumably caused fifty thousand Jews to depart. His efforts were viewed with great interest by Hagen in Berlin's Security Main Office. In November 1938, the Vienna "model" was recommended by Heydrich for Germany. Hans Safrian, *Eichmann und seine Gehilfen* (Frankfurt a.M., 1995), 38, 47.

33. For the establishment of the Reich Association, see Shaul Esh, "The Establishment of the 'Reichsvereinigung der Juden in Deutschland' and Its Main Activities," *Yad Vashem Studies* 7 (1968): 19–38.

34. Central Archive for the History of the Jewish People (henceforth CAHJP), DAL 76.1, from Hilfsverein to HICEM, Harbin, February 10, 1939, signed by A. Prinz,

F. Bischofswerder, and V. Loewenstein. Copy sent to the Council for German Jewry, London. HICEM was an amalgamation of three Jewish agencies founded in 1927 and concerned with the emigration of Jewish refugees. See also American Joint Distribution Committee (henceforth JDC), RG 33/44, file 457, Theodore C. Achilles, chairman, Departmental Committee on Political Refugees to George C. Warren, President's Advisory Committee on Political Refugees, March 31, 1939. Achilles quoted from Mr. Pell's talk with Berlin Jewish leaders who, above all, needed to get people out and were "ready to yield to the pressure of the secret police and enticements of the shipping companies."

35. Chinese consulates of the Guomindang Nationalist government continued to function in Europe. A number of Jews obtained visas there to immigrate to Yunnan province, which was under Nationalist control. See CAHJP, 86.3, Birman to Reichsvereinigung, August (?), 1940; DAL 99, from M. Birman to HICEM, Marseilles, August 1, 1941.

36. YVA, 051/oSo/41, copy of a letter to the Japanese consulate in Berlin, sent to Herbert Hagen from Hanseatic Travel Office, February 17, 1939. In his cover letter, Schlie states that the Japanese reception was cool because, according to them, the Chinese use the Jews for espionage.

37. YVA, 051/oSo/41, report from Schlie, March 5, 1939.

38. YVA, 051/oSo/41, Schlie to (?), June 28, 1939; Eichmann to Hagen, June 2, 1939.

39. See Claus Rothke, *Deutsche Ozean-Passagierschiffe, 1919 bis 1985* (Berlin, 1987), 47. The *Usaramo* of the *Deutsch-Ostafrika Linie* had a 250-passenger capacity. With nearly double the number, the refugees must have been packed in tightly. The 459 figure is according to SMP, D 5422 (c), police reports on ship arrivals, January–July, 1939. According to *The China Press*, June 28, 1939, 2, there were only 339 passengers on board. I assume that the police report is more accurate.

40. Mark R. Peattie, "Japanese Treaty Port Settlements in China, 1895–1937," in *The Japanese Informal Empire in China, 1895–1937*, ed. Peter Duus et al. (Princeton, NJ, 1989), 181, 184.

41. *The North China Herald*, August 24, 1938, 328.

42. *Newspaper Directory of China (Including Hong Kong) and Advertising Manual, 1937* (Shanghai, n.d.), 121.

43. F. C. Jones, *Shanghai and Tientsin, with Special Reference to Foreign Interests* (London, 1940), 1–2.

44. "Influx of Refugees to the International Settlement," SMP, D 8039A/7, folder no. 1, February 16, 1938, lists 34,204 refugees in numerous settlement camps.

45. *The Shanghai Evening Post and Mercury*, October 28, 1940, 2.

46. Jones, *Shanghai and Tientsin*, 22.

47. For pre-occupation Chinese Shanghai, see Jian Shenghuang, "Yu Hongjun yu Shanghai shizheng, 1927–1938" (Yu Hongjun and the Shanghai administration, 1927–1938), *Guoshiguan guangkan (The Academia Sinica Historical Journal)*, no. 5 (December 1988): 101–130.

48. Peattie, "Japanese Treaty Port Settlement," 200. The Japanese Special Naval Landing Party was stationed in Hongkou since 1927. In fact, the Japanese had increasingly made inroads in Shanghai's trade and government ever since 1932. See William C. Johnstone, *The Shanghai Problem* (Stanford, 1937), 288–289.

49. Robert W. Barnett, *Economic Shanghai: Hostage to Politics, 1937–1941* (New York, 1941), 14–17. See also Jonathan D. Spence, *The Search for Modern China* (New York–London, 1990), 446–447.

50. *The China Press*, November 18, 1938, 1. The Japanese vowed to keep the river closed until the Nationalist government was destroyed.

51. Public Record Office (henceforth PRO), FO 371/22129, report ending December 31, 1937.

52. Barnett, *Economic Shanghai*, 26.

53. For example, PRO, FO 371/2350, report ending September 30, 1939.

54. YVA, 078/85, "Consular Body Unable to Halt Refugee Flow from Europe to S'hai," *Shanghai Times*, February 5, 1939.

55. JDC, RG 33/44, file 457, M. Speelman, "Report on the Jewish Refugees Problem." Speelman emphasized that the Japanese military authorities could assume passport control "only at the unanimous request of the whole Consular body. Such a request is entirely out of the question."

56. Japan Ministry of Foreign Office, S series, reel no. 414, frame 903–904, Foreign Minister Arita to Consul-General Goto, Shanghai, December 30, 1938. My thanks to Professor Avraham Altman for making the translation available to me.

57. In addition to the Chinese refugees, there was also a considerable number of Russian, Iraqi, and British Jews made homeless by the 1937 hostilities in Hongkou and Yangzipu. For these, the Shanghai Jewish community shouldered the burden. See JDC, RG 33/44, file 457, report from Shanghai, dated March 2, 1939, forwarded from JDC, Paris to New York.

58. YVA, RG 078/85, Shanghai Municipal Archives, December 23, 1938.

59. PRO, FO 371/24079, W519, 5, Foreign Office cable to the ambassador in Shanghai, January 10, 1939.

60. SMP, D 5422, police report dated December 13, 1938. See also Günter Nobel and Genia Nobel, "Erinnerungen: Als politische Emigranten in Schanghai," *Beiträge zur Geschichte der Arbeiterbewegung* 21, no. 6 (June 1979): 882–890, who mention a group of around a dozen German party members.

61. YVA, RG 078/85, Shanghai Municipal Archive, unsigned to Sir Herbert Phillips, December 28, 1938.

62. PRO, FO 371/24079, W5686/519/48, Randall to the Board of Trade, May 16, 1939.

63. PRO, FO 371/23509, political report ending December 31, 1938. See also *China Press*, October 2, 1938, 2, which describes the anti-Semitic content of one such pamphlet. Marxism and Bolshevism had been coupled with Jews even earlier in Shanghai's German newspapers. See SMP, D-6961-D-6964, translation from the *Deutsche Schanghai Zeitung*, September 6, 1935.

64. The daily began publication in 1938 and was started by a Japanese journalist as the Chinese translation of the daily *Shanghai godo*. See *The China Yearbook, 1938–1939* (Chungking, 1939), 700–701; Frederick Wakeman Jr.,

Badlands, Wartime Terrorism and Urban Crime, 1937–1941 (Cambridge, 1996), 10.

65. "Chise Youtairen lai Hu hou, Bai'e shengji beiduo" (After red Jews come to Shanghai, White Russians are deprived of their livelihood), *Xin shenbao (New Shenbao)*, December 18, 1938, 7.

66. "Zhongguo he Youtairen wenti" (China and the Jewish problem), *New Shenbao*, September 29, 1939, 2.

67. PRO, W 2061, to the ambassador at Shanghai, February 4, 1939.

68. PRO, FO 371/24079, L. M. Robinson, British consulate general, Hamburg, to Sir George Ogilvie-Forbes, British Embassy, Berlin, January 10, 1939, who wrote that Italian ships are booked full until June and July.

69. YVA, 078/86, Shanghai Municipal Archives, memorandum received by the SMC secretariat August 9, 1939. This is an unsigned copy of the memorandum.

70. PRO, FO 371/24079, W 12030, to the British ambassador, Shanghai, August 15, 1939.

Translating the Ancestors

CHAPTER 4

A Critical Survey of Classical Chinese Literary Works in Hebrew

Translating literature written in Western languages was part and parcel of the development of modern spoken and written Hebrew.[1] But together with these translations, new readers of Hebrew, from their humble beginnings in nineteenth-century Europe and in British Mandate Palestine (1920–1948) to large numbers of present-day Israelis, have demanded translations from other works of literature as well. Chinese works began to be translated into Hebrew via intermediary languages around seventy years ago. This translating activity continues into the present day, as in the last ten years both translators and publishers have been exploiting an increasingly large market for foreign and, more recently, "exotic" or mystic literature.

More important, however, are direct translations from the original Chinese into Hebrew, which have become increasingly available during the last three decades. These translations—from philosophy, fiction, and to a lesser extent, poetry—are the work of a small and dedicated group of Hebrew speakers and native-born Israelis. The latter acquired mastery of Chinese at Israeli and foreign universities as well as in China (Eber 1996). Because of the excellence of these renditions directly from Chinese, these translators have been welcomed by a growing academic community of students and teachers. Their translations are, however, generally aimed at a larger public, and the popularity of their publications is also due to extraliterary factors: the establishment of diplomatic relations between Israel and China in 1991, subsequent tourism to China, and greater exposure to China on

Israeli television in recent years. Distorted as these media images often are, fueling an appetite for the exotic rather than providing accurate information, they nonetheless create a demand for better and more sophisticated information about China and the Chinese people.

In the following survey, I shall discuss works translated from intermediary languages as well as those translated directly from Chinese. In both cases, their quality as translations or literary works will be evaluated. Some translations of modern writers are included in this essay to highlight the changing interests of Hebrew readers, on the one hand, and the commercialization of translating, on the other. But first, some brief remarks are necessary regarding two major problems connected with written Hebrew and Chinese. Standard written Hebrew omits vowels, which, if they were written, would appear in the form of diacritical marks below the consonants. Hebrew speakers readily recognize unvoweled words when they are familiar with them. Non-Hebrew names and terms, however, often cause confusion. With the absence of vowels, a Hebrew reader does not always know how to pronounce unfamiliar Chinese names and concepts.

A second problem concerns the question of transliterations. Hebrew translators of thirty or forty years ago, most of whom did not know Chinese, rendered names and concepts according to the Wade-Giles system, thus distorting their pronunciation in Hebrew. Although more recently pinyin transliteration has come into use, the translator who does not know Chinese and is translating from an intermediary language also commits blunders. Hebrew script, furthermore, has no capital letters, which other written languages can use to highlight certain terms (*Dao* as Way, for example), so a translator must (or ought to) weigh carefully whether to transliterate or to translate.[2] Aside from these technical problems, there is, of course, the question of how to transpose specific concepts from one cultural context into another. This topic is discussed in greater detail below.

HEBREW SOURCES ON CHINA AND CHINESE HISTORY

The Hebrew reader's first stop to obtain some background information about China would be volume 25 of the *Hebrew Encyclopedia* (*Ha'Enziklopedia Ha'ivrit* 1974: 806–938). In well over one hundred pages, the reader can find excellent essays on major aspects of Chinese history, society, literature, and philosophy, as well as geography and climate. Aside from these essays (many of which are, unfortunately, dated by now), there is a near total lack of examples of Chinese historical writing. Except for the brief biography of Lü Buwei (d. 235 B.C.E.), reputed to be the father of the first emperor of the Qin dynasty (Daor 1995: 75–80),[3] an authentic sampling, such as some of Sima Qian's biographies, chapters from the *Zuozhuan*, or the *Han Shu*, remains untranslated. More as a curiosity than anything else, mention should be made of what is most likely the first history of China in Hebrew, S. M. Perlmann's *The Chinese* of 1911. The author, described as a scholar-merchant in Shanghai (Pollak 1980: 214), wrote the book in modern Hebrew, though by today's standards the language is rather quaint. Arranged topically and not chronologically, the short book is interesting as an early attempt at explaining China and the Chinese in a newly developing language (see Perlmann 1911).

In contrast to the lack of historical writing, Mao Zedong's works, the Chinese Communist revolution, and Mao's China, including the Cultural Revolution (1966–1976), were apparently of great interest to the Hebrew-reading public of thirty to forty years ago, when considerable portions of Mao's works were translated from Russian and English. There was also a thoroughly documented biography by the Hungarian Soviet expert George Paloczi-Horvath, which introduced the reader to Mao's childhood, the Long March, and the Sino-Soviet rift; it was translated by Shimshon Avidel (1964).[4] Accounts of China's revolution were translated from English (Smedley, Snow, Moravia),[5] Russian (Simonov), and German (Mehnert; see Hen 1936; Tevat 1946; Dori 1971; Raban 1950; and Kornfeld 1972).

Emphasis on the present, and on what was assumed to be the miraculous transformation of Chinese society, took precedence over interest in such subjects as China's early history, literature, and art. A small book by Kaltenmark-Ghequier on the history of literature includes both philosophy and fiction, and its one hundred and twenty-three pages hardly do justice to either subject (Kaltenmark-Ghequier 1963). Except for a small booklet published at least two decades ago (Chen and Lanzman n.d.), the history of Chinese art was similarly neglected. At the close of the twentieth century, Mao's China became historically interesting, and a published catalog of an exhibition of woodcuts harkened back to a politically more engaged era (Wachs and Chang 1999). The splendidly produced catalog includes, in addition to its excellent reproductions, useful articles by several authors on modern Chinese woodblock art.

In addition to reflecting literary trends, translations also reflect social phenomena. In the first twenty-odd years of the Israeli state, Mao Zedong and revolutionary China had the reading public's attention. At that time, the dominant trends in Israeli society were secularism and the socialist economic ethos of the labor movement. These were also the years of the successes of the *kibbutz* (agricultural collective) movement, together with the *kibbutzniks'* intellectual interests, which may not have transcended time but certainly transcended place. Seemingly successful revolutions like China's probably also appealed to those Marxists and leftists whose apocalyptic vision included a world free of hunger and want. But even if imperceptibly at first, Israeli society has drastically changed in the last twenty-five to thirty years. The enthusiasm for Mao's China waned even before post-Mao China began, and as will become obvious further on, Hebrew readers' tastes in translations also changed.

TRANSLATIONS FROM CHINESE PHILOSOPHY

Daoism has fared quite well in Hebrew, with several complete and partial translations of the *Daode jing*, two partial translations of the *Zhuangzi*, and one complete translation of the *Liezi*. The first *Daode jing* text in Hebrew was probably translated from Richard Wilhelm's (1921) German version by A. E. Aescoly (1937) and published in five hundred copies. This was followed by Martin Buber's (1878–1965) translation of eight chapters (1942). Buber did not know Chinese, and his chapters were, no doubt, prepared from either German or English (Eber 1994).

The first partial translation of seventeen chapters the *Daode jing* directly from Chinese was by Donald Leslie (1964: 30–43), and this was finally followed by the complete text from Chinese by Yuri Grause (Grause and Kalai 1973). Rendered by someone fluent in Chinese, this version of the *Daode jing* deserves some comments. The translator was not a native Hebrew speaker (he was raised in Harbin); therefore, it was coauthor Hanokh Kalai who supplied the stylistic refinements that resulted in an elegant and poetic Hebrew text. Aspects of philosophical Daoism are explained in the introduction, and selected chapters are briefly annotated. Yet this version often sacrifices fidelity to elegant phrasing, and the terse Chinese text is excessively wordy in Hebrew.

Other problems arose because at times the translator opted for a consistent use of Chinese terms in the target language when he would have done better by using several different expressions as dictated by context. This is, for example, true for the Chinese *shen* and *gui*, which in most instances may be translated as *ruah* (spirit) but for which at other times different Hebrew terms would have been more appropriate. Occasionally a chosen Hebrew term is too literal and obscures the meaning—for example, Grause's consistent translation of *ziran* as *derekh hateva* (way of nature).

It is useful to compare this translation with another prepared by two scholars who are native Hebrew speakers with degrees in Chinese philosophy. Daor and Ariel (1981) have given the Hebrew reader a translation of a high scholarly standard in a straightforward literary Hebrew style. The thoroughly annotated text provides useful explanatory materials in addition to an excellent introduction. In comparison with Grause, these translators invariably opted for flexible idiomatic Hebrew rather than attempting literal equivalence or a consistent use of terminology. However, where Grause had chosen not to translate *Dao*, transliterating the concept instead into Hebrew, Daor and Ariel translated it as *derekh* (way), which, they claim in a note, is "simple and exact." But I would argue to the contrary that despite the philosophical implications of the Hebrew term, it lacks the cosmological connotations of the Chinese.

One final translation, intended for the more mystically inclined,[6] is curiously entitled *The Dao of the Yijing and the Laozi*, hoping perhaps to catch both *Yijing* faddists and believers in the Dao (Ben-Mordekhai 1996). The translator claims to have rendered the Chinese text into Hebrew, which is highly unlikely.[7] Aside from the catchy title and the glossy cover, this is not a satisfactory translation. Finally, for those Hebrew readers who prefer pictures, there is even a Hebrew comic book *Daode jing* version (Saragusti 1995), translated together with the drawings from a Taiwan publication (Cai 1987).

There is as yet no complete Hebrew translation of the *Zhuangzi*. Yoel Hoffman (1977), a scholar of Japanese and Western philosophy and author of Hebrew fiction, translated considerable portions of the story materials but not whole chapters. Well versed in Zen writings, Hoffman skillfully captured the spirit and frequent playfulness of Zhuangzi's ideas, if not always the intricacies of the Chinese text. Another, much shorter selection was translated by Leslie (1964: 44–51). This has the advantage of presenting the chapters in their entirety. Also, what might be termed "Zhuangzi made easy" exists for the popular market and consists of some of the stories, termed "lectures," printed as if they were poetry (Yosling 1995).[8]

The *Liezi* has had a better fate in Hebrew. Translated by Dan Daor (1982), one of the most gifted translators from Chinese, this is an annotated text with a brief postscript in which the reader is helpfully informed about sources (133). The excellent rendition of the *Liezi* text is evident in several areas. Daor has transliterated Chinese names both consistently and in accordance with Hebrew linguistic usage, also supplying vowels for them at first mention. He has, in addition, chosen a graceful yet simple literary prose style to express the *Liezi*'s often enigmatic ideas. This is particularly evident at the very beginning of a passage presumably spoken by Huzi, who explains the nature of creation, production, and change (Daor 1982: 7). Daor has translated the *Liezi*'s delightful stories with facility without imposing on them a quaintness they certainly do not have in the original (see *Zhuzi jicheng* 1957: 3.1–101).

Confucian texts still await translators. The *Lunyu* was translated in 1969 by Leslie with an extensive thirty-five-page introduction and fourteen pages of notes (Leslie and Porat 1969). Although this is a solid scholarly rendition (printed with vowels throughout), the language is often clumsy, interspersed with archaisms, and lacks the elegant precision of Daor's prose. The major difficulty is, however, Leslie's often questionable translation of the *Lunyu*'s important concepts. Does not the text become distorted, for example, when the important term *li* with its many implications is translated into the target language as *minhag* (custom)?[9] There is a similar difficulty with the term *ren*; Leslie uses *hatov* (the good), perhaps under the influence of Arthur Waley's (1956) translation.[10] Leslie's text once more raises the question of how to transpose culture-specific philosophical concepts. Ideas in the target language are easily distorted when fixed meanings are attributed to terms where flexibility is called for and when Western philosophical assumptions get in the way (see Katz 1998a: 99). Should translators strive for hard-and-fast equivalence or uniformity, or is it desirable to express Chinese concepts with several terms depending on the context?

The popular (or is it the mystic?) market has not neglected Confucius. Presented to readers not as a translation but as a text directly from Confucius, a recent publication strings together rewritten random sentences from the *Lunyu* reminiscent of the messages diners find in fortune cookies (Ofek 1996). In a brief introduction, the author assures us that more than anyone alive, Confucius's wisdom has influenced human culture. The book is adorned with random illustrations of Buddhist statues, calligraphy, portions of paintings, and rubbings.

In contrast, Andrew Plaks's (1997) translation of the *Daxue* has established a new high standard for translating classical texts into Hebrew.[11] First and foremost is its innovative format: the Hebrew text is printed with the Chinese on the facing page so that the two versions can be read together by those who know both languages. Each translated sentence is numbered, allowing easy reference to the notes that follow the text. The notes, in effect a commentary on every sentence, include numerous references to Chinese commentaries, which, in turn, are listed in the extensive bibliography. The text is introduced in considerable detail and is prefaced by a general essay by Eber on the nature and function of the classics in the Chinese tradition.

With this translation and commentary, Plaks joins what Daniel Gardner (1998) has termed "the Confucian interpretive community"—that is, those scholars throughout the centuries who have interacted with the text in order to interpret it always anew and in accordance with their times (417). His choice of Hebrew terms for specific concepts is in most cases excellent. Thus, for example, the troublesome *ren* is translated as *enoshiyut* (humaneness). In rendering the title as "The Teaching of Great Men," Plaks decides to follow those Chinese interpreters who took *da* to be a noun rather than an adjective. Although an unusual interpretation, it is not unknown. The only drawback of this translation (and not everyone would agree with me) is Plaks's use of a mixed archaic style of Hebrew he believes is appropriate for a canonical text. Even if the translator's mastery of this beautiful style is exemplary, it may very well present difficulties for those laypeople and students who are not sufficiently conversant with premodern Hebrew.

There are two translations of the *Yijing* in Hebrew. Considering the antiquity and the difficulty of this classical text, together with the long and intensive engagement Chinese philosophers have had with it, it comes as no surprise that neither translation is satisfactory. The first, by Nitsan Visman (1983), is obviously based on the Wilhelm-Baynes version (1950) and is incomplete. The second and complete translation was prepared by Yuri Grause from the Chinese (Grause and Alon 1993). This version is an improvement over Visman's and has generally helpful annotations. Following Wilhelm's example, Grause also divides the commentaries, adding portions to the hexagrams, but leaves the "Da chuan" and "Shuo gua" as separate essays. However, neither translation even attempts to convey the long-established scholarly and philosophical significance of the *Yi*, nor do the translators dispel its popular image as a soothsaying book.[12]

No other Chinese writer was as popular as Lin Yutang in the 1940s and 1950s, with six novels and one volume of short stories translated into Hebrew. However, aside from Lin, Chinese fiction was apparently not on the agenda of translators in the first three decades after the Second World War, and the only other literary, though nonfictional, work translated was Xie Bingying's *Yige nübing de zizhuan* (Autobiography of a woman soldier). Like Lin's works, this too was translated from English.

An entirely new era began in 1983, when two literary works translated directly from Chinese appeared in print. The first was the famous work by Shen Fu (1763–?), *Fusheng liuji* (Six chapters of a drifting life; Daor 1983), and the other was a selection of ten modern short stories (*Pirhei* 1983).[13] In Dan Daor's translation, Shen Fu's account comes alive in Hebrew. As in his other renditions, he manages to cast the delightful book in a simple yet dignified literary style. Ample annotations elucidate difficult passages, and an excellent postscript supplies historical and other background information helpful for a better understanding of the text. The second book includes short stories by several well-known May Fourth writers and is the work of five translators, three of whom are graduates of the Hebrew University's Department of East Asian Studies.

Amira Katz, who translated five of the short stories in the above volume, also translated the first full-length novel from Chinese, Lao She's *Luotuo Xiangzi* (Camel Xiangzi; Katz 1985). Since 1983, she has published three volumes of translated short stories: one by Lu Xun (*Nahan* [Battle Cries]), one by Shen Congwen (*Biancheng* [Border Town]), and a selection by Feng Menglong from the *Gujin xiaoshuo* (Tales past and present; Katz 1986; 1989; 1993). Her most recent contribution is a selection of stories written between 1980 and 1997 by contemporary authors (Katz 1998b). Published in a pleasing paperback format of between 200 and 250 pages by Am Oved, these books are not only popular with a more demanding reading public but also used in university courses due to their excellent style and fidelity. Over the years, several more of her short story translations have also appeared in widely read literary journals.

Like Daor, Katz translates classical and modern texts with equal facility. That she has tended to translate more of the latter may be due to publishing pressures, as an increasing number of professional translators with little or no knowledge of China are turning out translations of Chinese fiction. But let us take a closer look at the title story from Feng Menglong's (1574–1646) collection *Jiang Xingge chong hui zhenzhu shen* (The pearl shirt returned to Jiang Xingge) and its several outstanding features. Both the story and the poems in it are rendered into graceful Hebrew. As in her other translations, Katz avoids strict literalism and instead casts the Chinese text into idiomatic modern Hebrew. Her renditions of poetry and couplets (or sayings) are especially successful, appearing with the economy demanded by Chinese poetic conventions. To choose one at random: "Painting a tiger's skin is easy, painting the bones is hard; to know a man's face is not to know his heart" is in Hebrew close to the Chinese, "Easier to paint a tiger's skin than to paint its insides; easier to get to know a man by his face than to know his heart" (Ma, Liu, and Hu 1979: 401; Katz 1993: 31).

Supplementing Katz's selection of six stories is one other long but less well-known story from Feng Menglong's *Jingshi tongyan* (Common words to warn the world) collection (Daor 1995: 17–41). But regrettably, only two of Pu Songling's (1640–1715) delightful stories from *Liaozhai zhiyi* (Strange stories from Leisure Studio) are thus far available in Hebrew (Daor 1995: 109–113; 127–138).[14]

Rather, different kinds of translations are aimed at readers with a craving for Eastern wisdom. An example of these is a word-by-word Hebrew version of Richard Martin's English text (itself from Franz Kuhn's German version) of Li Yu's (1611–1680) *Rouputuan* (Prayer mat of flesh; Deutsch 1998; Martin 1963). One might have looked more kindly at this effort had the publisher at least demanded that the full text in the superb translation by Patrick Hanan (1990) be made available to the Israeli reader. The same press also published a translation of Arthur Waley's highly abridged (and often mysteriously selective) translation of *Xiyou ji* (Journey to the West; Waley 1943; Visman 1995). This too is an exact replica of the English, reading rather like English in Hebrew. But far worse, and obviously intended for the pornographic market, is a hopeless jumble of excerpts from unidentified sources, entitled *Love of the Golden Lotus* (Ben-Mordekhai 1995). The book's introduction attempts (unsuccessfully) to explain sexual ideas in China. It is profusely illustrated.[15]

TRANSLATIONS OF CHINESE POETRY

Chinese poetry, read and appreciated in several intermediary languages, undoubtedly inspired some Hebrew poets and writers to attempt translating it. Over the years, their efforts have resulted in several books (perhaps better called booklets) of highly uneven quality. In addition, either the translators or the publishers, or both, seem to have assumed that the visual appeal is as important as the written word. They have used pink, deep-red, or yellowed paper; illustrations vary from abstract splashes of color to the customary pagodas and clouds; and one book is printed in foldout accordion format. Without any indication of sources for the translated poems, together with the frequently odd transliteration of the Chinese poets' names, it is in some cases hard to tell if the poem is an actual translation or a reworked version.

The earliest effort at translating Li Bai (699–762) seems to have been made by Dov Stock (Dov Sadan) and is a selection of eighteen untitled poems, none of which I was able to identify (Stock 1930).[16] The well-known and gifted poet Aharon Shabtai translated thirty-two poems from different periods (Shabtai 1960). Included are several from the *Shijing*, Li Bai, Du Mu (803–852), and the Manchu poet Nalan Shengde (1655–1685), as well as poems from Japanese. Shabtai gives no indication of his source texts, of which he probably had several. But even a poet as sensitive as Shabtai will miss important aspects of Chinese poetry if his sources lack explanations. For example, Du Mu's lovely poem "Qiuye" (Autumn nights), which consists of two couplets, is rendered in five lines. Moreover, the melancholy allusion to the stars by the herd boy and the weaving maid of Du Mu's last line (*Tang shi* 1976: 379) is completely lost in Shabtai's version because he omits the stars and has the distraught lovers laugh (Shabtai 1960: 20).

A more substantial poetry translation was published in 1970 (Ben-Zakai 1970); the author claims it is a rendition of *yuefu* poetry, assumed to be, according to the preface, love and nature poetry. Ben-Zakai's more than two hundred verses are almost certainly a reworking of materials from an intermediary language, consisting of uniform eight-line poems and what he calls "limericks" of five lines. Love was on the translators' minds, for this is also the theme of an otherwise undistinguished 1990 publication of twenty-one poems (Garin 1990). The transliteration of Chinese names is highly erratic, and in the absence of any other information, it is hard to say what was translated here.

Yuri Grause's and Dan Daor's translations of Chinese poetry stand in marked contrast to the efforts discussed above. Grause translated twenty-six poems by a number of Tang poets, including Li Bai, Du Fu (712–770), and Wang Wei (699–759), as well as lesser-known poets like Chang Jian (fl. 727). Grause, who passed away early this year, was especially fond of Tang poetry, which he taught students at the Hebrew University to recite by heart, and one would have liked to have more of his renditions than merely this slim booklet (Grause and Alon 1977). With uncommon sensitivity, he both translated and interpreted. At first sight, changing Chang Jian's title "Tipo shansihou chanyuan" (Meditation hall behind a broken mountain temple; *Tang shi* 1976: 184) to "Bitan hahitbonenut" (Meditation pavilion) seems unjustified. But when we read the title and poem as a Hebrew reader would, we find that the change allows us more easily to enter Chang's tranquil landscape.

The most serious effort to date is Dan Daor's anthology (Daor 2001).[17] The poetry selections include the best-loved Tang dynasty poets, in addition to poems from the *Shijing* and *Chuci*; poems by Jia Yi (200–168 B.C.E.); Cao Cao (155–220); Tao Qian (365–427); as well as the later Su Shi (1037–1101). The volume includes his previously published poems (Daor 1977). Despite some mistranslations that might not escape the punctilious reader, the translations are uniformly excellent and are accompanied by brief explanations. In the hands of one as sensitive to both language and poetics as Daor, these poems have assumed a new life in the Hebrew language. Although many examples could be given, one, a brief poem by Du Fu—"Chun wang" (Spring gazing), in which the poet contemplates the consequences of the An Lushan rebellion of 755–763—will have to suffice here.

The poem has five-character lines; each line is divisible into groups of two and three characters, and every two lines form a couplet. Daor's first two lines repeat this pattern, not with syllables (impossible in Hebrew), but with polysyllabic words that nonetheless preserve the rhythm. A literal translation of these lines from Hebrew into English reads, "States fall, mountains rivers eternal; spring [within] walls, trees grass deep." The first two lines are balanced by the last two, where the translator has managed to express Du Fu's shift of mood about his own aging self, again in two five-word lines (Daor 2001: 85; *Tang shi* 1976: 192).

CONCLUDING REMARKS

Three different kinds of translation are under way at present. One aims to give the Hebrew reader literary texts translated from Chinese sources. Another caters to readers with currently fashionable notions of the "East." The third is somewhat different by providing informative texts of contemporary Chinese fiction. But except for those translated by Amira Katz, these are translated by professional translators who do not know Chinese.

Obviously, the translations prepared directly from Chinese texts have received higher marks in this essay than those translated from intermediary languages. But should such mediated translations be rejected outright? Can some of them nonetheless serve a purpose, despite inaccuracies, distortions, or omissions? Might one not also argue that for readers who know little or nothing about China, they convey at least some information, accessible only in this way, thus helping build bridges between peoples? In the 1950s, Mao Zedong's writings and utterances about war and revolution may very well have seemed a bridge to the outside world for leftists (and dreamers) in the newly established state of Israel. We therefore need, no doubt, to distinguish between the political interest in the Chinese Revolution of forty years ago and the surge of a latter-day apolitical Orientalism. But what about the literary value of fictional works translated from intermediary languages? Zhang Xianliang's fiction may indeed provide interesting information about the Chinese gulag and Maoist China's politics, helping Hebrew readers toward a better understanding of China. But is this enough? Is the Hebrew reader also able to appreciate the fine literary quality of Zhang's texts?

Translators of philosophical texts encounter problems different from those of translators of fiction. As pointed out earlier, cultural assumptions more often than not get in the way of creating a satisfactory text in the target language. Both Grause and Leslie had, however, an additional problem by not being native Hebrew speakers. Despite their unimpeachable expertise in Chinese philosophical texts, each translator had to resort to other persons for Hebrew linguistic refinements. Thus I believe that when linguistic considerations in the target language took precedence, the philosophical content frequently suffered. Attempting a strictly literal translation misses the point of translating; as Eugene Eoyang reminds us, perfect translations are a myth, for the text in the target language can never be like the original.

The successful translation is at once an interpretation of the original text (Eoyang 1993: 44, 170).

How true Eoyang's observations in fact are is apparent in Plaks's, Katz's, and Daor's Hebrew renditions, be they of philosophy, fiction, or poetry. Literal translations, they know, are out of the question, and the search for equivalence is futile. Whether transposing Chinese philosophical vocabulary, poetry, or the fictional foreign culture into Hebrew, these translators are aware (as was Grause) that they must interpret and even at times misinterpret so that the source text can be appropriated into the new cultural setting (Eoyang 1993: 187). For this to happen, more than linguistic adeptness is required. The successful translator, though immersed in his own culture, must also be conversant with the culture of the text's origin.

REFERENCES

Aescoly, A. Z., trans. 1937. *Sefer hadereh ve'orah meyesharim* (Book of the way and way of honesty). Jerusalem: Reuven Mas.

Avidel, Shimshon, trans. 1964. *Sin beyadei Mao Zedong* (China in Mao Zedong's hands). Tel Aviv: Am Hasefer.

Ben-Mordekhai, Elisha, trans. 1995. *Ahavat lotus hazahav, Dao ve'ahava* (Love of the golden lotus, Dao and Love). Hod Hasharon: Astrolog.

———, trans. 1996. *Dao haYijing, Laozi* (The Dao of the *Yijing* and the *Laozi*). Hod Hasharon: Astrolog.

Ben-Zakai, J., trans. 1970. *Perah halotos: Shirei ahava beSin hakeduma* (Flower of the lotus: Love poems from early China). Jerusalem: Kiryat Sefer.

Buber, Martin, trans. 1942. "Laozi al hashilton" (Laozi on government). *Hapo'el hatsa'ir* 35, no. 31–32 (May): 6–8.

Cai, Zhizhong. 1987. *Laozi shuo, zhizhi de diyu* (Laozi says, the sage's whispered words). Taibei: Shenbao wenhua.

Chen, Qibing, and Eli Lanzman. n.d. *Sin, omanut, vehistoriya* (China, art, and history). Taibei: China Publishing Co.

Daor, Dan, trans. 1977. *41 shirim Siniyim: Antologiya ketana* (41 Chinese poems: A small anthology). Tel Aviv: Hakibbutz Hameuchad.

———, trans. 1982. *Lie yukou, Liezi*. Jerusalem: Keter.

———, trans. 1983. *Hahayim hasehufim* (The drifting life). Tel Aviv: Sifriyat HaPo'alim.

———, trans. 1995. *Hamelumad vehazona: Antologiya shel sipurim Siniyim* (The scholar and the whore: Anthology of Chinese stories). Jerusalem: Keter.

———. 2001. *198 Shirim min haklasika haSinit* (198 poems, anthology of classical Chinese poetry). Tel Aviv: Khargol.

———, and Yoav Ariel, trans. 1981. *Laozi: Sefer haderekh vehasegula* (Laozi: Book of the way and virtue). Israel: University Publishing Projects.

Deutsch, Avi, trans. 1998. *Dao ha'ohavim* (Dao of lovers). Ein Harod: Astrolog.

Dori, Asher, trans. 1971. *Masa beSin ha'aduma* (Journey in red China). Tel Aviv: Am Oved.

Eber, Irene. 1991. "Introduction." In *Martin Buber: Chinese Tales*, ix–xxiii. London: Humanities Press.

———. 1994. "Martin Buber and Taoism." *Monumenta Serica* 42:445–464.

———. 1996. "Sinology in Israel." *Revue Bibliographique de Sinologie* 29–35.

Enziklopedia Ha'ivrit (Hebrew encyclopedia). 1974. Jerusalem-Tel Aviv.

Eoyang, Eugene Chen. 1993. *The Transparent Eye: Reflections on Translation, Chinese Literature, and Comparative Poetics.* Honolulu: University of Hawaii Press.

Gardner, Daniel K. 1998. "Confucian Commentary and Chinese Intellectual History." *Journal of Asian Studies* 57, no. 2: 397–422.

Garin, Doron, trans. 1990. *Nahar ha'ahava: Shirei-ahava Siniyim* (The river of love: Chinese love poems). Jerusalem: Piyut.

Grause, Yuri, and Yona Alon, trans. 1977. *Migdal hanezah: Shirat Tang* (Tower of eternity: Tang poems). Tel Aviv: Eked.

———, and Yaffa Alon, trans. 1993. *Sefer haTemurot, Yijing* (The book of changes, *Yijing*). Jerusalem: Carmel.

———, and Khanokh Kalai, trans. 1973. *Laozi, Dao De Jing.* Jerusalem: Bialik.

Ha'Enziklopedia Ha'ivrit (Hebrew encyclopedia). 1974. Jerusalem-Tel Aviv.

Hanan, Patrick, trans. 1990. *The Carnal Prayer Mat.* New York: Ballantine.

Hen, Ya'akov, trans. 1936. *BeSin hamitoreret* (In awakening China). Tel Aviv: Alnov.

Hoffman, Yoel, trans. 1977. *Kolot ha'adama* (Sounds of the earth). Jerusalem: Masada.

Inbari, Assaf. 1999. "The Underground of Yearning." *Ha'aretz Magazine* 10 (September): 8–13.

Kaltenmark-Ghequier, O. Sh. Sagiv, trans. 1963. *Hasifrut haSinit* (Chinese literature). Tel Aviv: M. Mizrahi.

Katz, Amira, trans. 1985. *Riksha, korotav shel gorer hariksha Xiangzi "hagamal"* (The biography of the rickshaw puller Xiangzi the "camel"). Jerusalem: Keter.

———, trans. 1986. *Kriyot krav* (Battle Cries). Tel Aviv: Am Oved.

———, trans. 1989. *Ayeret hagvul* (Border town). Tel Aviv: Am Oved.

———, trans. 1993. *Ketonet hapninim* (Pearl shirt). Tel Aviv: Am Oved.

———. 1998a. "In Search of a Text: Translating the Analects." In *Autumn Floods: Essays in Honour of Marián Gálik*, edited by Raoul D. Findeisen and Robert H. Gassmann, 96–110. Bern: Peter Lang.

———, trans. 1998b. *Ke'ilu hitbonenu bahem atsmam: Mivhar sipurim Siniyim* (As if looking at themselves: Selection of Chinese contemporary stories). Tel Aviv: Am Oved.

Kornfeld, Edna, trans. 1972. *Sin ahar hase'ara* (China after the storm). Tel Aviv: Schocken.

Leslie, Donald D., trans. 1964. "Datot Sin" (Chinese religions). In *Yalkut hadatot* (Religions collection), edited by Yosef Bentwich, 7–60. Tel Aviv: Joshua Chachik.

———, and A. Porat, trans. 1969. *Kong Fuzi (Confucius): Ma 'amarot* (Sayings). Jerusalem: Bialik.

Ma, Youyuan, Liu Shaoming, and Hu Wanchuan, eds. 1979. *Zhongguo chuantong duanpian xiaoshuo xuanji* (Collection of traditional Chinese short stories). Taibei: Lianjing chubanshe.

Martin, Richard, trans. 1963. *Jou Pu Tuan* (The prayer mat of flesh). New York: Grove Press.

Ofek, Binah. 1996. *Omer hakhaham, Kong Fuzi (Confucius)* (The wise (man) speaks). Tel Aviv: Ofarim.

Perlmann, S. M. 1911. *HaSinim, darkhei hayei haSinim uminhageihem.* (The Chinese, Chinese life, manners and customs, culture and creeds, government system and trade). London: Hayehoody.

Pirhei gehinom ketanim: Mivhar hasipur haSini bamea ha20 (Small flowers of hell: A selection of Chinese stories from the twentieth century). 1983. Tel Aviv: Sifriyat Hapoalim.

Plaks, Andrew, trans. 1997. *Torat hagadol* (The teaching of great men). Jerusalem: Bialik.

Pollak, Michael. 1980. *Mandarins, Jews, and Missionaries.* Philadelphia: Jewish Publication Society of America.

Raban, N., trans. 1950. *Sin halohemet* (reportage) (Fighting China). Tel Aviv: Sifriyat Hapoalim.

Saragusti, Yosef, trans. 1995. *Laozi omer, dvarav hashketim shel ha'hakham* (Laozi says, silent words of the sage). Tel Aviv: Parog.

Shabtai, Aharon, trans. 1960. *Shirei ahava Siniyim* (Chinese love poems). Tel Aviv: Hadas.

Shai, Aharon. 1981. *Mimilhemet ha'opium ad yorshei Mao: Sin bazira habein-leumit 1840–1979* (From the Opium War to Mao's heirs: China in the international arena 1840–1979). Tel Aviv: Zmora Beitan.

Stock, Dov, trans. 1930. *Mishirei Li Taipe* (From Li Bai's poems). Warsaw: Hako'operativ haShomrei haMerkazi.

Tang shi sanbai shou (300 Tang poems). 1976. Taibei: Sanmin chuju.

Tevat, S., trans. 1946. *Kokhav adom bishmei Sin* (Red star in China's heaven). Tel Aviv: Hakibbutz Hameuhedet.

Visman, Nitsan, trans. 1983. *Yijing: Sefer haTemurot* (*Yijing*: The book of changes). Jerusalem: Elishar.

———, trans. 1995. *HaDao shel kof* (The Dao of monkey). Ein Harod: Astrolog.

Wachs, Iris, and Chang Tsong-zung. 1999. *Hamishim shana shel hedpesei ets Siniyim* (Fifty years of Chinese woodblock prints). Ein Harod: Museum of Art at Ein Harod.

Waley, Arthur, trans. 1943. *Monkey*. New York: Grove Press.

———, trans. 1956. *The Analects of Confucius*. London: George Allen and Unwin.

Wilhelm, Richard, trans. 1921. *Laotse, vom Sinn und Leben* (Laozi about meaning and life). Jena: Eugen Diederichs.

———, and Cary F. Baynes, trans. 1950. *The I Ching or Book of Changes*. Princeton: Princeton University Press.

Yosling, Hara, trans. 1995. *Keshehana'al mat'ima* (When the shoe fits). Hertseliya: Gal.

Zhuzi jicheng (Collectanea: The philosophers). 1957. 8 vols. Beijing: Zhonghua shuju.

NOTES

I gratefully acknowledge the partial support of the Truman Research Institute and the Frieberg Research Fund of the Hebrew University of Jerusalem. My thanks to Dr. L. Yariv-Laor for bringing to my attention several works discussed in these pages and to Professor A. Altman for his thoughtful comments on this paper.

1. Hebrew belongs to the Canaanite branch of Semitic languages. Biblical Hebrew (or pre-exilic Hebrew) was subject to many changes and influences during the two thousand years of the Jewish diaspora, since Hebrew continued in use as a written language. The nineteenth-century Jewish Enlightenment (*Haskala*) included the revival of Hebrew as a modern written as well as spoken language. Hebrew was one of the three languages recognized under the British Mandate in Palestine and it became, together with Arabic, one of two official languages of the State of Israel in 1948.

2. The major essays were written by the faculty of the Department of East Asian Studies at the Hebrew University, and several were translated from English.

3. Daor's book is a heterogeneous collection of twenty-two stories of varying length, apparently chosen for no other reason than the translator's fondness for them.

4. The original title of the book was *Mao Tse-tung, Emperor of the Blue Ants* (London: Secker and Warburg, 1962).

5. Moravia's title in Italian is *La rivoluzione culturale in Cina*. This was transformed into the English title *The Red Book and the Great Wall* and then into the Hebrew *Journey into Red China*.

6. Perhaps a tendency toward mysticism has been there all along in Israeli life, though it has only become more noticeable in recent years (see Inbari 1999, 8–13).

7. Ben-Mordekhai writes that he used "the famous Shanghai edition" of 1930, which was translated into English by the London Buddhist Association. The reference seems to be to Zhu Dagao's English translation of 1937.

8. Yosling's version is based on a similarly titled English version published by the Osho International Foundation.

9. *Minhag* has rather different implications from *li* where religious customs are concerned

and is often contrasted to *halakha,* or law. Custom varies and is not prescriptive; law is.

10. In distinction, the nineteenth-century James Legge opted for flexibility, using several terms like "humanity," "benevolent actions," or "the good" to express *ren.*

11. This is the first book in the Bialik Institute's project of the *Four Books (Si shu).* The *Mengzi,* translated by Daor, is in press, as is the *Zhongyong,* translated by Plaks. Amira Katz's translation of the *Lunyu* is nearing completion.

12. So pervasive is this image that Orthodox Jewish students often refuse to learn anything about the *Yi.*

13. The title of the book was taken from one of Lu Xun's short pieces, "The Good Hell That Was Lost" (*Shidiao de hao diyu*).

14. Little known, though noteworthy, is the fact that the uncommonly perspicacious Martin Buber remarked in 1909 on the sophistication of the *Liaozhai* stories and how they expressed certain Chinese philosophical assumptions (Buber 1991, xiii).

15. Next to these two kinds of translations are still others of contemporary Chinese fiction prepared from English sources. Among the authors translated are Mo Yan, Zhang Xianliang, and Ah Cheng, with only the last translated from Chinese.

16. Another early translation by Lichtenboim in 1943 was not available in the library and therefore could not be examined.

17. Over the years, Daor's translations of Chinese poetry have also appeared in the literary pages of major Hebrew newspapers.

CHAPTER 5

The Peking Translating Committee and S. I. J. Schereschewsky's Old Testament

Protestant missionaries in nineteenth-century China considered one of their most urgent initial tasks translating the Bible into Chinese. The translating enterprise encountered, however, numerous obstacles, including language mastery, finding the indispensable Chinese scholars willing to work together with foreign missionaries, and the choice of language—classical (*wenyan*) or colloquial—and the appropriate style. Whether working alone or in cooperation with others, missionaries could expect additional difficulties. The labor of many years might, in the end, prove unacceptable to other Protestant denominations; a cooperative undertaking might founder on disagreement on the principles of translation. Agreement was not always easily attained: for example, when the Delegates' Bible translators were unable to reach an agreement, the group was dissolved.[1] The difficulties of rendering the Union Bible into vernacular Chinese, which was eighteen years in preparation, provide another example.[2] Against such a background, the work of the Peking Translating Committee seems especially remarkable. For the years it took to translate both the New Testament (NT) and Old Testament (OT), the committee worked together in apparent harmony despite the differing backgrounds of its members. Furthermore, the task was completed within a reasonably short time.

Although mentioned in the available literature on Bibles in Chinese,[3] the committee's Chinese Bible, the so-called Mandarin Bible, deserves special attention for being the first translation into the spoken language of northern China. It was therefore accessible to a much larger audience (of either readers or listeners) than any previously translated Bible in classical Chinese or one of the spoken southern languages. As the first translation into northern vernacular (called *guanhua* then and later *guoyu*), the Mandarin Bible served as a prototype to the translators of the Union Bible, still in use in many Protestant churches. And finally, whereas the NT was translated from the Greek, the OT—the work of Bishop S. I. J. Schereschewsky—was rendered from the original Hebrew and included his explanatory notes, which were largely based on the Jewish commentary tradition. This essay explores the relationships among the Peking group of translators and their method of work. Special attention will be devoted to some of the characteristics of the OT translation. In conclusion, the Peking group's attempt at a nonpartisan stand in the hotly debated "term question" will be discussed.

THE PEKING TRANSLATING COMMITTEE AND ITS WORK

The committee that began work in 1864 consisted of Henry Blodget (1825–1903), American Board of Commissioners for Foreign Missions; Samuel I. J. Schereschewsky (1831–1906), Episcopal Church in the United States of America, Domestic and Foreign Missionary Society; John S. Burdon (d. 1907), Church Missionary Society; and Joseph Edkins (1823–1905), London Missionary Society. W. A. P. Martin (1827–1916), Presbyterian Church in the United States of America, Board of Foreign Missions, participated only intermittently. Thus the committee was more or less equally represented by Americans and Englishmen. All four had been in China for some time and were proficient in Chinese. Edkins had arrived in 1848, Burdon in 1853, Blodget in 1854, and Schereschewsky in 1859. They came to Peking between 1862 and 1863. Burdon came as a "quasi chaplain" to the British Legation, Schereschewsky as "translator" to the American Legation. Of roughly the same age, the four men were drawn together by their novel situation in the capital newly opened to foreigners.[4] They shared the problems of settling in: whether to build, rent, or purchase living quarters; and where to preach and how best to make converts. In the first half of the 1860s, the foreign community in Peking numbered no more than sixty people, including missionaries and customs officers.

The newly arrived missionaries were not oblivious to the grandeur and beauty of the capital, the seat of the emperor and his court, or its Asian cosmo-politanism. Blodget wrote admiringly, "Here is the concourse of nations of northeastern Asia, embracing Coreans [*sic*], Manchurians, . . . Mongolians, Eastern and Western Thibetans [*sic*], and Russians from the frontier of Mongolia. The Chinese language is the medium of intercourse with all these nations."[5] Even if Martin highly disapproved of the pervasive "idolatry," he too was impressed by the city's great size, its imposing walls, and the color and liveliness of its urban scenes.[6]

The conviviality developed over two years of sharing experiences and information undoubtedly included discussions on the need for a Chinese Bible. As early as 1861, while still in Tianjin, Blodget had proposed translat-ing the Bible into northern vernacular, which was spoken, as he recognized, by more than half of China's population.[7] By 1864, having recruited Chinese coworkers for the task at hand, the four men were sufficiently encouraged to start the project. Although they had remained for the most part nameless in the missionaries' letters, these Chinese scholars were an integral part of the translating process. Ultimately it was up to them to choose an acceptable style and proper Chinese characters, neither too classical nor too collo-quial, with meanings that would not be misunderstood or misinterpreted in the written text. Blodget has given us a vivid description of the committee's work:

> Our method is to apportion to each of the five members certain chapters, or books, that he may prepare a draft. This draft is sup-posed to be the *best translation he can produce*. Then this draft is criticized most truly by each of the remaining four, working in his own study, with his teacher. The author . . . receives these criticisms and . . . makes out a second draft. . . . This second draft is sent around to each of the other members who notes every thing, whether in the style, or in the sense, which he wishes to see changed. When this has been done, we meet for discussion . . . two or three native teachers being present to assist.[8]

A visitor who sat in on the discussion of the final draft expressed his admi-ration for the fact that decisions were made by majority vote, including the participation of the coworkers. The Chinese, he wrote, discussed points of the Chinese text as earnestly as the others and were "no less vexed by them, than were the translators themselves by the niceties or the difficulties."[9] The visitor's occasionally patronizing tone may be dismissive, but the description shows a continuing dialogue between Westerners and Chinese, during which knowledge about Chinese culture and language was inevitably imparted by the latter to the former. An open and tolerant spirit apparently prevailed, and differences of opinion, which surely must have arisen, never reached the point of impeding the work.

Differences would have invariably existed over interpretation but were more likely to occur over how to translate specific biblical terms and expressions. The committee had to decide whether to use neologisms or coin new words for such crucial terms as *baptism*, *circumcision*, and *soul* and whether to transliterate names or translate their meanings. It was also necessary to critically examine previous translations for usages, especially those that circulated widely in classical Chinese.[10]

Among the Peking missionaries, Samuel Schereschewsky stood out.[11] Of Jewish parentage, he hailed from Lithuania, where he had received a traditional Jewish education followed by advanced study in a secondary progressive rabbinic school. After several years in Breslau (Wroclaw), he went to the United States at the age of twenty-three. There he converted to Christianity in 1855 and attended several seminaries. Schereschewsky's knowledge of Hebrew together with a thorough acquaintance with both Jewish and Christian biblical scholarship persuaded his Peking colleagues to entrust the entire OT translation to him. According to Blodget, "[His] early studies in the Old Testament eminently qualify him for the work of translation. He is a man of extensive and varied learning, especially in studies bearing upon philology. That his work will be able, and thoroughly idiomatic, I have no doubt. His Jewish background was an asset to the profession of translator . . . and it was acknowledged as such by his missionary colleagues and superiors."[12] Schereschewsky accepted the challenge with delight.[13]

For the next ten years, the four (sometimes five) men often worked feverishly to complete the translation. Their efforts had the support of both the British and Foreign Bible Society and the American Bible Society, which had committed themselves to the Bible's printing. Work on the NT progressed more rapidly, with some portions being printed as they were completed. The entire NT appeared in 1872.[14] Genesis and Psalms were printed by the American Bible Society in 1866 and 1867, respectively, and the entire OT appeared in 1874 and 1875.[15] The Mandarin Bible came to be the Bible most widely used in China until the appearance of the Union Bible in 1919, forty-five years later. The Mandarin Bible's sales soared many years prior to the adoption of northern vernacular, or *guoyu*, as China's official language. Figures for the period 1911–1922, when by the latter date the Union Bible was already on the market, indicate that 45,985 Mandarin Bibles had been sold in comparison with 9,481 Bibles in literary and classical Chinese.[16]

TRANSLATION STRATEGIES

Closer examination of features of the OT text reveals the problems encountered and how they were solved. Willis Barnstone has noted, "Translation is not a mirror, nor is it mimetic copy. It is another creation. Of course every translation owes form and content to its source, yet it has become a new text."[17] The biblical text had to be transposed from one cultural context into another, and in the receptor language, the new text had to both appropriate the source and render it readable. While revising his translation of fifteen years earlier, Schereschewsky wrote in 1890 that literal translation is mistranslation; it is never idiomatic. A translation must be felicitous without attempting to be literal; its style must be clear, using the idiom of the target language.[18]

Such felicity can be seen especially in Schereschewsky's technique of supplying a more explicit rendition in the Chinese where the Hebrew text tends to be suggestive. Psalm 43:1 refers to the nation without piety (*goi lo hasid*) among whom the exile finds himself. In Chinese this is rendered "a people without benevolence and justice" (*buren buyi*).[19] "And the dust returns to the earth as it was; and the spirit returns unto God who gave it" (Ecclesiastes 12:7) is rendered more explicitly: "The body (*shen*) came from dust, again returns to dust; the soul (*linghun*) again returns, goes to God who bestowed the soul." My literal retranslation from Chinese sounds clumsy and repetitious, but it is not so in Chinese, where it has to be clearly stated that the body was dust and where the sequence has to be added by inserting "again." The Hebrew "spirit" (*ruah*) was translated here as "soul" to indicate that the soul is bestowed by God.

Aside from adding a word or phrase to render the text more intelligible, the translator also occasionally opted for omissions. God's covenant with Abraham included circumcision of male children (Genesis 17:10), and verse 11 specifies what is to be cut in the act of circumcising. The translation omits this portion and simply repeats the injunction to circumcise. Neither to missionaries nor to converts would that line have been important; the omission eliminated the need for awkward explanations.

Written idiomatic Chinese is frequently enhanced by the use of *chengyu*, four-character idiomatic phrases that enrich the text and add emphasis. "My soul failed when he spoke" (*nafshi yatsah be'dabro*, Song of Solomon 5:6) is recaptured with *shenbu shoushe*, meaning roughly "the soul left the house unguarded" (often used to imply absentmindedness). In Psalm 106:48, the Hebrew "from everlasting to everlasting" (*min ha'olam ve'ad ha'olam*) is perfectly reproduced with *chengyu*, *wanshi wuqiong* (ten thousand worlds inexhaustible).

Dealing with proper names and whether to translate their meaning (thus abandoning pronunciation) or transliterate (thus abandoning meaning) was a major problem. Schereschewsky opted for the latter, in most cases glossing the meaning. He justified the decision by referring to Buddhist, Muslim, and Roman Catholic precedents. Sanskrit terms, he pointed out, were also transliterated in Buddhist sutra translations and eventually became an integral part of the Chinese language.[20] He evidently assumed that the spread of Christianity would promote the entry of these terms into the Chinese language.

Finding a proper term for *God* in Chinese was a major issue not only for the Bible translators but for the missionaries to China generally. Doubtless with the approval of his colleagues on the committee, Schereschewsky decided on a course of flexibility. Instead of translating a term consistently with the same Chinese word, he chose different terms depending on context and perceived meaning, a strategy that involved interpreting the text. Indeed, Eugene Chen Eoyang's remark that "the translation becomes a pivotal text which comments on and interprets the original, either explicitly or implicitly,"[21] is especially applicable to Schereschewsky's OT translation.

Among a number of examples that could be cited, the "soul" (*nefesh*) especially required interpreting the meaning. Generally, *linghun* was adequate for the soul of a living person (Genesis 2:7). But sometimes more spiritual aspects of the human being were implied, as in Psalm 42:3, where the soul (*nefesh*) thirsts for God, or in Psalm 19:8, where the soul is restored. *Linghun* in these places would make no sense to a Chinese reader, and *xin* (heart/mind) was used instead, a term weighted with Confucian philosophical significance. *Nefesh*, however, can also mean simply the life of a person (Exodus 21:30 and Judges 9:17, for example), in which case neither of the above two terms was appropriate. In these places, Schereschewsky instead used the Chinese word for life (*ming* or *xingming*).

What might have been Schereschewsky's guides or references for choosing one or another interpretation? His years in Breslau had apparently acquainted him with German biblical criticism. Schereschewsky had also brought with him to Peking a number of works by such important scholars as W. M. L. De Wette, Heinrich F. W. Genesius, and Ernst F. K. Rosenmüller.[22] He consulted these works in a number of instances. However, his major guide for interpreting the biblical text was Rashi (Solomon Yitzhaki ben Isaac, 1040–1105), the French rabbinic scholar whose commentary on the Pentateuch has been considered authoritative for centuries. The evidence for Rashi's interpretations is for the most part contained in Schereschewsky's glosses and notes (these were almost completely deleted from the Union Version) but is also apparent in the text itself.

After the Mandarin Bible was published, the Peking Translating Committee terminated its function. Except for Schereschewsky, the other men continued to have distinguished careers in other areas. John Burdon became bishop of Victoria (Hong Kong), an office he filled with distinction. Henry Blodget continued to pursue an active career in the mission field, and Joseph Edkins wrote a number of books on Chinese culture and religion, which were still read to good benefit in the first half of this century. Elected bishop of Shanghai with jurisdiction in China in 1876, Schereschewsky suffered a sunstroke in 1881 and was for the next twenty-five years confined to a wheelchair. He continued his work, however, first revising the Mandarin OT (published in 1899) and then translating the entire Bible into literary Chinese (published in 1902). With the Union Bible under way, however, Schereschewsky's literary Bible never achieved the popularity of the Mandarin Bible.

THE "TERM QUESTION"

Determining which Chinese term best expressed the word *God* as well as the Christian idea of God was a major problem for Bible translators. The controversial issue was first discussed by the Jesuit missionaries in China in the seventeenth and eighteenth centuries and by some of their Chinese converts.[23] Never a dispassionate exchange of views, the question was finally settled by papal decree in 1742. Henceforth Catholics were to use *Tianzhu* (Lord of Heaven) for God.

For Protestant missionaries in the nineteenth century—who had no final authority to whom they could appeal and who were, moreover, represented by a variety of European and American denominations in China—there was no easy solution. Several terms in the Chinese religious vocabulary came under consideration: *Shangdi* (High Lord, a term of great antiquity), *Tian* (heaven, an equally ancient term), *Shen* (deity, spirit; also used adjectivally as divine, spiritual), and *di* (deity). There was also the Catholic neologism *Tianzhu*, which Protestants were, however, reluctant to use. Robert Morrison (1782–1834), when launching his translation of the Bible into Chinese, recorded in his journal the quandary of expressing God in Chinese. Morrison wrote in January 1808 that he liked *Tianzhu*, but the resemblance of Catholic saints and martyrs to Buddhist divinities was too great. He therefore decided to use *Shen* while attempting to get his converts to change the meaning of the term.[24]

But *Shen* was certainly not acceptable to everyone, and in the mid-1840s, an often vociferous controversy erupted that engaged theologians outside missionary circles.[25] Choosing the proper term posed larger questions of importance to the missionary enterprise in China, such as the nature and practice of Chinese religion, whether the Chinese ever were monotheists, and how the Chinese considered creation. In the 1850s, the major antagonists were William J. Boone (1911–1864), bishop of the Episcopal mission in Shanghai, and James Legge (1815–1897) of the London Missionary Society. Boone supported *Shen*, Legge *Shangdi*. Although by the time the Peking translators got down to work, the controversy had subsided somewhat, it resumed again in the later 1860s with a different set of participants, including a new generation of Chinese Protestants.[26]

At the very start of their work, the Peking group decided on *Tianzhu*, the term used by the Catholic Church. The record of the Peking Committee's discussions is not preserved, and precisely how the four (or five) men were persuaded to adopt *Tianzhu* in their translation is not clear. Some of their arguments can be gleaned, however, from their correspondence. Apparently a major consideration was that the men did not want to be allied with either the *Shangdi* or *Shen* party, evidently hoping to rally the missionary community, or at least the northern missionaries, to the use of the Roman Catholic term. Blodget objected to *Shangdi* because, according to him, it was long used "in a pantheistic sense" and could not be equated, therefore, with the Tetragrammaton (the "incommunicable name" of God, YHVH; Exodus 3:14).[27] According to Edkins, *Tianzhu* was especially appropriate in Mandarin-speaking areas, and nearly one million Catholics were already accustomed to it.[28] Schereschewsky agreed with Blodget that *Shen* had pantheistic associations. But he was also concerned about the term's multiple meanings: it can be plural for gods, it can designate goddesses, and it can be an adjective. Neither *Shen* nor *Shangdi* conveys the idea of the Creator: "The more I have examined native authorities as to the meaning of this term [*Shangdi*], the more I am convinced that to render God by *Shangti* . . . is to obscure, if not wholly to obliterate the cardinal doctrine of Revelation; namely the existence of an absolute personal living God, independent of and above nature."[29]

Apparently the committee hoped that their choice would end the frequently bitter squabbling among the missionaries, end divisiveness, and end the controversy. In retrospect, their expectations strike us as naive. Did they really anticipate rallying a majority of the missionaries behind their term? Even if their position was fairly strong—their Mandarin version had a much larger potential audience than any other translation—they completely underestimated the growing opposition to *Tianzhu* among missionaries in South and Central China. In those areas, Protestant missionaries more than once expressed concern that the Chinese might mistake Protestants for Catholics. In the end, neither *Tianzhu* nor *Shen* and *Shangdi* were unanimously accepted, and the British and Foreign Bible Society printed its Bibles with *Shangdi*, while the American Bible Society printed its Bibles with either *Shen* or *Tianzhu*. Apparently Chinese converts were not persuaded to adopt one term in preference to another. When articles by the first generation of Chinese Protestants began to appear, their arguments tended to be framed in far broader terms, suggesting that Westerners insufficiently understood the implied meanings of the Chinese terms. Most, however, saw no difficulty in using more than one term.[30]

But for Schereschewsky, translating the OT involved additional difficulties. The Chinese version had to indicate that in the Hebrew text different terms for God occur. In Genesis he followed a consistent course, translating Elohim (God) with *Tianzhu* and using Lord (*Zhu*) for the Tetragrammaton.

For YHVH Elohim he transliterated the Tetragrammaton as *Yehehua* and added *Tianzhu*.[31] Lord God (Adonai YHVH) was rendered as *Zhu Yehehua*.[32] In other OT books, Schereschewsky was, however, less consistent. Lord God (Adonai YHVH) was sometimes translated as *shang Zhu Yehehua* (High Lord YHVH; Exodus 23:17; Daniel 9:8; Isaiah 1:24) and at other times only with *Zhu Yehehua* (Psalm 8:2, 10) or *Tianzhu Yehehua* (Judges 16:28; Isaiah 3:1). When Schereschewsky translated the most-high God (*El Elyon*, Psalm 78:35; Genesis 14:19, 20) with *shang Tianzhu*, he invited a charge similar to the one he himself had made—namely, if there is one God (*Tianzhu*) who is superior (*shang*), there must be others who are not.[33]

Schereschewsky consistently translated the god or gods of other peoples as *shen*, whether he meant strange gods, other gods (*bieshen*, Exodus 34:14; Psalm 44:21), or foreign gods (*yishen*, Psalm 81:2). For teraphim, he used "images of gods" (*shenxiang*, Genesis 31:34, 35; Judges 17:5). But relegating *shen* to mean false gods must have been offensive to those missionaries who were using this term for God in preference to *Shangdi*, and it may have come to haunt him later.

The fiercely argued "term question" did not address the many problems of translating the OT. New decisions had to be made where Adonai occurred or when the Tetragrammaton was combined with descriptive appellations. Did Schereschewsky decide unilaterally, or had there been consultations? Are the inconsistencies intentional, or are they due to haste? According to James A. Muller, the OT translation was not subjected to the same rigorous criticism as the NT translation. Only Blodget went over the translation, and Schereschewsky made the final revisions.[34] The success of the Mandarin Bible in its transcultural journey was due to a variety of factors: the amicable relationships among the translators, their excitement over and dedication to their unique undertaking, and the coworkers' ability to help evolve a literary style in spoken Chinese. I have highlighted here Schereschewsky's special contribution to translating the OT. His skill as a translator in particular was significant. As a scholar of Chinese, he had few equals at the time, and his background in Hebrew, the Jewish commentaries, and the state of biblical criticism of his day were widely recognized. Also important were his astute views on the translator's task and his decision to produce a felicitous but also interpretive OT rendition. Regarding the controversial "term question," however, the Peking Translating Committee was not successful. In the end, *Tianzhu* proved to be the least popular term, and neither the missionaries nor the Chinese converts took to it. To render the Bible into present-day spoken Chinese is an ongoing task now carried on by Chinese translators. In this continuing effort, the work of the Peking Translating Committee stands as a monument for starting the process and creating the groundwork.

NOTES

1. The plan to cooperate on a Bible translating project was developed in an 1843 Hong Kong meeting. In 1847, delegates from both American and British missionary societies met in Shanghai, and work began thereafter on translating the Bible into classical Chinese. The New Testament was published in 1852; the Old Testament appeared in 1854. An alternate OT version by Elijah C. Bridgman and Michael S. Culbertson was published in 1862.

2. Jost Zetzsche, "The Work of Lifetimes: Why the *Union Version* Took Nearly Three Decades to Complete," in *The Bible in Modern China: The Literary and Intellectual Impact*, ed. I. Eber, S. K. Wan, and K. Walf, (Nettetal, 1999).

3. For example, A. J. Garnier, *Chinese Versions of the Bible* (Shanghai, 1934); and the more recent book by Zhao Weiban, *Yijing siyuan, xiantai wuda Shengjing fanyi shi* (Tracing Bible translations, a history of the translations of five modern Chinese versions of the Bible) (Hong Kong, 1993).

4. As a result of China's defeat in the first Anglo-Chinese War of 1839–1842, the so-called Opium War, five treaty ports were opened to Western penetration south of the Yangzi River. The renegotiation of the treaties ended with the forced opening of all of China in 1858 to Westerners, including their presence in the capital.

5. Henry Blodget, "The City of Peking," *The Church Missionary Gleaner* 13 (May 1863): 54–55.

6. W. A. P. Martin, "Scenes in Peking," *Foreign Missionary* 24 (January 1865): 196–197.

7. American Board of Commissioners for Foreign Missions (hereafter ABCFM), "Letters and Papers Addressed to the Board," Houghton Library, Harvard University, vol. 302:1,

Blodget to R. Anderson, November 4, 1861, ms. 127.

8. ABCFM, vol. 302:1, Blodget, Occasional Notes, March 20, 1867, 6, ms. 181.

9. "Peking Mission—N. China," *Foreign Missionary* 7 (December 1868): 169.

10. ABCFM, vol. 302:1, Blodget, Occasional Notes, March 20, 1867, 6, ms. 181.

11. For my study of Schereschewsky and his OT translation, see *The Jewish Bishop and the Chinese Bible: S.I.J. Schereschewsky, 1831–1906* (Leiden, 1999).

12. ABCFM, vol. 302:1, Blodget to R. Anderson, December 22, 1864, ms. 165.

13. Domestic and Foreign Missionary Society, China Records, 1835–1951 (hereafter DFMS), the Archives of the Episcopal Church, USA, Austin, Texas, RG64-28, Schereschewsky to Denison, October 14, 1864.

14. "Shengjing yi guanhuaben gaocheng" (Translation of the Bible into *guanhua* is completed), *Jiaohui xinbao* (Church news) 14 (July 13, 1872): 225.

15. I was unable to locate the 1866 and 1867 editions. They are also not in the archives of the American Bible Society. The two printings of 1874 and 1875 were in two different sizes, according to personal communication from Mary Ellen Gleason, Archives of the American Bible Society, July 18, 1995.

16. Milton T. Stauffer, ed., *The Christian Occupation of China* (Shanghai, 1922), 453. Although Stauffer's figures have to be accepted with caution, the fact is that vernacular Bibles by far outnumbered those in classical Chinese.

17. Willis Barnstone, *The Poetics of Translation: History, Theory, Practice* (New Haven–London, 1993), 261–262.

18. DFMS, RG64-29, "Translation of the Scriptures into Chinese," photocopy, 2. I do

not have the publication data for this article, which is dated March 17, 1890.

19. I am using the *Jiuyue quanshu*, printed with *Tianzhu*. The full English title is *The Old Testament in the Mandarin Colloquial, Translated from the Hebrew by the Reverend J.I.S. Schereschewsky, D.D. of the American Episcopal Mission, and Printed for the American Bible Society at the Press of the ABCFM, Peking, China, 1875*. For the Hebrew, I use the standard Masoretic text.

20. S. I. J. Schereschewsky, "Terminology in the China Mission," *The Churchman* 57, no. 6 (January 14, 1888): 34–35. For the question of biblical transliterations, see Jost Zetzsche, "Bibel in China (I, III): Transkriptionen in den Chinesischen Bibelueberset-zungen," *China Heule* 13, no. 6 (76) (1994): 178–185; no. 2 (78) (1995): 46–55.

21. Eugene Chen Eoyang, *The Transparent Eye: Reflections on Translation, Chinese Literature and Comparative Poetics* (Honolulu, 1993), 170.

22. DFMS, RG64-28, Schereschewsky to the Rev. S. D. Denison, July 21, 1865.

23. The Chinese contribution to the term question controversy is at last receiving notice. For its earlier beginnings, see the excellent discussion by Nicolas Standaert, *The Fascinating God: A Challenge to Modern Chinese Theology Presented by a Text on the Name of God Written by a 17th Century Chinese Student of Theology* (Rome, 1995).

24. Eliza Morrison, *Memoirs of the Life and Labours of Robert Morrison* (London, 1839), 1:201.

25. Douglas G. Spelman has provided an excellent summary of the first twenty years of the controversy in "Christianity in Chinese: The Protestant Term Question," *Papers on China*, East Asian Research Center, Harvard University, 22A (May 1969): 25–52.

26. The polemical literature on the term question—pamphlets, articles, and books—is enormous. For a summary of the issues, see I. Eber, "The Interminable Term Question," in *The Bible in Modern China*, ed. Eber, Wan, and Walf.

27. Letter cited in Margaret T. Hills, "Text and Translation, Languages of China: 1861–1900," ABS Historical Essay, #16, IV-G-3, unpublished ms., 17. Courtesy of the American Bible Society, New York.

28. The Archives of the Council for World Missions, including the London Missionary Society, London University, School of Oriental and African Studies Library (CWM), Edkins to Dr. Tiedeman, May 14, 1866.

29. Letter in *Spirit of Missions* 31 (May 1866): 268–270; (June 1866): 326–328.

30. See the review article by Zhou Shungui, "Yuege shenghao lunjin chenbi jian" (Review essay of articles on holy appellations), *Wanguo gongbao* (Globe magazine) 10, no. 491 (June 1, 1878): 562a–63b (5025–5027).

31. The inconsistency of both transliterating the tetragrammaton and translating it as *Zhu* was criticized by John W. Davis, "Jehovah," *Chinese Recorder* 7, no. 6 (December 1876): 399.

32. Like Elohim, Adonai is morphologically plural, but according to the content, it is singular, of which Schereschewsky was well aware.

33. Some of the terms were changed in the 1899 revised version, printed by the British and Foreign Bible Society. The American Bible Society version was not available to me.

34. James A. Muller, *Apostle of China: Samuel Isaac Joseph Schereschewsky, 1831–1906* (New York–Milwaukee, 1937), 88.

CHAPTER 6

Translating the Ancestors

S. I. J. Schereschewsky's 1875 Chinese Version of Genesis

Partial and complete Bible translations into classical Chinese existed well before Protestant missionaries actually began to work actively among the Chinese. Translation work accelerated once missionaries gained a foothold in the newly opened treaty ports after 1842, and the entire Bible or portions of it were translated into Fuzhou, Amoy, Canton, Hakka, Suzhou, Ningbo, and Shanghai dialects.[1] S. I. J. Schereschewsky's (1831–1906) translation of the Old Testament (OT) into the northern vernacular in 1875 opened a new chapter. His translation was accessible to larger numbers of people and, in contrast to the OT in classical Chinese, was readily understood when read to the illiterate. Moreover, unlike previous translations, it was prepared entirely from the Hebrew original.

The purpose of this essay is to examine some of Schereschewsky's views on translating and several of the techniques he employed in rendering the Book of Genesis into Chinese. My basic assumption is that translation is an interpretative activity. When a text is transposed from one language into another, changes are introduced that are consonant with the receiving languages and culture. Translation is affected by interpretations from within the receptor tradition, which, in turn, makes possible the acceptance of the translation and the ideas it contains. Thus the Old (as well as the New) Testament translations represented one of the initial steps in the Sinification of Protestant Christianity.[2]

Schereschewsky's OT translation is of considerable interest. It was prepared by a person who was thoroughly familiar with the original Hebrew text and its Jewish commentary tradition. In addition, first the 1875 translation and then the revised 1899 version were widely used until the appearance of the 1919 Union Version, which is still in use. Although the latter represented a new translation effort, even a superficial comparison of Schereschewsky's OT and the Union text reveals close correspondences both in style and in the use of terms.[3] Earlier printings of the Union text, furthermore, retained portions of the explanatory notes Schereschewsky had appended to his translation. Precisely when these were deleted in some, though apparently not all, printings must still be ascertained.

My aim here is not, however, to establish the relationship between Schereschewsky's OT and the Union text's OT. It is rather to examine how the translator transposed the text from one cultural context into another. To this end, I shall first take up Schereschewsky's Jewish background and how he viewed the translation enterprise. This will be followed by a brief summary of the "term question" and uses of transliteration and techniques of translating. The essay will conclude with a discussion of the notes he appended to the text to clarify terms and obscure passages.

BIOGRAPHICAL SKETCH

Details about Schereschewsky's early life are scarce, since he apparently did not talk much of his childhood and youth.[4] Yet it is obvious that his Jewish education, first in his hometown and later in the Zhitomir rabbinic school, uniquely equipped him to undertake the OT translation. His lack of strong family ties combined with the stirrings of the Eastern European Jewish Enlightenment (Haskala) also played a role in leading him at an impressionable age to search for meaning outside Judaism. At a later stage in his life, he joined, as it were, his Jewish past with his new faith by making the translation enterprise his life's work.

He was born into a Jewish family in Tavrik (Tauroggen, Taurage) in Russian Lithuania. It was a small town, then near the Prussian border, numbering among its inhabitants 410 Jews in 1847. He was orphaned early and was brought up in the home of his well-to-do half brother (probably from his father's previous marriage), who was in the lumber business. As an orphan, dependent on the goodwill and care of relatives, he seems in his early years to have been quite unhappy. Like other Jewish boys, however, he was sent to a *heder* (lit. "room"), a school where generally underpaid and overworked teachers inculcated in their unruly charges the basics of Jewish learning. He left home, such as it was, in 1846 or 1847, when he was fifteen years old.[5]

The next three to four years were crucial in the life of the adolescent boy and must be seen against the background of the Jewish Enlightenment in Europe. Starting in eighteenth-century Western Europe, the Enlightenment had as its aim Jewish emancipation, participation in Western education and culture, the study of the sciences, and a loosening of the hold of Orthodox traditions. By the nineteenth century, this movement had spread throughout Central and Eastern Europe, leading to widespread educational ferment and open hostility between Orthodox Jews and Enlightenment supporters. The former opposed a nontraditional education for Jewish youths, and the latter supported the establishment of "modern" educational institutions. Hardly a Jewish community throughout Eastern Europe remained untouched by the controversy.

During Tsar Nicholas I's reign (1825–1855), a number of significant educational innovations took place in Russia and in the lands under Russian rule. Among these were government-sponsored rabbinical seminaries, one located in Vilna, Lithuania, and the other established in 1847 in Zhitomir, Ukraine. By offering instruction in both traditional and secular subjects, the two seminaries, though they were abhorred by their elders, made themselves extremely attractive to reform-minded youths.[6]

With no immediate family in Tavrik and no further educational opportunities nearby, it seems no accident that the fifteen-year-old orphan decided to go to Zhitomir to attend the seminary.[7] There he could choose between a rabbinic or a teaching curriculum, and there he found a window on the world that was not available in Tavrik. In Zhitomir he was for the first time exposed to non-Jewish teachers who taught secular subjects (there being no qualified Jewish teachers for these), and he probably also encountered the New Testament (NT) in a Yiddish or perhaps Hebrew translation.[8] Schereschewsky's long journey to conversion and high church office in China quite likely began at this early point.

His encounter with Christianity in Breslau, where he arrived in 1851 or 1852, was certainly a fact. There he came under the influence of a Dr. S. (or J.) Neumann, "a learned Jewish convert" who taught at the Breslau University and was revising the Hebrew (?) NT translation.[9] Neumann no doubt introduced him to German biblical criticism of the time.[10] Whereas in Zhitomir Schereschewsky was initiated into the Jewish commentary tradition, in Breslau he was introduced to "modern" methods of criticism.

From Breslau, his road led to the United States in 1854, conversion, and seminary study. He was ordained a deacon in 1859 at the age of twenty-eight and immediately sailed for China, having decided already in 1857, according to an interview many years later, that he wanted to translate the Bible into Chinese.[11]

Translation of the OT and NT began in 1864 in Peking together with a group of other missionaries and was completed eleven years later. In the six years that followed, Schereschewsky engaged in raising funds for and in founding what eventually became St. John's University in Shanghai. He was also elected missionary bishop of Shanghai, a post he actively filled only until 1881. That summer he suffered an attack of sunstroke, which left him completely paralyzed. He spent the last twenty-one years of his life revising the complete vernacular Bible and producing a new translation in classical (easy Wen-li) Chinese.

THE TRANSLATING ENTERPRISE

Missionaries emphasized rendering the Bible into Chinese in order to place the "word of God" into the hands of the people. The Bible, they argued, was an essential tool for their work. Translating it was sometimes described in extravagant terms and likened to "what Luther did for Germany" and what the King James Version had done for the English-speaking part of the world.[12] But translation as an integral part of the missionary effort was, above all, concerned with the recipient culture. Lamin Sanneh's argument on translating the Bible into African languages also holds true for Chinese. He writes, "That mission was not the instrument for sifting the world into an identity of cultural likeness, with our diversities being pressed into a single mold in preparation for some millennial reckoning. So obedience to the gospel was distinguished from loyalty to a universal cultural paradigm. Translatability presupposed cultural pluralism by assuming that linguistic variety was needed for the word of God." Far from demanding cultural conformity, missionaries, by means of translation, encouraged cultural pluralism.[13]

Schereschewsky expressed similar views in 1877, in his consecration address as bishop of Shanghai. The aim of the mission, he stated, was the creation of a native and thoroughly Chinese Christianity, "trained on the soil and for the soil." At a time when ethnicity and identity were hardly subjects of discourse, he argued that nothing must be done to destroy Chinese "ethnic characteristics"; "foreign traits" must not be grafted onto the Chinese character. Dislocating Chinese "from all their social and civil articulations with the body politic in which they were born" must be avoided. "Instead of weaning him from the dress, the dwellings, the food, the habits and customs, the family circle and the civil obedience due from him . . . his whole status should be preserved intact."[14]

However, Schereschewsky and other missionaries also recognized that in China they encountered a highly literate civilization that attached great importance to the written word. Referring to Chinese schools and the examination system, he said that "no nation on earth has such a multiplicity of histories, anthologies, encyclopedias and standard works on archeology, law and letters, as the Chinese." He described the Chinese as a "highly civilized and well-educated people."[15] His wife wrote in a similar vein that the literature of the Chinese was "both ancient and immense. Systems of religion, high standards of morality, philosophical treatises composed by the best minds of the nation are theirs."[16] This respect for China's literary tradition led Schereschewsky, no doubt, to an increased awareness of the importance of the Bible's literary merits in translation.

China's literary heritage was intimidating, but so was the diversity of spoken languages and the question of the translators' target audience. Did they want to reach readers as well as listeners? And where, in sheer numbers, was their largest audience?

The importance of vernacular translations to be read to illiterate audiences, in addition to those in classical Chinese, was recognized early on. Hence by 1860, when Henry Blodget (1825–1903) arrived in Tianjin, he at once realized that aside from the several translations into southern Chinese languages, a translation of the Bible into northern vernacular was a major priority. It would be understood by more than half the population of China, he wrote, and in its written form would be understood by everyone.[17] At a later time, he again explained that the northern vernacular is "read everywhere throughout the Empire by all educated men . . . [and it is] the language of daily life. It is called the Mandarin colloquial because it is the language of all who are in office, spoken in all their official transactions. It is also the language of the common people. . . . All the provinces north of the Yangtzu river, Yunnan and Kweichow south of it, speak this dialect. It is intelligible to nearly all the people . . . [and] may be regarded as the general colloquial language of China."[18]

Although a northern vernacular translation could be understood by many millions of Chinese, Schereschewsky was nonetheless aware that a vernacular text would not be highly thought of by the educated Chinese. Therefore, he was eventually convinced that separate Bibles were needed for each audience and that both the vernacular and the classical translations were equally important.[19] This was especially so after 1879 and the founding of St. John's in Shanghai, when he realized that to educate the boys by means of a vernacular work—which was, moreover, in idiomatic northern Chinese—was impossible.

Professor Fairbank has rightly stressed the importance of close collaboration with Chinese assistants and teachers as indispensable partners in the translating enterprise. No matter how good a missionary's Chinese—and Schereschewsky's was acknowledged to be superb[20]—the assistants often rescued translators from embarrassing blunders and outright errors.[21] Blodget's description of the Peking Translating Committee's working method[22] with their teachers is worth quoting in full:

> Our method is, to apportion to each of the five members certain chapters, or books, that he may prepare a draft. This draft is supposed to be the *best translation he can produce* [underlined in original]. Then his draft is criticized most truly by each of the remaining four, working in his own study, with his teacher. The author . . . receives these criticisms and . . . makes out a second draft. . . . This second draft is sent around to each of the other members who notes every thing, whether in the style, or in the sense, which he wishes to see changed. When this has been done, we meet for discussion . . . two or three native teachers being present to assist.[23]

Apparently each missionary had his own teacher or teachers. I was not able to ascertain who Schereschewsky's teachers in Peking were. Mrs. Schereschewsky mentions two (unfortunately not by name), one of whom, an older man, had "served with foreigners for many years."[24] Blodget mentions Lang Yunshong, a forty-five-year-old "literary man" whom he converted and who became his teacher. Another, Si Xiansong, disappointed him, however, when he smuggled opium into Peking.[25] As a group, the

Chinese teachers presumably were "the most competent Chinese scholars such as Peking could afford," in the words of a later commentator.[26]

What was deemed desirable in a translation of the Bible, and how did Schereschewsky see his task? In the introduction to the 1875 OT, he wrote, "The original Holy Scripture was written by the Jews (*Youtai*). Afterwards all Western countries (*qinxi*) translated [it] into each language. The present translation into Mandarin (*guanhua*) is profound in meaning and is prepared in accordance with the original. [I] . . . did not dare add or subtract one word."[27]

At a later time he wrote, "Idiom and clearness should not be sacrificed to literality. To translate literally Hebrew or Greek into Chinese is often mistranslating." And he also said, "It is possible to be faithful to the original without being slavishly literal." On the other hand, he believed that it was possible to preserve the "biblical diction" in Chinese, especially the unique characteristics of Hebrew poetry. Hebrew parallelisms could be reproduced in Chinese, and it was essential to retain the differences between the OT prose and poetry portions.[28] Above all, he was convinced already during the initial stages of the translation work that even if other translations were consulted, he was "resolved to adhere to the Hebrew original as much as the nature of the Chinese language . . . will possibly admit. I believe that the Hebrew text is to be preferred to any version old as it may be."[29] His principal objections to the two earlier translations were that whereas the one was idiomatically sound, it deviated from the biblical text, and the other was too literal and therefore not idiomatic.[30]

Finally, although the translators throughout their eleven years of labor felt that they were engaged in one of the most significant tasks of their time, the appearance of the northern vernacular Old and New Testaments was but briefly noted in missionary circles. *The Church News* (*Jiaohui xinbao*) praised both scriptures for their careful attention to detail, calling them a "meritorious effort." *The Chinese Recorder* stated the price and assured potential buyers that they now could gratify their desire for a Bible in the "Mandarin dialect."[31] The significance of Schereschewsky's accomplishment was fully acknowledged only many years later. Frederick R. Graves, then bishop of Shanghai, wrote that after its appearance in 1875, Schereschewsky's vernacular OT was immediately adopted: "Before the publication of the Union Version . . . Schereschewsky had no rival, and if it has been replaced by the Union Version, his Old Testament in Mandarin in the judgement of the best qualified critics preserves a special value which will be lasting."[32]

THE "TERM QUESTION"

In China, the Bible translators' major problem was which term to use for God. The issue was debated at length in numerous publications,[33] and it was raised time and again in the translators' correspondence home. There was (and still is) no easy solution. Not only did British and American missionaries disagree, but Baptists, Methodists, and Presbyterians were also unable to find common ground.

Should an entirely new term be coined, or should an already existing term be chosen? In the first case, it was feared that the Chinese Bible reader would have no idea who or what was being referred to, while in the second case, he would assume that the Christian message and this God were, after all, no different from the gods he had known all along. Was there in the Chinese vocabulary, others asked, a term that most closely approximated the meaning of God? Although the missionaries' knowledge of the various forms of Chinese religion was far from profound (their teachers were probably also not overly helpful on this subject), they were nevertheless aware that such terms as *Tian, Shangdi,* and *shen* had significantly different connotations in Chinese religious beliefs. Both those missionaries who knew the language well and their teachers invested much effort in searching the Chinese classics and dictionaries to establish meanings and usages of the Chinese terms. They cited examples from the *Shujing* and the *Lunyu,* and they defined the terms on the basis of the Kangxi dictionary in trying to pinpoint the "generic" name for God.[34] Others, however, rejected the notion of a "generic" term—James Legge, the translator of the Chinese classics, among them. Bringing his impressive knowledge of the classics to bear on the subject, he supported the use of *Shangdi* for God by citing from the *Shijing* and the *Yijing,* as well as the Chinese histories.[35]

Recourse to learned references did not, however, produce a definitive solution, because as George Staunton pointed out, actual worship in temples was of numerous gods (*shen*) and not of one god (*Shangdi*) only.[36] Since the *shen* were many, those who supported this term suggested prefacing it with "true" (*zhen*). But this was rejected on the grounds that even a *zhen shen* can cease to be *zhen* when it is invaded by a "wandering spirit" (*cao mu shen*).[37]

Schereschewsky employed a more sophisticated argument in pressing for his term for God, which was *Tianzhu* (Lord of Heaven). *Shangdi* was not satisfactory, he argued, because of *Shangdi*'s identification in some quarters with the Jade Emperor (*Yuwang*) or with heaven (*Tian*), the latter conveying a pantheistic idea. The search for a generic name for God may in itself not be mistaken, he wrote, but *shen* cannot serve the purpose. The term can be used in the singular or plural, and it can also denote female deities. Therefore, it cannot be used for a monotheistic religion. To preface it with *zhen* contributes nothing. A god is meant to be true; otherwise, he is not a god.

His own solution, which he employed in his 1875 OT translation and which had been approved by the Foreign Committee in 1865, was to use *Tianzhu* for Elohim (God), *Zhu* (lord) for YHVH, and *shen* for (other) gods because *Tianzhu* had "never been used in an idolatrous sense," as none of the Chinese gods are referred to as *Tianzhu*.[38] Schereschewsky's OT translation maintained these distinctions strictly, using, in addition, *Yehehua* (YHVH) *Tianzhu* whenever YHVH Elohim occurred in the original. Two other terms were also scrupulously differentiated: Almighty God (El Shadai) was translated as *quan neng di Tianzhu*, and YHVH, the Everlasting God (Yehova El Olam) was translated as *Yehehua yongsheng Tianzhu*.

Tianzhu was, of course, used by the Roman Catholic Church, he conceded, and there was the danger that Chinese Bible readers would confuse Protestants with Catholics. He also admitted favoring for a time the use of *Shangzhu* (Supreme Lord), but Blodget persuaded him otherwise. Yet Schereschewsky by no means dogmatically insisted on his choice of *Tianzhu* as the only possible term. Although in printed matter God was to be rendered as *Tianzhu*, in 1878, while serving as bishop of the Episcopal mission, he told his clergy to use any term they preferred when preaching.[39]

In 1893, Blodget presented the most cogent argument yet in favor of *Tianzhu*. He believed that the entire Christian church—Protestant, Roman Catholic, and Greek—should use uniform terminology. Like Schereschewsky, he felt that it was necessary to distinguish between many gods and the One God. *Shangdi* was not the proper term because of its association with the "national cult," he wrote. *Tianzhu* was suitable on two counts. The term is mentioned by Sima Qian in connection with the *feng* and *shan* sacrifice, when the first emperor of the Qin dynasty is said to have worshipped eight gods (*shen*), among them *Tianzhu*.[40] Second, "no word in the

Chinese language has more of religious reverence attached to it than the word T'ien, Heaven." *Zhu* adds the personal element.[41]

Even so, until the appearance of the Union Bible in 1919, which uses *Shangdi,* the "term question" was not resolved, and echoes of the problem continue to linger. In the early years of this century, after Schereschewsky completed both the OT revisions and the translation into classical Chinese, the OT and NT Bibles were printed in three different editions, using *Tianzhu, Shangdi,* and *Shen.*[42]

THE TRANSLATION TECHNIQUES

Schereschewsky had the choice of either translating or transliterating names and terms. Whatever method he employed, he and his teachers had to exercise extraordinary care in choosing acceptable Chinese characters so as not to expose themselves to ridicule for using characters with improper connotations. For the transliteration of sounds, Schereschewsky saw a precedent in Buddhist, Muslim, and Roman Catholic translations, and he pointed out that Sanskrit terms especially, though first transliterated, eventually became an integral part of the Chinese language. Hence, aside from the OT translation, he frequently resorted to transliterations, especially of terms connected with church practice and church ritual,[43] assuming perhaps that as China became Christian, these terms would also enter the Chinese language.

In Genesis, he transliterated names of plants, place names, and personal names. Place and personal names in Genesis generally refer to attributes or characteristics; in transliterated form, some semblance of their sound was retained, but not of the meaning. Since he transliterated from the Hebrew, he obviously followed the Hebrew pronunciation. Thus, for example, the Hebrew Hava (Eve) is transliterated as Xiawa (Gen. 3:20), and the city Amora (Gemorrah) is Emala (Gen. 18:20). Notes are frequently appended to the names explaining their meaning.

I will discuss the notes separately, turning first to a number of terms for which there were no equivalents in Chinese and terms for which equivalents existed.[44] In both cases, the translator had to balance carefully interpretation and terminology. Several examples will serve to demonstrate how interpretation, together with the demands of the Chinese language, has left its imprint.

In Genesis, the potential for life commences with the creation of a firmament (*rekia*) that divides the waters above and below it (Gen. 1:6–7). God called the firmament heaven (Gen. 1:8). Later, after the great and lesser lights (e.g., sun and moon) as well as the stars were created, they were set onto the firmament (Gen. 1:17).

Schereschewsky had two problems here. First, how to translate *firmament*, and second, what to do with it once it was said to be the same as heaven. He translated firmament, which in the Hebrew suggests space, expanse, and emptiness,[45] as *kongqi* or air. This was neither an accurate nor a happy choice, leading to confusion for the serious Chinese reader, since air is not heaven. Possibly to avoid compounding the problem and opting for consistency, Schereschewsky then had God place the lights on heaven (*tianshang*, Gen. 1:17) rather than on air. The fact that no equivalent for firmament could be found in Chinese led to necessary changes in the text.

Circumcision, which is included in God's covenant with Abraham (Gen. 17:10–11), presented a similar problem but was handled differently. The term used for the Hebrew word was *geli*, which may be defined as ritual cutting. In the translation, Abraham is told to circumcise, but the first part of verse 11, specifying what is to be cut, is omitted, and the injunction to circumcise is simply repeated. Verse 14 is handled similarly. The omission was of no consequence to either missionaries or converts, and Schereschewsky's decision—based, no doubt, on avoiding embarrassing explanations—is perfectly understandable.

Even where Chinese equivalents could be used, interpretation played an important role. The most obvious examples of the way interpretation influenced translation concern the concepts associated with the three covenants and how they relate to the process that identified the people of Israel as a separate group. The covenant with Abraham, Isaac, and Jacob includes God's promise to each of the Patriarchs of offspring, nationhood, and land (Gen. 12:1–3, 15:5, 7; 17:5–9; 26:3–4; 28:13–14; 35:11–12). Covenant (*brit*), *yue*, or establishing a covenant, *liyue*, was easily translated, as the Chinese clearly indicates that the person who enters the covenant obligates (binds) himself to do certain things.[46] Similarly, the Hebrew term *seed* for progeny was translated with various synonyms signifying sons and offspring and also presented no problem.

The promise of land was, however, a different matter because the translator had to interpret whether the world, a country, or a locality was meant.

In the majority of cases, Schereschewsky translated land or country (*eretz*) as *di*. God tells Abraham that He will give him this land (Gen. 12:7), and to Jacob He says similarly that the land that was given to Abraham and Isaac will be given to Jacob and his posterity (Gen. 35:12). Sometimes also *difang* is used (Gen. 12:1, 17:8), but whether *di* or *difang*, the Chinese terms indicate land as real estate, a place, but not a country. On the other hand, "all the nations of the earth" (Gen. 26:4) is translated as *tianxia*. The translator's avoidance of more politically slanted vocabulary is especially obvious in Genesis 17:8, where God promised Abraham "all the land of Canaan," which is translated as *quandi* (the whole land).

The question of the Israelites' peoplehood versus that of other peoples reveals a similarly cautious use of terminology with possible political implications. Genesis has two distinct terms for differentiating people as followers of a ruler or person (*am*) and people in the sense of a nation (*goi*). Schereschewsky was clearly intent on retaining the distinction, translating people in the first sense as *min* (Gen. 26:10) or *renmin* (Gen. 14:16, 35:6) and occasionally as *zhongmin* (Gen. 19:4).

When *goi*, or nation, is used in the singular, the Chinese reads *zu*, with its meaning closer to tribe or clan.[47] God's promise to Abraham (Gen. 12:2), Ishmael (Gen. 21:18), and Jacob (Gen. 46:3) that they each will become a "great nation" reads that they each will become a great *zu*. In contrast, the translator used *guo* (Gen. 17:4–5, 35:11) when *goi* occurs in the plural (*goiim*). The distinction between the singular as tribe or clan and the plural as states or nations is deliberate, and there are few exceptions to the rule. One of these is in Genesis 27:29, where Isaac blesses Jacob: "Other peoples (*guo*) will serve you, many nations (*wan zu*) will kowtow to you." A more faithful translation should have used *min* for the people in the first phrase and *guo* for nations in the second. The other example is Genesis 25:23, where God explains to Rebecca, Isaac's wife, that two nations (*guo*) are struggling within her (Jacob and Esau), and "two sons (*zi*) will be born from your stomach," even though the Hebrew text states that two nations (*goiim*) and two peoples (*le'umim*) are involved.[48] Hence in Schereschewsky's translation, the epic struggle of the brothers does not begin in the womb— Rebecca is merely having a difficult pregnancy. These translations in what must be considered central portions of Genesis (because they contain God's promise of future greatness) are not easily explained. The translator seems deliberately to avoid a politically linked vocabulary, which may be a result of the way Schereschewsky interpreted these portions. However, it may also be the result of intentionally eschewing an explicitly political vocabulary in order not to arouse the suspicion that subversive literature was being produced.[49]

The Chinese text often tends to be more explicit than the original. Following the creation of Adam, for example (Gen. 2:7), the Hebrew reads that "man was a living soul (*nefesh*)," whereas the translation states that he was a "living man having a soul (*linghun*)." Translating *nefesh* as *linghun* raises the complex question of what is implied by *ling* and *hun* and *nefesh*. It cannot be discussed here in all its ramifications, but suffice it to say that where *nefesh* denotes life, the *linghun* combination denotes the spirit, or the spiritual and yang component of the human being. Although obviously a person with a *linghun* is alive, the life of the person is not attributable to the *linghun* alone. For the Chinese reader, the text therefore had to state clearly that he was a living man having a soul.

On the subject of Eve's creation (Gen. 2:23), the Chinese text states more precisely than the Hebrew that "she came out from man's body." According to the Hebrew, "she was taken from man (*ish*)." In regard to Adam, Schereschewsky drops the impersonal *ren*, man (*adam*) already in Genesis 2:19. Thereafter, he switches to the named man, Adam (*Yadang*), thus leaving no doubt who is being discussed. In the original, man as *adam* occurs until Genesis 3:17, changing from then on to the named man, Adam.

By making the Chinese text more explicit, the ideas conveyed themselves become different. God tells Abraham to leave his country, his birthplace, and his father's home to go to the land that He will show him (Gen. 12:1). The Chinese is overly emphatic by adding that God ordered (*fenfu*) Abraham to go. The verse together with the command assumes a harshness in the Chinese that is not present in the original, reading now that Abraham must forsake his "native place (*bendi*), kinfolk (*qinzu*), [and his] father's home (*fujia*)."

A more radical change in meaning occurs in Genesis 17:14. Part of God's covenant with Abraham concerns the circumcision of male children. Abraham is told the consequences of not abiding by the agreement to circumcise: the soul will be cut off from his people because he broke the covenant. As pointed out above, the connotations of soul (*linghun*) being different from the Hebrew *nefesh*, Schereschewsky had to opt for a different translation, which, in turn, led to a different interpretation from that implied by the

Hebrew text. The soul being cut off meant expulsion. Thus the translation reads, "The male child who is not circumcised, he will be renounced, he will not be permitted (*rong*) among the people, because he abandoned (*fei*) my covenant." In the 1899 revised version, this passage is interpreted still differently: "The male child who is not circumcised, abandoned (*fei*) my covenant, he will certainly be destroyed (*miejue*) among his people."

Both versions omit the word *soul*, punishing the person directly; the 1875 version mercifully threatens only ostracism, whereas the 1899 version foretells death and destruction. Was he overly influenced by interpretations of a wrathful God? Or did Schereschewsky in this place disagree with the Hebrew commentaries? The Onkelos commentary implies that the uncircumcised will be excluded from the community. Rashi, on the other hand, interprets this passage to mean that the person will die childless and before his time.[50]

These examples are not evidence of a flawed translation. To the contrary, in the interpreted text, Schereschewsky abandoned suggestiveness for the unambiguous statement: Abraham responds to an explicit order; breaking the covenant entails dire consequences.

After 1864, the Peking group of translators had several Bible translations available to them that they could consult for their own work. Even if in classical Chinese, these could serve at least as points of reference. The most recent OT versions were the so-called Delegates' Version, published in 1854, and the variant translation by E. C. Bridgman and M. S. Culbertson, published in 1863.[51] Some of Schereschewsky's transliterations, like *Yehehua*, were quite likely based on the earlier translations. Furthermore, not all of Schereschewsky's terminology was new or different from previous translations. *Geli*, for example, for circumcision was probably also borrowed from the Bridgman and Culbertson translation, since earlier versions tended to use only *ge*, to cut.[52]

THE NOTES

Schereschewsky's notes are possibly the most interesting part of this translation enterprise. They do not attempt to present theological interpretations, and they are not a vehicle for the Christian message in the OT. Rather, they exemplify the translator's concept of a Chinese Christianity "trained on the soil and for the soil," as Schereschewsky had put it. The notes provided the reader with technical tools for understanding the text and the Bible reader and teacher with the means of explaining it. Above all, the notes demonstrate Schereschewsky's erudition and his profound familiarity with the biblical text and the Jewish commentary tradition.

They generally deal with technical matters of translation, such as the meaning of place and personal names, and they explain or reword enigmatic and obscure passages.[53] The notes are always placed within the text and follow directly the word or phrase that they explain. The elucidation in many cases is based on Rashi's commentary, although there is also evidence that Schereschewsky resorted to Midrashic materials aside from those included in Rashi.[54]

Following are a number of random examples. Among those notes intended to clarify the text, there is the creation from Adam's rib of Eve, who, according to the translation, "can be called woman" (Gen. 2:23). The note reads, "According to the original Hebrew text, the pronunciation of the two [words] 'ish' and 'isha' [man and woman] indicates the meaning of woman being obtained through man." It is quite questionable that this explanation was satisfying to an inquiring mind, considering that the crucial issue, the question of that rib, is being evaded.

Another note concerns Lemech, the fifth-generation descendant of Cain. In Genesis 4:23 the following enigmatic sentence appears: "I have slain a man to my wounding, and a young man to my hurt." The Chinese translation reproduces the Hebrew, but in the appended note, Schereschewsky reworded the sentence: "If I kill a warrior I harm myself, [if] I harm a youth I damage my [own] body." The note reflects Rashi's explanation (obtained from a midrash) that Lemech inadvertently killed Cain, his forebear, and, utterly distraught, then killed his own son, Tubal-Cain.[55]

Almost as faithfully as Rashi had done eight hundred years earlier, Schereschewsky glossed minute points of the text. In Genesis 31:46–47, Laban and Jacob, after the latter's successful flight, erect a cairn to seal their agreement. Laban calls the cairn Yegar Sahaduta; Jacob calls it Galed. For both names there are notes. The first, Schereschewsky explained as an Aramaic (*Yalan*) word meaning a stone heap as testimony; the second, he wrote, was a Hebrew word with the same meaning.[56]

Plants, fruit, types of wood, animals, or fabrics for clothes—all these Schereschewsky tried to explain in notes. A few examples will suffice. Pharaoh dresses Joseph in "*shesh* clothes" (*bigdei shesh*, Gen. 41:42).

Schereschewsky, not differentiating between the name of the cloth (*shesh*) and the Hebrew construct for clothes (*bigdei*), transliterated both words as *bishu*. In the appended note, he explained that the fabric was of the whitest and finest kind; in antiquity, it was most expensive and was worn only by the highborn. Schereschewsky knew that descriptions of this fabric (a fine wool?) occur elsewhere in the OT, and his note was based on these.

At harvest time, Reuben brings home mandrakes (*duda'im*), a plant or fruit (Gen. 30:14) widely thought to have been an aphrodisiac but unknown today. The name of the plant is transliterated in the text as *dudai*, and the appended note explains it as the name of a plant. Some of the extensive literature on mandrakes must have come to Schereschewsky's attention in the next two decades, for in the revised 1899 edition, there is the added information that this is a kind of tomato. Indeed, mandrakes, which were said to have erotic qualities and enhanced the charms of women, were identified with tomatoes after the latter became known in Europe.

A somewhat different kind of explanation concerns Genesis 47:21, which reports rather laconically that during the famine, Joseph moved his people from Egypt's borders to the cities. Rashi's lengthy explanation that Joseph wanted to remove from the people the stigma of emigrants by settling them in the cities[57] is only partly reproduced. According to the note, Joseph caused his people (*min*) to be removed to and to settle in cities from one border to the other.

Finally, the meaning of transliterated names of people is frequently given. Thus Hava's name (Gen. 3:20) is explained as meaning "life." The name Cain (Gen. 4:1) refers to his occupation. Schereschewsky here probably had Rashi's explanation of Genesis 4:22 in mind, which states that Tubal-Cain, a worker of metals, "refined Cain's craft."[58] Noah (Gen. 5:29) means "peaceful." Abraham (Gen. 17:5) means that he is the ancestor (*zu*) of many nations (*guo*). Jacob's name (Gen. 27:36) can be translated as "cheating" (*qipian*).

The appended notes attest to Schereschewsky's intimate acquaintance with the OT and its Jewish commentary tradition. But the notes also add a new dimension to the text. Names that in transliteration can be considered devoid of all meaning become concrete when explained; passages that are otherwise obscure often make more sense in the receptor language. By means of the notes, the translation became a teaching tool that could be used by the newly converted to instruct others.

This examination of Schereschewsky's Chinese Genesis translation has shown that aside from other considerations, the background of the translator is important. In the attempt to determine what kind of a translation he produced, Schereschewsky's Jewish antecedents and early training are evidently also significant factors. Moreover, that Jewish scholarship had a role in the incipient beginnings of Chinese Protestant Christianity has serious implications. These cannot be explored here, but they are surely an element in the reception of the OT in nineteenth- and twentieth-century China.

By the same token, the assumptions that inform the translating enterprise must be considered. Schereschewsky profoundly respected Chinese civilization, and it is a pity that his extant correspondence reveals so little on this subject. Still, it is this respect, I would suggest, that led to his firm belief that becoming Christian did not mean becoming Westernized, that a genuinely Chinese Christianity was both possible and desirable. His belief was, no doubt, reinforced by his own experience of becoming a Christian. Conversion had not changed him into an Anglo-Saxon. His respect for Chinese civilization and learning was, however, not some vague notion of what China was about. Although there is no evidence that he was widely read in the Chinese classics or histories, he seems to have had a deep appreciation for the Chinese language and a highly unusual grasp of its complexities. He never doubted the translatability of scripture or the suitability of the Chinese language as its vehicle.

Perhaps for this reason, the "term question," which so exercised most missionaries, did not seem to trouble him once he decided that the use of neologisms was unavoidable. Yet I find that aside from God and a few other key terms, these are kept at a minimum in Genesis, and he preferred to use standard, idiomatic Chinese together with the device of explanatory notes. Schereschewsky was above all interested in creating a standard, unified, and consistent terminology, eliminating the arbitrary usages of earlier translations. The "term question" may not have bothered him, as it did others, for still another reason. In his translation work, he was concerned with understanding a text and with conveying this understanding and not with questions of theology. The absence of theological overtones in Genesis either in the choice of vocabulary or in the notes has been noted earlier.

Schereschewsky's translating techniques have been described in some detail. As concerns the transliterating of place and personal names, the obvious drawbacks, as noted by Arthur Wright, are that transliterations are awkward, uncouth, and destructive of rhythm.[59] There is no quarreling with this judgment; the biblical names look and sound supremely clumsy and must have given difficult moments to readers and listeners alike. Yet short of translating names according to their meaning, which would have led to the loss of their sound, Schereschewsky had no alternative.

It is to Schereschewsky's credit that he confined transliterations to place and personal names, translating everything else, whether Chinese equivalents existed or not. As a result, he did not make good on his promise in the introduction to neither add nor subtract a word. Quite the opposite is true. The examples cited from Genesis show that the translation is not literal; there are omissions, and the choice of language and idiomatic expressions often changes the text's connotations. There is, in addition, the tendency to transform opaque passages into explicit statements, which is in part, at least, due to the linguistic peculiarities of northern vernacular. However, precisely because literalness was not attempted and omissions, changes, and vocabulary choices were made, the transposed text was not merely a translation into another language. More than any other early translator of scripture, Schereschewsky recognized and tackled the problem of Chinese cultural and linguistic factors in the expression of foreign ideas.

NOTES

The present essay is based on a paper read at the Thirty-Third International Congress of Asian and North African Studies, Toronto, 1990. I wish to thank Dr. Steven Kaplan of the Hebrew University, Jerusalem, for his constructive comments, and Uri Melammed for guiding me through some of the more complex biblical passages. Research for this essay was partially supported by the Louis Frieberg Fund for East Asian Research.

1. For a fairly comprehensive listing of translations, see Hubert W. Spillett, comp., *A Catalogue of Scriptures in the Languages of China and the Republic of China* (British and Foreign Bible Society, 1975). See also Alexander Wylie, *Catalogue of the Chinese Imperial Maritime Customs Collection at the United States International Exhibition, Philadelphia 1876* (Shanghai: Statistical Department of the Inspectorate General of Customs, 1876),

appendix, "Catalogue of publications by Protestant missionaries in China"; and H. R. Hykes, *Translations of the scriptures into the languages of China and her dependencies, tabulated to December 31, 1915* (New York: American Bible Society, 1916), iv, 1–11, courtesy of the Burke Library of the Union Theological Seminary in the City of New York.

2. John Fairbank notes the importance of the Chinese collaborators in the signification process in addition to the Chinese vocabulary that came to be used for religious terms. John K. Fairbank, introduction to *Christianity in China: Early Protestant Missionary Writings*, ed. Suzanne W. Barnett and J. K. Fairbank (Cambridge: Harvard University Press, 1985), 7–9.

3. The Union Version continues to be used widely and has not been replaced by other versions in the Protestant churches of the People's Republic. See Thor Strandenaes, *Principles*

of *Chinese Bible Translation* (Stockholm: Almqvist & Wiksell, 1987), 15n. A recent effort by the Bible Societies of Taiwan and Hong Kong, *Shen jing: xiandai Zhongwen yiben* (The Holy Bible: Today's Chinese version) (Hong Kong Bible Society, 1975), although widely used, has not replaced the Union Version. This recent translation, however, differs greatly from the Union Version. For what we know of the process whereby Schereschewsky arrived at his final version of his translation of Genesis, see n. 50 below.

4. James A. Muller, *Apostle of China: Samuel Isaac Joseph Schereschewsky, 1831–1906* (New York: Morehouse, 1937), is a biographical account that emphasizes his missionary career. Most of the documentary sources used by Muller, including Muller's correspondence with a number of valuable informants, are now housed at the Archives of the Episcopal Church in Austin, Texas. I have resorted to the archival collection rather than to Muller's account. I would like to express my deep appreciation to Dr. V. Nelle Bellamy, Eleanor Hearn, and the staff of the archive for their generous help and hospitality.

5. Domestic and Foreign Missionary Society (hereafter DFMS), China Records, 1835–1951, RG64-185, Caroline Schereschewsky's biographical statement, which had been in possession of Sister Emily Faith and was forwarded to J. A. Muller, MS, 5 pp. In the above, I have enlarged somewhat on C. S.'s bare facts.

6. Among the Russian, Hebrew, and Yiddish literature on the subject of the Jewish Enlightenment, Azriel Shochat, *Mosad Harabanut Mita'am, Parasha Bama'avak-Hatarbut bein Haredim levein Maskilim* (The "Crown Rabbinate" in Russia, a chapter in the cultural struggle between Orthodox Jews and "maskilim") (Haifa: University of Haifa, 1975), details the arguments on both the Orthodox and enlighteners' side. Michael Stanislawski, *Tsar Nicholas I and the Jews: The transformation of Jewish society in Russia, 1825–1855* (Philadelphia: Jewish Publication Society of America, 1983), explores government policies and their effects on Jewish life.

7. Neither Caroline Schereschewsky's written statement, DFMS, RG64-185, nor Muller's notes on his talk with her, DFMS, RG64-185, January 5, 1929, mention the Zhitomir seminary. The sole evidence is found in DFMS, RG64-185, James A. Kelso, president, Western Theological Seminary, Pittsburgh, Pennsylvania, letter to Muller, December 16, 1933. Kelso wrote that according to Schereschewsky's registration, he studied at the Zhitomir Rabbinical Seminary.

8. NT translations were prepared by the London Society for Promoting Christianity Amongst the Jews. Their intensive proselytizing activities began after 1818 in lands under Russian control. The translation of the Hebrew NT was completed in 1817; the Yiddish in 1821. William T. Gidney, *The History of the London Society for Promoting Christianity Amongst the Jews from 1809 to 1908* (London: London Society for Promoting Christianity, 1908), 55–56. Although I have found no evidence in the yearly published reports of the London society about active missionaries in Zhitomir, from their stations in Warsaw, Lublin, and Kalish, the missionaries covered considerable distances to other towns. However, the NT need not have been brought to Zhitomir by missionaries. New and Old Testaments were liberally distributed throughout the areas of the missionaries' activities, and pupils could have easily brought copies to the seminary from elsewhere.

9. London Society for Promoting Christianity Amongst the Jews, 19th Report (1827), 36.

10. DFMS, RG64-28, Schereschewsky, letter to the Reverend S. D. Denison, July 21, 1865. For his translation of the OT, Schereschewsky mentions consulting works by De Wette, Rosenmüller, Eichhorn, and Genesius. See John W. Rogerson, *Old Testament criticism in the early 19th century: England and Germany* (London: Anchor Press, 1984), for a discussion of these authors and the German scholars' controversies.

11. [Bishop McKim and Bishop Partridge], "How the Bible Has Been Translated for the Millions of China," *Spirit of Missions* 68, no. 4 (April 1903): 233.

12. DFMS, RG64-29, John R. Hykes (?), 1903 (?).

13. Lamin Sanneh, *Translating the Message: The Missionary Impact on Culture* (Maryknoll: Orbis Books, 1990), 170, 205.

14. "Consecration of the Missionary Bishop of Shanghai," *Spirit of Missions* 42 (December 1877): 672.

15. Ibid., 670, 673.

16. DFMS, RG64-30, Mrs. Schereschewsky, letter to the Reverend S. D. Denison, January 21, 1876.

17. American Board of Commissioners for Foreign Missions (hereafter ABCFM), vol. 302; *North China Mission, 1860–1871,* "Letters and papers addressed to the Board," vol. I, Houghton Library, Harvard University; Henry Blodget, letter to the Reverend R. Anderson, November 4, 1861, Tianjin, MS. 127, by permission of the Houghton Library, Harvard University, and the United Church Board for World Ministries.

18. Ibid., Henry Blodget, letter to the Reverend N. L. Clark, October 12, 1867, Peking, MS. 186.

19. DFMS, RG64-29, Schereschewsky, letter to Dr. Langford, May 18, 1895.

20. DFMS, RG64-185, Sister Emily Faith, Deaconess, Sisters of the Transfiguration, St. Lioba's Convent, Wuhu, letter to Muller, December 19, 1933. She wrote that Max Muller ranked Schereschewsky as one of the six most learned Orientalists in the world.

21. Fairbank, introduction to *Christianity in China,* 7.

22. The committee was formed in 1864 and consisted of three Americans (Henry Blodget, W. A. P. Martin, and Schereschewsky) and two Englishmen (Joseph Edkins and John Burdon).

23. ABCFM, *North China Mission,* vol. I, Henry Blodget, "Occasional notes," March 20, 1867, MS. 181.

24. DFMS, RG64-30, Mrs. Schereschewsky, letter to (?), December 27, 1871.

25. ABCFM, *North China Mission,* vol. I, Henry Blodget, letter to (?), December 28, 1861, Tianjin, MS. 129; and letter to the Reverend R. Anderson, January 29, 1863, Peking, MS. 147.

26. Marshall Broomhall, *The Bible in China* (London: China Inland Mission, 1934), 83–84.

27. *Jiuyue quanshu* (Peking, 1875). The full English title is *The Old Testament in the Mandarin colloquial, Translated from the Hebrew by the Reverend J. I. S. Schereschewsky, D.D. of the American Episcopal Mission, and printed for the American Bible Society at the press of the ABCFM, Peking, China, 1875.*

28. DFMS, RG64-29, "Translation of the scriptures into Chinese." See also *Bible Society Record,* April 1890.

29. DFMS, RG64-28, Schereschewsky, letter to S. D. Denison, July 21, 1865.

30. DFMS, RG64-29, 4–5, "The Bible, Prayer Book, and terms in our mission," addressed to the House of Bishops, pamphlet. Schereschewsky was referring to the Morrison translation and the Bridgman and Culbertson OT.

31. "Shengjing yi guanhuaben gaocheng" (Translation of the Bible into *guanhua* is completed), *Jiaohui xinbao* 14 (July 13, 1872): 225; "Missionary News," *The Chinese Recorder* 5, no. 4 (August 1874): 223–224. *Mandarin* and *guanhua* were synonymous before 1911. When the latter term was abolished, *Mandarin* continued to be used for *guoyu,* as the Peking dialect was referred to before 1949. In both cases, the spoken northern Chinese language is meant. See Strandenaes, *Principles of Chinese Bible Translation,* 15n.

32. DFMS, RG64-29, Frederick R. Graves, letter to John H. Wood, June 30, 1937. Although Bible sales generally had sharply increased in the second decade of the twentieth century, Mandarin Bibles (i.e., northern vernacular Bibles) outstripped all others. Most of the OTs sold must have been in Schereschewsky's translation. See Milton T. Stauffer, ed., *The Christian Occupation of China* (Shanghai: China Continuation Committee, 1922), 453.

33. How to translate the Holy Spirit was equally vexing. But since this is a NT problem, it will not be discussed here. For a summary of the term question, see Douglas G. Spelman, "Christianity in Chinese: The Protestant Term Question," *Papers on China* 22A (May 1969): 25–52.

34. For example, B. Helm, "Shen and Shang-Ti," *The Chinese Recorder* 7, no. 6 (December 1876): 436–442; and Sir George Thomas Staunton, *An inquiry into the proper mode of rendering the word "God" in translating the sacred scriptures into the Chinese language . . .* (London: Lionel Booth, 1849), 5–6, 34.

35. James Legge, *The notions of the Chinese concerning God and spirits: With an examination*

of the defence of an essay, on the proper rendering of the words Elohim and Theos, into the Chinese language, by William J. Boone, D.D. (Hong Kong: Hong Kong Register Office, 1832), 7–64 (Ch'eng Wen reprint, 1971).

36. Staunton, An inquiry, 18.

37. The Chinese Recorder 7, no. 4 (August 1876): 294–297.

38. DFMS, RG64-28, Schereschewsky, letter to S. D. Denison, July 21, 1865.

39. "The Bible, Prayer Book and Terms," 9–11; and "Terminology in the China Mission," The Churchman 57, no. 6 (January 14, 1888): 34–35.

40. Shi Ji, 28, in Ershiwu shi (Twenty-five histories) (Kaiming edition, 1934), vol. I, 115.

41. Henry Blodget, The Use of T'ien Chu for God in Chinese (Shanghai: American Presbyterian Mission Press, 1893), 1, 4, 10, 20. Pamphlet by courtesy of the Burke Library of the Union Theological Seminary in the City of New York.

42. DFMS, RG64-29, John R. Hykes, letter to John Fox, August 29, 1903.

43. "Terminology in the China Mission," 60–62.

44. I am using the Jiuyue quanshu, 1875 edition, although I will sometimes refer to the Jiu xinyue Shangjing (The Old and New Testament Holy Scriptures), 1899 revised edition as well. For the Hebrew, I am using the standard Masoretic text.

45. See M. Rosenbaum and A. M. Silbermann, trans., Pentateuch with Targum Onkelos: Haphtaroth and Rashi's Commentary (New York: Hebrew Publishing Co., n.d.), vol. I, 3–4 (hereafter Rashi). Rashi (Solomon Yitzhaki ben Isaac, 1040–1105) was a French rabbinic scholar whose authoritative commentary on the Pentateuch has been universally studied for centuries past. Schereschewsky apparently often consulted Rashi both for translating the text and for the appended notes.

46. Compare, for example, the Lun yu, 6:25; Yue zhi yi li, "bind oneself with li."

47. Rashi, 115, explains goi with le'um, or "nation."

48. The 1899 revision corrects sons (zi) to read clan (zu), which is, however, also not in keeping with the Hebrew. The 1899 reading is retained in the Union Version.

49. DFMS, RG64-30, Mrs. Schereschewsky, letter to the Reverend S. D. Denison,

August 22, 1870, and October 25, 1870. The tragic incident involving the Catholic mission in Tianjin and the subsequent massacre in June 1870 had apparently led to considerable tension in the capital, and relations between Chinese and foreigners were severed. By 1870, Schereschewsky was well along in the translation of the entire OT. Genesis, which had been almost completed in 1864, as he wrote in a letter to Denison (DFMS, RG64-28, October 14, 1864), was published separately in 1866. I was not able to examine this version. The 1872 version, Chuang Shi ji (Beijing: Meihua shu guan shuyin, 1872), in the ABCFM collection of the Harvard-Yenching Library that I was able to examine is identical with the Genesis published in the complete OT in 1875. Therefore, Schereschewsky made no revisions between 1872 and 1875. Unless the 1866 Genesis is compared with the later versions, one cannot know definitely if he decided to revise certain terms after 1870. However, I tend to think that he did not make changes between 1870 and 1872, being eager to forge ahead with the entire OT and given the relative calm of the capital in the months following the Tianjin massacre.

50. Rashi, 67.

51. See Spillett, A Catalogue of Scriptures, 21. Part 2 of the Bridgman and Culberton version was published in 1861; the other parts in 1863. I have consulted the 1865 edition, Jiuyue quan shu (The Old Testament) (Shanghai: Meihua), 3 vols., in the ABCFM collection at the Harvard-Yenching Library.

52. For example, Robert Morrison, Chuang-shi lidai chuan (Genesis), 1832, in the ABCFM collection at the Harvard-Yenching Library.

53. Most of the notes were retained in the 1899 revised version, and in some instances, new notes were added or briefer ones expanded. The Union Version reduced the number of notes.

54. Midrashic literature refers to a large collection of writings dealing with interpretation, and it includes a rich body of imaginative works.

55. The English wording is according to the Masoretic text, which is not faithful to the Hebrew. However, because of the terse and obscure nature of this sentence, a faithful translation is practically impossible.

For the story, see *Rashi*, 20–21. I thank Uri Melammed for pointing out that Lemech's statement is probably a line from a long poem, perhaps a dirge, which he addressed to his two wives.

56. The note is based on *Rashi*, 153.

57. Ibid., 236.

58. Ibid., 20.

59. Arthur F. Wright, "The Chinese Language and Foreign Ideas," in *Studies in Chinese thought*, ed. Arthur F. Wright (Chicago: University of Chicago Press, 1953), 296.

Modern Literature in Mutual Translation

CHAPTER 7

Bridges Across Cultures

China in Yiddish Poetry

The poet as traveler is a familiar figure. He wanders through the landscape like Du Fu or stops at an old tomb or historic site or, like Li Bai, at an impressive panoramic view and relates what he sees. He is an observer of the sites he visits, though he may not always be a stranger to them. He often knows the history of the places he sees and the stories associated with them. For the sake of convenience, I shall call such poems "travel poetry." Some present-day examples of travel poems may be found in a recent volume by Wolfgang Kubin. Like his Chinese counterpart of centuries ago, the poet-traveler goes to Warsaw, Vienna, Chicago, Leipzig, and Jerusalem and tells of oceans and cities, of mountains and graves, and also about the people he encounters.[1]

This essay deals with poet-travelers who are both similar and different. They came to China from Poland in the 1930s and 1940s as strangers, knowing little about the country or its past and recent history, and they wrote in Yiddish, a kind of lingua franca spoken and read by the majority of Jews in Central and Eastern Europe before World War II.[2] Their travel poetry is in many ways unique, not only because of the language in which the poets recorded their impressions and feelings, but especially because of the compassion expressed in their poetry about China's plight and their response to human suffering. As strangers and observers of the places and sights, their verses captured the unfamiliar scenes of a cruel and indifferent world of a particular time.

Among the poems that will be discussed in this essay are several by Meylekh Ravitch (Zekharia Khone Bergner, 1893–1976), who traveled in China in 1935. Others are by Polish refugees (involuntary travelers, as it were) who came to Shanghai in 1940 and 1941. They did not expect to remain long but could not leave until years later. These poets' subjective impressions, translated into moving and often powerful verse, are compelling, for they wrote at a time when they themselves experienced poverty and hardship.

Ravitch, well known for his poetry in Yiddish-speaking circles, came to China in 1935 as an emissary of an organization that supported vocational training for Jews. He was also "helped," as he put it, by PEN, being the founder and secretary of the PEN Yiddish section in Warsaw.[3] He began his China journey in Moscow on the Trans-Siberian Railway, which probably took him to Manzhouli, the Manchukuo border town, from where he continued to his first stop in Harbin. The tedious journey of seven or eight days and around eight thousand kilometers through the vast and nearly empty Russian countryside is beautifully captured in his long poem "Trans-Siberian Winter Journey." Repeatedly the poet reminds us of the passage of time by prefacing his couplets intermittently with "day," "night," "again day," and "again night" until even the locomotive seems exhausted:

> Again night. With final strength, deeply breathing:
> "save me" is heard from the tired locomotive.

But from within the train, Ravitch keenly observes the endless landscape:

> Again day. Forests and sun—white porcelain.
> Evenings the sun dims like an old copper pan.

Or

> Again day. Ice-cold, sharp and briefly glittering sun,
> Its beams broken on a red Kozak rider's lance.

Scenes rush by the window as the train speeds through the wintry countryside, disappear, give way to others: horses, a village, boys and girls on skis, an abandoned church, a caravan of sleighs. He hears the sleigh's bells, hears dogs barking "while wind trembles in wintry trees."[4]

Ravitch may have known about Manchukuo, the Japanese puppet state, before he embarked on his journey, but certainly more information would have been conveyed to him by his hosts in the Harbin Jewish community. This community, though much shrunken by 1935 due to growing economic difficulties, consisted mostly of Russian and a smaller number of Polish Jews.[5] The poem Ravitch wrote about Harbin did not deal with the Jews, however. Rather, in his "Lord Lytton from Geneva and the Coolie Mei Wanfu from Chefoo: A Harbin Ballad," he presents a stark juxtaposition between the politics of the League of Nations and the life and death of a poor opium addict (though Ravitch writes "heroin," not opium). The opening verse summarizes the political situation:

> Manchuria there, Manchuria here
> And Henry Pu-yi sits already on the throne
> And Japanese ships are already anchored
> in Harbin on the river Sungari.

In two subsequent verses, Ravitch juxtaposes Lytton and the addict, but it is not comparisons he is after; it is the futility of Lytton's mission as well as the futility and waste of the coolie's addiction that haunts the poet.

> And the Lytton Mission in the hotel "Moderne"
> Partakes of the final great banquet.
>
> .   .   .   .
>
> In his yellow hand Mei Wanfu clutches
> His last three fen, throws himself on the [wooden] plank.
> "I want to write the truth in my report,
> A truth from Genf to New York, to Chefoo!"
>
> .   .   .   .
>
> Mei Wanfu thinks: from Genf to New York
> To Chefoo, such truth does not exist in the world.

While Mei Wanfu is taken to die next to the railroad tracks, where already other corpses are laid out, Lytton leaves Harbin to tell the world the truth. And in Harbin,

> It'll be spring—when the Sungari thaws,
> Gaoliang and soya will blossom green.[6]

In couplets like these, Ravitch seems to express the hope that with time passing and similar to nature's renewal, there might be the promise of a better future as well, despite life's brutalities, politicians' lies, and death.

We might compare the couplet to another where he wrote about Beijing students who are executed after a demonstration. In the last verse, the dead girl's skin seems to turn greener, and

> It renders green the hope of China
> On the stones of Peking.[7]

In April 1935, Ravitch came to Shanghai, where he was welcomed by both the Russian and Baghdadi Jewish communities and where he gave a number of well-attended lectures.[8] Similar to his Harbin poem, he again chose the theme of tragedy and death when writing about Shanghai. In both poems, Ravitch's deft handling of detail is impressive, and his stories of living and dying betray an emotional involvement far beyond that of a casual observer. "A Rickshaw [Coolie] Dies on a Shanghai Morning" tells the story of a man who, having injured his foot, knows he is about to die. With his last strength and clutching a few pitiful coins, he runs to a Buddhist temple to plead with Buddha:

> I'm still Zhan Zungui—soon I'll be nothing—
> I'm still one of five hundred million.
> From you I want nothing, not even an easy death,
> I merely want to remind you of myself.
>
> .   .   .   .
>
> Spit woodenly on me, on Zhan Zungui, worse than a dog,
> In my face that had never lain under a roof,
> I don't even know it, never seen it in a mirror,
> Only in street puddles, in rain water.
>
> *   *   *
>
> And I don't want Nirvana. I—worse than a stray dog,
> Now with torn foot from a rusty iron,
> Am burning with heat, [but] no one
> Will even shoot me compassionately.

Zhan tells the statue to stretch out its wooden hand so that he can place the money and his life in it:

> Buddha hears, extends his hand, soon smiles again,
> Zhan Zungui stretches out, smiles at Buddha,
> On his face a first and last smile
> That was always only mirrored in rain puddles.[9]

Zhan dies believing that Buddha recognized his existence. Yet this is not the last verse. The poem concludes with the temple servant coming to collect the coins and the dead man, whom he drags away by his uninjured foot. Is there a ray of hope here, as Ravitch had apparently expressed in the previous two poems? Or is there no hope at all, only the man's illusion at the moment of death? Possibly, I would prefer to assume, Ravitch wanted to indicate that if a man's life is worse than a dog's (not even deserving a bullet), by dying with dignity, he has reclaimed his humanity. By smiling a last smile, the rickshaw coolie assumed the individuality he did not have while alive. And this smile, though never seen by him, was seen in the moment of death by the wooden divinity.[10]

Meylekh Ravitch was a tourist in China. He came and left with a valid passport, visas, and a return ticket. The small group of Polish poets and writers who arrived in Shanghai in 1940 and 1941 were not so fortunate. They had fled from Nazi-occupied Poland to neutral Lithuania and fled that country when the Soviet army occupied it in the summer of 1940. Like Ravitch six years earlier, they boarded the Trans-Siberian Railway in Moscow, going together with other refugees to Vladivostok. From Vladivostok, they crossed over to Japan by ship and then went to Kobe, where large numbers of Central European refugees were being cared for by the Kobe Jewish community. But if they had hoped to sit out World War II in Japan, they were sorely disappointed. In 1941, the Japanese authorities decided to ship the refugees to Shanghai, where already between eighteen thousand and twenty thousand German and Austrian refugees had found a haven after being forcefully expelled from their native countries.

The Kobe arrivals, most of whom came in one shipload after another in August and September 1941[11] and whose languages were Yiddish and Polish, were yet another group in Shanghai's Jewish communities, which consisted of English-, Russian-, and German-speaking Jews. None of the different groups of Jews had much in common with the others. Inevitably, there was friction between old-timers and newcomers, and even among the Polish newcomers, who were ultra-Orthodox religious Jews (referred to as "Talmud Scholars" by the press) and secular intellectuals.

Having traveled more than twelve thousand kilometers to Shanghai since leaving his native Poland, E. Simkhoni (Simkha Elberg) expressed his dismay in a succinct history of his journey. The poem "Three Countries

Spat Me Out" must have been written shortly after he arrived in Shanghai. First Poland spat him out, and he worried about the fate of those left behind. Then Lithuania spat him out:

> As one who is tubercular spits
> His last drop of blood.

And finally,

> On a humid day,
> When Japanese tie up their nose
> And step with wooden feet
> Japan spat me out
> Into Shanghai.[12]

The pervasive irony of this poem is softened, however, by the imagery of landscapes and colors. There is the red of blood; the black of the ocean, which he uses for ink; and the white of heaven from where he obtains the paper to write a note.

Simkhoni's poem is an angry one. Unlike Ravitch, he had not intended to come to Shanghai had it not been for the misfortunes of war. But on the whole, the poets did not lament their fate. They were, to be sure, involuntary travelers, yet the Shanghai scene, so unlike any they had ever seen (more specifically, the International Settlement and the French Concession), held their attention. Ya'akov Fishman's (1891–1965) impressions of Shanghai are captured in three brief prose poems entitled "Miniatures." Following is a translation of one of these:

> An elegant and highly satisfied couple, a gentleman and a lady, sit at a cafe window. Politely they drink their coffee, swallow and glance into the street. Speaking to them from outside is a ragged Chinese, he pleads with his mouth and eyes, with his eyebrows and his hands, no more than a few cents. And they, the pair—a swallow and a glance, a swallow and a glance....
>
> All three, the elegant couple and the Chinese beggar together leave the window. The couple to the taxi, and the Chinese . . . ?[13]

A small vignette, yet how sharp is the moment, caught as if with a camera, showing within and without inequality, social injustice, and indifference to human misery.

Yosl Mlotek came to Shanghai at the age of twenty-three. He was a lonely young man, as is evident from some of the poems he wrote in Shanghai. But he too took note of those who were even more unfortunate than he—the abjectly poor among the Chinese people. Throughout his long poem entitled "Shanghai," he contrasts rich and poor and literally one kind of life above and another below. Here is a portion of Mlotek's impressions of what then was Nanking Road:

Shanghai—
The city beckons
With a thousand passionate eyes.
Neon lights dazzle
A marvellous rainbow.

Changing colors, moving
Glittering mercury.
Up and down, down and up—
An electric thunderstorm.

"Buy, buy these cigars
The brand 'Two times F'!
Women don't be fooled
Silks, socks, the brand 'Blef.'"

On houses
Roofs
Chimneys
And still higher
"Buy! Buy!"

Lights signal
Messages
Call and pull, allure
Remind and caress
Buy! Buy!

And at the side
Runs
A man in harness—a horse,
Feet barely touch the ground.

Behind him—hauling, hundreds more
Run, hurry, noisily.
They must run faster, faster—
Otherwise how to be sure
Though at night they run
Even twenty times in a circle!
Whether there'll be a small bowl of rice.

  *   *   *

Above—jazz music
And drunken laughter.
Below a tight cluster
China's daughters

Stand at the wall
Together with their mothers
And above mocking them
A large advertisement:
Buy! Buy!

Shanghai
Nanking Road
The city screams
From a thousand throats

And from a thousand eyes.
Ever louder, shriller
Shouts resound
Scream China! Scream Shanghai![14]

Ravitch was in China for less than one year. The three Polish poets and others departed as soon as they could, toward the end of the 1940s. Shanghai had been a way station in their long journey from home to elsewhere, their poems those of travelers who would be moving on. But while they were in Shanghai, they built "paper bridges"[15] between the destitute and desperate among the Chinese people with whose condition they identified and their Yiddish readers.

NOTES

I gratefully acknowledge the partial support of the Truman Research Institute and the Frieberg Research Fund, both of the Hebrew University of Jerusalem. I also thank Professor A. Altman of the Hebrew University for his careful reading of this essay and his comments. All translations from Yiddish are my own.

1. Wolfgang Kubin, *Das neue Lied von der alten Verzweiflung* (Bonn: Weidle Verlag, 1999).

2. Yiddish is written with Hebrew letters and consists of Hebrew, Old French, Old Italian (Loez), Slavic, and German components, of which medieval German of the Middle Rhine area is most important.

3. *Israel's Messenger* 32, no. 2 (May 1935): 23.

4. Meylekh Ravitch, "Trans-Sibirishe winter rejze," in Ravitch, *Kontinentn un Okeanen: Lider baladn un poe* (Continents and Oceans: Songs, Ballads and Poems) (Warsaw: Literarishe Bleter, 1937), 24–26. Credit for the pioneering work on the topic of China in Yiddish writings belongs to Chang Shoou-Huey, and I am indebted to her for bringing Ravitch to my attention. See Chang, "China und Jiddisch, jiddische Kultur in China—chinesische Literatur auf Jiddisch," in *Jews in China: From Kaifeng to Shanghai*, ed. Roman Malek (Sankt Augustin: Institut Monumenta Serica, 2000).

5. For a brief survey of the Harbin Jewish community, see I. Eber and V. Gilboa, *China and the Jews. A Sampling of Library Resources for the Study of Jewish Life in China and Chinese-Jewish Relations* (Cambridge: Harvard University Library, 1992), 37–43.

6. "Lord Lytton fun Genf un der coolie Mei Wanfu from Chefoo, a kharbiner balad," in *Kontinentn un Okeanen*, ed. Ravitch, 27–30. The Lytton Commission of the League of Nations came to Manchuria in early spring 1932. Its report later in the year condemned Japanese aggression in Manchuria. In March 1933, Japan withdrew from the league.

7. Ibid., 43. The poem is entitled "He Naiwan and Li Guanyu: A Peking Love Ballad."

8. *Israel's Messenger*. The so-called Baghdadi Jews hailed for the most part from Iraq, many of whom had come to Shanghai via India after the Opium War. The majority of the Russian Jews came after the Bolshevik Revolution. For a brief survey of Shanghai's Jewish communities, see Eber and Gilboa, *China and the Jews*, 16–21, 22–23.

9. Ravitch, "A rickshaw shtarbt in a Shanghai fartog," in *Kontinentn un Okeanen*, 44–46.

10. I thank Amira Katz for bringing to my attention Ba Jin's story, "Gou" (Dog), which he wrote in 1931. Although the theme and the author's intent in this allegorical story are quite different from Ravitch's poem, it is nonetheless worth noting that both authors used similar symbols to express degradation and futile expectations of help. "Dog" (trans. Tong Dzuo) first appeared in *Voice of China* 1, no. 1 (March 15, 1936): 18–20. A revised version was included in Edgar Snow, ed., *Living China: Modern Chinese Short Stories* (London: George G. Harrap, 1936). Might Ravitch have had access to the story and written the poem shortly before publishing his book in 1937?

11. These are reported, for example, in *The China Press*, August 24, 1941, 2; August 31, 1941, 2; and September 18, 1941, 2. By then, only around seventy ill, elderly, and children remained in Kobe.

12. E. Simkhoni, "Drei lender hobn mikh oisgeshpign," *Unzer Lebn* (Yiddish supplement of *Nasha Zhizn*) 20 (September 12, 1941). The Russian-language Jewish paper, *Nasha Zhizn*, commenced publication in 1940 and ceased in 1946. The last Yiddish supplement was printed in August 1944.

13. Ya'akov Fishman, "Miniaturen," *Unzer Lebn* 40 (February 6, 1942).

14. *Unzer Lebn* 38 (January 23, 1942). A partial translation of Mlotek's poem also appeared in German translation, "Auf einer einsamen Insel: Jiddische Dichter in Schanghai," in *Jüdischer Almanach 2001*, ed. Anne Birkenhauer (Frankfurt: Jüdischer Verlag, 2000).

15. I borrow this apt term from the title of Kathryn Hellerstein, trans. and ed., *Paper Bridges: Selected Poems of Kadya Molodowsky* (Detroit: Wayne University Press, 1999).

CHAPTER 8

Sholem Aleichem in Chinese?

A world without translated philosophical and literary works is unimaginable. Unable to learn the many languages in which the masterpieces of world literature have been and are written, we are dependent on translations. Without them, we would know little about the cultures beyond our circumspect lives.

My own interest in translating and translation was awakened many decades ago by an offhand remark by my then professor, Chen Shouyi, who asked if I knew that Yiddish fiction was translated into Chinese. I answered, incredulously, "Why would Chinese writers translate Sholem Aleichem, I. L. Peretz, or Solomon Libin? And how would a Chinese reader relate to their stories in the target language?"

Reading these stories in the original Yiddish and then rereading them in Chinese, I realized, of course, that they had been translated from secondary languages—Esperanto or English. Most of those translations dated from the 1920s, the years when modern Chinese literature emerged, a literature in the spoken rather than classical language. Yiddish literature thus provided models for the new literature about the common people—workers, peddlers, shopkeepers—and fidelity to the original was hardly a concern. Moreover, Jews were one of the "weak and small peoples" (*roxiao minzu*) who would resonate with Chinese readers, a people who did not belong to the strong and exploiting powers.

Although Chinese translators rarely encountered Jews, Jews did not remain entirely unknown. And while Chinese writers were translating

Yiddish fiction, Yiddish writers were translating Chinese poetry and literary works. Like their counterparts in China, the Yiddish translators worked from intermediate languages. And they used translation—as the Chinese translators did—as a window into another world; the Yiddishists were looking for a way to know the "other," a bridge leading beyond their own lives.

Martin Buber was an important translator who brought Chinese thought and literature to German readers as early as 1910 and 1911. Moreover, he was the first to introduce Hebrew readers to Confucian writings by means of translation after settling in Jerusalem in 1938.

Translating is complicated. While translators used to exercise great fidelity to the source work, attention has now shifted to the target text: how to evaluate a text in a new cultural environment. This, in turn, raises the question of a work's afterlife or, in fact, the afterlives of an original text. Thus we're finding that classics are often in need of retranslation. Cultures and linguistic expressions change, and what was clear and acceptable at one time is surely not so at a later period. A work lives on precisely because it is translated and retranslated many times, as inevitable changes occur. For example, the first translation of the Tanakh into Chinese was published in 1874 and prepared by Samuel Isaac Joseph Schereschewsky (1831–1906), a Jew from Lithuania. Schereschewsky's superb translation raises many questions: How is a text so far removed in time and place transposed into another culture of another time? How is the human drama that infuses so many of the biblical stories conveyed? How are the many poetic portions rendered? Translating can be understood, then, as an interpretative art form, the product being both identical to and different from the original. In the end, should a text be faithful to the original text? Should it be literally translated?

These are the questions that have inspired my work for the past thirty-odd years as a translator; my task has been to serve both literary and intellectual history, to give new life to foreign works. Through translation, I hope to introduce readers to the peoples and cultures who inhabit the original text. Sometimes, when I translate Chinese poetry of long ago, I try to imagine the world of the poet and where he wrote the poem. Similarly, I believe translators anywhere attempt to see the world in which the text began life before being able to imbue it with a new life of a different place and time.

CHAPTER 9

Translation Literature in Modern China

The Yiddish Author and His Tale

Translation literature—the product of different cultures and different perspectives—has played a significant role in modern China's intellectual life. This body of translation work, which began in the latter part of the nineteenth century, is concerned broadly with scientific, humanistic, behavioral, and literary subjects. The group of translations from literary works is a particularly fascinating subject.

Translating from another people's literature poses several highly interesting problems. First there is the question of the selection of works for translation, for what a translator will choose is invariably related to specific values, concerns, and even goals of his own period. Second, the translator's ideological, philosophical, or political point of view is bound to influence the choices he makes. And third, when a translator translates from a literature with whose language he is not familiar—thus using a secondary translation—his selection is in fact already preselected.[1] Notions gained and views developed regarding other peoples on the basis of translations are, therefore, sometimes distorted. Another people may be idealized or condemned. Similarities may be seen where none exist, and differences may be glossed over because they are not understood.

Translations from Yiddish literature have a place in the translation literature generally. Although numerically not large—forty-eight stories and plays in all[2]—the importance of these translations stems from the fact that they supported a variety of ideas current among Chinese intellectuals, particularly in the twenties. Among these was the idea that Chinese intellectuals ought to be concerned with the plight of the so-called small and oppressed peoples (*hsiao pei ya-p'o min-tsu*). And of course Jews, in addition to Poles, Hungarians, and Czechs, were such a people. Perhaps more important, however, was the idea concerning the use of Yiddish, for it was thought that Yiddish was the true vernacular of the Jewish peoples. Chinese writers, wanting to use their own vernacular, were urged to take note of what the use of Yiddish had done for the Jewish people.

Chinese writers did not translate from original Yiddish, a language that, for obvious reasons, they did not know. Rather, the translations, with some exceptions, show that English or Esperanto sources were used. Of the forty-eight known translations, eighteen were prepared from English, five from Esperanto, and twenty-five from unidentified sources.[3] English translations of Yiddish literature were readily available in China, and English, moreover, was apparently favored by many as a language of translation.[4] More interesting is the considerable use of Esperanto works, for these were used for the preparation of translations not only from Yiddish but also from Polish and other minor European languages.[5]

The bulk of the translations from Yiddish literature appeared in the 1920s. A few translations were, however, published in the first half of the 1930s, and thirteen stories appeared in the late fifties. There also appeared alongside the translations a number of articles discussing either the nature, history, or content of Yiddish literature or individual authors and their works. The last such article dates from 1959. When the stories and plays are grouped into patterns of themes, the basis of the selection process as well as current concerns emerges; the critical and descriptive articles in turn indicate how interest in Yiddish literature was related to Chinese intellectual problems and changes.

The purpose of this essay is to attempt to answer several questions. What did Chinese writers know of Yiddish literary history and of Yiddish authors, and how did they evaluate them? What kind of stories were chosen for translation, who were the translators, and from whence came their interest in Yiddish literature? And finally, what sort of problems did the translators encounter with the frequently specifically Jewish idiom?

I

The interest in translating Yiddish literature must be understood within the general context of China's literary revolution, which was initiated in 1917 but blossomed fully only after 1919. As part of the general intellectual ferment, the literary revolution was a complex phenomenon.[6] Its two central issues were, first, the abolition of the written literary language (*wen-yen*) and the use of vernacular (*pai-hua*) and, second, the creation of a new literature in vernacular, which would be original in form as well as in content.

In 1918, Hu Shih (1891–1962), the "father" of the literary revolution, described these twin goals as the development of tools and the development of methods. The first involved a thorough acquaintance with vernacular usage and also practice in writing in vernacular. The second consisted of new methods of collecting materials, new methods of composition, and new methods of description. In order to use new methods for collecting materials, wrote Hu Shih, old themes must be discarded. Materials for writing literature should be drawn from the lives of the common people—farmers, workers, storekeepers, and the impoverished strata of society. In order to use new methods of description, writers must describe people, their environment, their affairs, and their feelings.[7]

The proponents of the literary revolution looked to Western literature as a model and guide. Reading Western literature led Chinese intellectuals to two conclusions. First, both China and some European nations faced similar political and social problems. Moreover, even China's intellectual ferment was also found elsewhere, though in a different form. And second, knowledge of foreign literature was vital in the creation of China's new and "human" literature (*jen ti wen-hsüeh*). Human literature must be concerned with the universal experiences of men and women; Chinese writers, in order to write this literature, must be able to "perceive humanity as a whole."[8]

But this was not all. The most important reason for the creation of a new literature was that literature could be used as a tool for the transformation of society. Chou Tso-jen (1885–1956), essayist and literary critic, writing in 1917, explained that he had planned to transform society through literature and art while still a student in Japan prior to 1912. Toward this end, he had been translating and publishing the new literature of foreign countries.[9]

Notions such as these concerning literary creativity were first publicized in *Hsin ch'ing-nien* (New youth magazine), the highly influential journal of the intellectual revolutionists, which was founded in 1915. By 1920 these tenets were further elaborated by the Literary Research Society (*Wen-hsüeh yen-chiu hui*), a loosely organized group of writers and scholars. From 1921 on, men like Shen Yen-ping (Mao Tun, 1896–1981), Cheng Chen-to (1898–1958), and Chou Tso-jen publicized their views in *Hsiao-shuo yüeh-pao* (Short story magazine), the organ of the Literary Research Society. Throughout the 1920s, this journal set the tone for the literary revolution and the new literature, and it became the major vehicle for the publication of Chinese translations of Western literature.

In the early 1920s, contributors to *Short Story Magazine* expressed increasing interest in the literature of the small and oppressed peoples. Chinese writers were struck by the fact that these small European peoples not only waged a desperate struggle for independence and identity but also had produced great literary figures who articulated this struggle—for example, the patriot-poet Adam Mickiewicz (1798–1855)[10] in Poland and A. Petöffi (1823–1849) in Hungary.[11] Apparently, Chinese writers not only felt a kinship to such nations, identifying with their struggle, but also found the literary figures very attractive personalities.[12] When, in October 1921, an entire issue of *Short Story Magazine* was devoted to the literature of the oppressed peoples, the "Introduction" quite specifically stressed this feeling of kinship.[13]

However, it was one thing to assume ties of kinship with people deprived of political independence and national identity and another to identify with a people without a land and without national cohesion, such as the Jews. As will be shown below, Yiddish literature had a somewhat different and specific appeal found only peripherally or not at all in the literature of other small and oppressed peoples. This attraction, as Chinese writers saw it, was, first, the portrayal of a society oppressed by its own tradition and a hostile environment. Second, it was the portrayal of a society faced with the necessity for change and modernization in order to survive. And third, Chinese writers saw the development of Yiddish literature as a result of a literary revolution similar to their own. And this literary revolution, according to Chinese writers, was related to a Jewish cultural renaissance.

II

In order to understand more clearly how Chinese writers arrived at these conclusions, it may be well to take a closer look at how informed Chinese writers were on the subject of Jewish literature. The following is a summary of the contents of descriptive and critical articles on Yiddish literature, which were published between 1923 and 1959.

From the available materials, it can be seen that pre-nineteenth-century literature in the Hebrew language was of little concern.[14] The literary developments that interested Chinese writers began only with the use of Yiddish. They ascribed to Mendel Levin (1741–1819, also called Lefin, Satanower, or Mendel Mikolayover) and Israel Axenfeld (1787–1866) the beginning of the revolution of the written language (*wen-tzu k'o-ming*). Of special importance was Levin, who, by translating the Psalms into Yiddish in 1817, created a new written language (*hsin wen-tzu*). According to Shen Yen-ping, both men discarded Hebrew, the dead language or the "old literary language" (*wen-yen*), and substituted for it the living spoken language. By using this new written language, Jewish writers made the Jewish national heritage available once more.[15]

By the end of the nineteenth century, Yiddish literature came into its own. The social works of Mendele Mocher Sforim (Shalom Jacob Abramovich, 1836–1917) are superb examples of the literature in the new language, and in the works of the prose writers I. L. Peretz and Sholem Aleichem, Yiddish literature reached its height. Peretz, declared Shen Yen-ping, was the best short story writer among the new Jewish writers, and his use of the method of realism was unequaled. Neither he nor Aleichem, who is described as the Jewish Mark Twain, indulged in obtuse or idealistic descriptions. Indeed, Aleichem's influence extended beyond Jewish literature to world thought and world arts.[16] Both Peretz and Aleichem first wrote in Hebrew but later switched to Yiddish, abandoning the "learned" language of the Jews.[17] Aleichem, moreover, came from among the people; he wrote of the small places and the small people, of oppression and the oppressed.[18]

David Pinski (1872–1962) is another writer primarily concerned with the oppressed. His works, wrote the Japanese author Chiba Kameo, reflected an exceptional bias and sympathy for the impoverished classes. His superlatively realistic descriptions portrayed all aspects of the lives of the laboring and destitute, their wickedness and their temptations. But Pinski did not presume to judge. He wept over man's weaknesses and his inability to relieve the distresses of the soul. Chiba Kameo saw in Yiddish writing a strong humanistic (*jen-tao chu-i*) trend as well as a oneness of mankind. No matter whether one spoke of men and women in Poland or men and women in the Far East, all basically acted alike.[19]

Other Jewish prose writers, whose works were known although not translated, were Leo Kobrin (1873–1946)[20] and David Frishman (1859–1922).[21] Shen Yen-ping rather approved of the fact that Kobrin's socialist leanings did not lead him to condemn Jewish culture and that he developed naturalistic and realistic descriptive techniques to a high point.[22]

Turning now to discussions of Yiddish poets and poetry, it should be noted that although Chinese writers were acquainted with some Yiddish poetry, they confined themselves to simply mentioning the existence of Yiddish poets and added little or no critical analysis. Thus there are discussions of Morris Jacob Rosenfeld's (1862–1923) *Songs of the Ghetto* and the work of Joel Linetzki (1839–1916), Jacob Dienesohn (1856–1919), and Simeon Frug (1860–1916). The latter's poetry was enthusiastically praised. Although for the most part unacknowledged among modern Jewish writers, Frug is perhaps the greatest Jewish poet of the past eighty years, wrote Shen Yen-ping. Frug spent his whole life among peasants, loved nature, and was a naturalist poet with a modern egalitarian outlook. Frug's poetry, therefore, consisted of a deep appreciation of nature and a profound sympathy for his fellow man.[23]

Closeness to the people or a feeling for the masses and their language was also stressed as a significant attribute of the work of Moishe Nadir (Isaac Reiss, 1885–1943). Nadir, stated one Chinese writer, was unlike others in his use of language. He avoided elaborations, used direct speech, and preferred common expressions.[24] The group of young Jewish poets (*di Yunge*) called the Insikhists (Introspectives) was not neglected, and the influence of French symbolism on such writers as A. Leyeless (Aaron Glanz, 1889–1966) was mentioned.[25]

Dramatists and dramatic literature were more closely scrutinized. In addition to the general historical development of Yiddish drama,[26] Pinski and Sholem Asch (1880–1957) were especially noted as dramatists. Pinski, wrote Shen Yen-ping, pointed out the illness of modern man. His ideas were particularly useful when he expressed his doubts regarding civilization and man's capacities and when he reflected on human existence. What is more, Pinski had been influenced by socialist thought, which could be seen in his utopian (*ta-tung shih-chieh*) leanings. Asch, in contrast, was completely Jewish. His thinking was Jewish, and some vestiges of the old Jewish literature—its obtuseness and symbolism—continued in Asch's writings. Both Asch and Pinski represented the two poles of contemporary world Jewry.[27]

Aside from these discussions about Yiddish literature, it seems fairly obvious that the social and political realities of Jewish existence were not completely unfamiliar in China. Hence Chinese writers could supply a certain, if limited, context for their analyses of Yiddish literature. Periodic notices of persecutions of Jews had been appearing in Chinese missionary publications toward the end of the nineteenth and in the early years of the twentieth century,[28] while Zionism and its role were discussed in the twenties and thirties.[29] An improvement in American Jewish life was also reported,[30] and one optimistic writer observed in 1921 that the former contempt for Jews was disappearing and that there was a great change in attitudes. He unhesitatingly suggested that this might have been due to the export of Jewish literature to the literary world at large.[31] In a more cautious vein, Shen Yen-ping felt that Jews were the only people in the world without a country of their own and whose religion, being different from that of other people, often subjected them to cruel treatment. Still, no matter where they were, they kept to their faith, their customs, and their Eastern thought.[32]

The foregoing discussion has revealed several highly interesting points related to the questions of language and literary creativity and to the significance of new literary methods. Before proceeding, however, it should be pointed out that Chinese writers held an entirely mistaken notion of the place of Yiddish in Jewish literature. Although the use of Yiddish certainly opened a new chapter in Jewish letters, Hebrew by no means fell into disuse, nor indeed can Hebrew be described in terms of China's ossified *wen-yen*, or classical language. In fact, together with Yiddish, Hebrew was itself assuming a new literary significance during this period. This impression, which was created in the early twenties in China—namely, that Yiddish had displaced Hebrew—was never corrected, in spite of an essay on Hebrew poetry published in 1924 that clearly speaks of a Hebrew literary restoration (*fu-huo*).[33] Thus the impression that Yiddish was the Jewish *pai-hua* continued to persist. The mistaken idea that the literary revolution of Yiddish led to the disuse of Hebrew offered, if nothing else, the comforting certainty that literary revolutions could succeed. But more significantly, it confirmed the relationship between language and literary creativity.

In addition, Yiddish literature was seen as socially relevant because the miserable lives of the common people were depicted by naturalistic and realistic methods that made it possible for readers to understand and identify with it. Hence the Chinese writer was comforted once more by the fact that his own efforts were taking place not in isolation but in conjunction with efforts elsewhere. Implied here is a kind of universalism—a universalism of the human condition, as it were, that writers everywhere describe and that writers everywhere can understand.

But what is naturalism, and what is realism? And why was Yiddish literature so consistently described in terms of method? Obviously it was not without reason that Peretz and Pinski were said to use the method of realism, that Kobrin was considered a naturalist and realist, and that Frug was described as a naturalist poet. The labels naturalism and realism were often used interchangeably (or together), especially by Shen Yen-ping.[34] Their use in relationship to Yiddish writers reflects both the intense discussions of literary criticism at that time and the attempt to understand Yiddish literature from the point of view of modern literary criticism. Literary naturalism was considered an ephemeral but necessary development. The creation of new literature necessitates that writers pass through a "naturalist baptism," as Shen Yen-ping put it. But a precise definition is lacking. Apparently, naturalism in 1921 and 1922 in China was considered simply truthful description based on thorough and minute observation. Discussions of Chinese writers show that realism was not much different from naturalism. It, too, is a method of truthful description based on observation. But in addition, there is the demand for finding the typical, and most frequently, realism in literature is didactic.[35] When Chinese writers referred to Yiddish authors as naturalists or realists, I think they wanted to indicate their modernity. By means of such criteria as naturalism or realism, they expressed their conviction that Yiddish writers were indeed within the mainstream of modern European literature.

Accordingly, Chinese writers saw a definite relationship between literary creativity and the use of new literary methods. Changes in language make possible increased literary creativity. Both language and literature can reflect the conditions and concerns of a period of change. The resort to new literary methods is due to the use of new language. And therefore the new literature rests, on the one hand, on new uses of language and, on the other, on the adoption of new methods of expression. Chinese writers saw the universality of literature when there was a confluence of these phenomena.

The question of universality is particularly significant. The Chinese writers seemed to imply that relevancy was equivalent to universality. New methods are relevant. Literary creation that utilizes new methods to create relevant literature is tantamount to the creation of universal literature. The universality of this literature consists in the fact that though a particular condition is depicted, it is universally accessible. Yiddish literature, it would seem then, confirmed, for those who became acquainted with it, the belief in a universality joined with a cultural identity and a communality of human values.

Within the context of pre-1949 Chinese intellectual history, these assumptions are both valid and acceptable. But how are we to understand the fact that writers after the establishment of the People's Republic have continued to translate and comment on Yiddish literature? What does it mean that Sholem Aleichem was lauded as a "people's" writer in 1959? The answer to these questions has once more much to do with the notion of universality. Relevant literature is still seen as universal literature in the People's Republic. But relevant literature is more narrowly "people's" literature. The writer who writes "people's" literature creates universal literature. Joseph Levenson's distinction here between the "people" in terms of an international class (*jen-min*) and the "people" as national entities (*min-tsu*) is particularly significant.[36] Aleichem, who comes from the people (*jen-min*) and writes of the people (*jen-min*), need not be relegated to ideological impurity. With a slight twist on the definition of universality, Aleichem was able to maintain his honored position.

III

The translations from Yiddish literature, as far as can be determined, include both short stories and dramas, but no full-length works. The thirty-three stories and plays that I have been able to identify can be grouped into the following thematic categories:[37]

A. *Social Criticism and Injustice*

Author	Title	Year	Translator	Language
D. Pinski	Forgotten Souls	1920	Chou Tso-jen	English
D. Pinski	Tale of a Hungry Man	1925	Ch'en Ku	English
D. Pinski	In the Storm	1924	Ch'en Ku	English

Author	Title	Year	Translator	Language
I. L. Peretz	The Fast	1921	Shen Yen-ping	?
I. L. Peretz	Sisters		Lu-yen	Esperanto
I. L. Peretz	The Devout Cat	1957	Hsi Tzu	Esperanto
I. L. Peretz	The Messenger	1957	Hsi Tzu	English
I. L. Peretz	A Weaver's Love	1957	Li Nien-p'ei	English
S. Libin	Picnic	1934	Chao Chung-ch'ien	English
Sholem Aleichem	Eternal Life	1957	T'ang Chen	English
Sholem Aleichem	Three Little Heads	1957	T'ang Chen	English
Sholem Asch	God of Vengeance	1936	T'ang Hsü-chih	English
Z. Wendroff	Zerach and Bulani	1921	Shen Che-min	?
Sholem Aleichem	Gymnazya		Lu-yen	?
D. Pinski	Down with the Burden		Lu-yen	?

B. *Philosophy of Life*

Author	Title	Year	Translator	Language
Sholem Asch	Winter	1921	Shen Yen-ping	English
Sholem Aleichem	A Pity for the Living	1929	Nan-ming	English
H. D. Nomberg	In the Mountains	1935	Yin Yen	?
I. L. Peretz	Seven Years of Plenty		Lu-yen	?
I. L. Peretz	What Is the Soul?	1924	Lu-yen	?
I. L. Peretz	Pidjon Shwuim		Lu-yen	?
I. L. Peretz	Ormuzd and Ahriman		Lu-yen	Esperanto
D. Pinski	Rabbi Akiba's Temptation	1922	Hsi Chen	English
?	The Jew's Dance	1931	?	?

C. *Entertaining*

Author	Title	Year	Translator	Language
Sholem Aleichem	Miracle of Hashono Rabo	1925	Lu-yen	Esperanto
Sholem Aleichem	Bad Luck		Lu-yen	?
Sholem Aleichem	The Passover Guest	1934	Huang I	English
Sholem Aleichem	Rabchik	1924	Lu-yen	Esperanto

D. *War*

Author	Title	Year	Translator	Language
D. Pinski	The Beautiful Nun	1921	Tung Fen	English
D. Pinski	Poland 1919	1922	Hsi Chen	English
D. Pinski	Diplomacy	1924	Hu Yü-chih	English

E. *Exile and Love of Land*

Author	Title	Year	Translator	Language
A. Szymanski	Srul from Lubartow	1921	Chou Chien-jen	English

F. *Jewish Existence*

Sholem Aleichem	Passover in a Village	1929	Nan-ming	English

Works for which no dates appear were published in Lu-yen's anthology *Yu-t'ai hsiao-shuo chi* (Collection of Jewish fiction; Shanghai, n.d.), which appeared before 1929. For the titles, I have generally followed existing English translations. Where English titles were unavailable, I have translated the Yiddish titles, and in one case, where I was unable to trace the Yiddish title, I have translated the Chinese title.

As can be seen from the above tables, translations from Yiddish were published between 1920 and 1957. Most appeared in the twenties, a few in the thirties, in the forties none at all, and five stories were published in 1957. The two largest categories by far are those dealing with social injustice and criticism (A) and with philosophy of life (B). The reason for category A's size is clear. The theme of social injustice found a strong echo in China in the twenties as well as in the fifties. On the other hand, stories dealing with a philosophy of life appear to have little relationship to the concerns that made themes of social injustice so popular. One explanation is that interest in this theme was somehow related to the concern with evolving a *Weltanschauung.* The protracted dispute among intellectuals, known as "the controversy on science versus philosophy of life" (*K'e-hsüeh yü jen-sheng-kuan*), was one expression of this concern.[38] The translation of literature on this theme may very well have been the expression of a similar concern on another level.

It is important that only one story can be described as dealing unequivocally with the problem of Jewish life (E). The absence of such purely "Jewish" stories or plays no doubt strengthens the conclusion that the Jewish content of the stories or plays was largely incidental to other messages conveyed.

Several other facts should be mentioned. First, only a small number of Jewish writers were translated into Chinese—nine or ten in all.[39] Second, the stories and plays translated deal with a restricted number of themes, indicating a high degree of selectivity. Third, a relatively large number of translators had an interest in translating Yiddish literature.

The last point requires further explanation. There were possibly fourteen or fifteen translators. However, since many writers translated pseudon-ymously, the exact number cannot be established with certainty. Most important among translators was Wang Heng (Wang Lu-yen, 1901–1940), who usually signed his stories as Lu-yen. He published two anthologies of translated Yiddish literature,[40] some of which appeared in journals. Wang, a writer in his own right, translated principally from Esperanto. Chou Tso-jen was an essayist and a well-known literary figure. Like his brother Lu Hsün, he was interested in Eastern European literature. He translated one, or possibly three, stories.[41] The third of the Chou brothers, Chou Chien-jen, translated one story. Shen Yen-ping, who was particularly interested in the literature of minority peoples, translated all together six stories, four of these under the pseudonyms Hsi Chen and Tung Fen.[42] Hu Yü-chih (1900–), who translated one drama, was a literary critic and translator. The remaining translators cannot be identified.

Chinese translators, as pointed out previously, did not translate at random. They seem rather to have carefully selected whatever they wanted from a variety of available works, omitting themes that did not serve their purposes. Thus there are no plays or stories that deal specifically with romantic love, industrialization, and problems of the working class (except for one 1957 translation, which, in dealing with social injustice, has a working-class setting). Furthermore, works whose content was totally unfamiliar and works that did not have a "familiar ring"[43] were not trans-lated. Although it has not been possible to trace all the translations to their sources, it might nonetheless be useful to list the few works that are known to have been used. The number of stories or plays that they contain and those actually translated will show more clearly that only certain examples were chosen for translation.

> Benecke, Else C. M., trans. *Tales by Polish authors*. Oxford, 1915. 6 stories all together; 1 story translated.
> Berman, Hannah, trans. *Jewish Children: From the Yiddish of Shalom Aleichem*. New York, 1922. 19 stories all together; 3 stories translated.
> Frank, Helena, trans. *Yiddish tales*. Philadelphia, 1912. 48 stories all together; 2 stories translated.

Frank, Helena, trans. *Stories and Pictures by Isaac Loeb Perez.* Philadelphia, 1906. 35 stories all together; 3 stories translated.

Goldberg, Isaac, trans. *Six Plays of the Yiddish Theatre.* Boston, 1916. 2 plays translated.

Goldberg, Isaac, trans. *David Pinksi: Ten plays.* New York, 1920. 3 plays translated.

Goldberg, Isaac, trans. *Temptations: A Book of Short Stories by David Pinski.* London, 1919. 8 stories all together; 3 stories translated.

"Jewish Life" Anthology, 1946–1956: A Selection of Short Stories, Poems and Other Essays, Drawn from the Magazine. New York, 1956. 43 stories, essays, and poems; 1 story translated.

Salem-Alehem, Mucnik, Is. trans. *Perec, Hebreaj rakontoj.* Leipzig, 1923 (Esperanto). 11 stories all together; 4 stories translated.

Turning now to the stories themselves, it will be useful to discuss briefly their contents in order to see the variety of treatments of the different themes. As it will be impossible to describe all the translations, some representative examples from each category will be chosen.

The theme of social criticism and injustice is discussed in the translations in many different ways, as either corruption, religious and secular bigotry, exploitation, or social oppression. Sholem Aleichem's "Eternal Life"[44] is an attack on the social system as a whole, the corruption and indifference of both the Jewish and the Russian establishment. A young man journeys to another town. At an isolated inn, overcome by compassion and lured by the promise of eternal life, he is persuaded by the innkeeper to take the body of his dead wife for burial to the next town. However, when he suggests that the town's burial society bury the dead woman, they begin to suspect that the dead woman was in fact his own wife, his mother-in-law, or worse. No one believes the truth. At last he is forced to fabricate a tale for the Russian authorities. The young man is swindled out of his money for burial expenses and put in jail. In the end, his mother-in-law is summoned and the affair is straightened out. Eternal life may be his in the next world, but in this world, there is only misfortune.

Criticism of the hypocrisy of religious piety forms a basic substratum of a number of the translated works by Peretz and Asch. Peretz's "The Devout Cat"[45] and Asch's "The God of Vengeance"[46] are superb examples of attacks on a superstitious and religiously bankrupt society. In the first story—a magnificently biting fantasy—a religious cat kills three singing birds in the name of piety. Filled by holy zeal, the first bird was killed in order to save it from committing further sins. The second bird was killed for the same reason, but now gently and kindly. The third bird, however, died because of the cat's pious breath, which was to instill in the bird remorse and repentance. In the stifling atmosphere of religious piety, the bird suffocated. Peretz indicts religious hypocrisy, and the message was not lost on the Chinese, for the story appeared in translation in 1957. Asch denounces religion and the religious Jew more forthrightly, showing mercilessly the clash of religious bigotry and human values. In "The God of Vengeance," the Jewish keeper of a house of prostitution has an only daughter whom he protects and educates in order to erase the sinfulness of his occupation. He commissions the writing of a Torah, which to him signifies a holy talisman that will protect his home from misfortune. To the leaders of the Jewish community, however, this commission means money in the form of various contributions. The drama ends on a distressing note, for in spite of the Torah's presence in the household, his daughter turns to prostitution. Though a simple and ignorant Jew, the father is overwhelmed by the human tragedy of his family's existence. On the other hand, the community leaders' single thought is to preserve the outward forms of Judaism and not let it be known that the daughter has strayed. Asch masterfully shows that this sort of Judaism is only an empty shell. Its outward forms do not coincide with human values.

The only story that may be considered proletarian literature—that is, one concerned with problems of the working class—is the 1957 translation of Peretz's "A Weaver's Love."[47] Written in the form of a series of letters, Peretz tells of the abysmal conditions of workers. Underpaid and overworked, the weavers try to organize in order to improve their lot. But they are no match for the powerful manufacturers, who simply fire workers when they become troublesome. In an ever-growing labor market, ten other workers are waiting to find one place. And even if a weaver gives no thought to collective welfare, slaves at his trade, and does not lose his job, he will still not earn enough money to marry and support a family.

Without a doubt, one of the most forceful and moving stories in this category is Pinski's "Tale of a Hungry Man."[48] Itsye, the subject of the story, is a total outcast. Hungry, filthy, and hopelessly impoverished, he goes inevitably to his doom. However, in spite of his total misery and degradation,

Itsye is neither compliant nor meek. Angry and quarrelsome, he strikes out at society. At last he quarrels with a policeman and lands in jail. Although he has reached the end of the road, Itsye does not give in to the oppressive society that has brought him to this state. Defiantly and mockingly, he will not let them kill him; instead, he hangs himself.

Preoccupation with social injustice apparently led Chinese writers to search for stories that would describe social oppression in its many different forms. Their concern, therefore, is always with the little man who suffers when religious law loses its human value, when factory owners exploit his labor, when a heavy-handed bureaucracy plays with him as with a pawn, or when rich landowners exhaust his last ounce of strength. The different situations described in this group of translations were all well known to Chinese writers. They ring as true in the Chinese as in the original. And they certainly reflect the concerns of the various periods when the translations appeared.

However, it would be interesting to know how a Chinese reader received, for example, "A Weaver's Love." To be sure, the story describes the exploitation of the proletariat. But woven into the narrative is also another theme—namely, Peretz's questioning whether this new world in the making is worthwhile. In a poignant passage, the weaver explains that in the factory, new cloth as well as new customs and standards are being woven. But more than that, shrouds for the old world are being made, for it is to be buried in them. Will this new world be a better place? No, says Peretz. In place of the old, there "will arise another world, rotten through and through." Such a strongly pessimistic statement definitely did not correspond to what was demanded from Chinese literature in the name of socialist realism, for socialist realism required—if not in actuality, then at least potentially—that a new world with new men be shown.[49] In one respect, the weaver is a "new man," since against many odds, he does attempt to organize the workers. But he does not succeed. And in the last letter, he announces his return home.

The stories in the next category are extremely diversified, all raising the question of human existence or the meaning of life from a different perspective. In "Ormuzd and Ahriman,"[50] Peretz deals with the dangers of excesses, whether nationalism, which turns into jingoism, or simple living transformed into some sort of ideal. Sholem Aleichem, in "A Pity for the Living,"[51] expresses concern for all life, whether it is a cock to be butchered, a bird killed by two boys, or a dog inadvertently scalded by the maid. This is a beautifully sensitive story, which, as told through the eyes of a child, points to the insensitivity of adults. Sholem Asch's "Winter"[52] raises two crucial problems, one concerning self-sacrifice for family and the other the perpetuation of customs. A matchmaker has persuaded a mother to marry off her younger daughter while the older remains unmarried. The mother's feelings are in turmoil, since this is contrary to traditional custom. The older sister, in touching self-denial, bows to necessity and helps prepare the younger for the suitor.

In contrast to the category on social injustice, it is no doubt indicative that those translations concerned with some aspect of the philosophy of life were all published between 1921 and 1935. This group of stories often verges on the sentimental; they are gentle and leisurely. In trying to understand the appeal of these contemplative stories, it may be suggested that part of their attraction consisted of the utilization of an interesting and imaginative literary device. Two of the stories are told through children's eyes, and four of the stories have a fairy-tale-like setting. Their appeal might have been, therefore, the result of combining a serious theme with a playful literary device. It is perhaps also significant that six out of nine pieces were translated in the twenties, when many intellectuals were precisely preoccupied with the question of the meaning of life.

Stories in the third category are entertaining, light in spirit, and all told by the master storyteller Sholem Aleichem. Whether about a runaway locomotive, as in "The Miracle of Hashono Rabo";[53] about a dog, as in "Rabchik";[54] or about a misfired business venture, as in "Bad Luck";[55] all the tales are charming but apparently have no deeper significance.

The translations concerned with war are a series of plays by David Pinski. "Poland 1919"[56] tells of suffering and death as a group of people is trapped in no-man's land between two opposing armies. "The Beautiful Nun"[57] portrays the ultimate dehumanization of men in war. "Diplomacy"[58] is somewhat different. In this drama, Pinski shows how unscrupulous politicians manipulate events. He describes growing war hysteria as the masses are incited to hate and kill. With superb irony, Pinski mocks the symbols of God, fatherland, honor, or religion, in the name of which wars are fought and people die.

Concerning exile, the fifth category, there is only one story, and this not by a Jewish but by a Polish author. The story has been included here, since, in accordance with its contents, Chinese writers and translators consistently labeled it a Jewish story. "Srul from Lubartow"[59] tells of a Polish exile in Siberia who has met a Jew. Far from home, in strange and unaccustomed surroundings, the exiles pine for their native land. But it is not only the Polish exile but also the Jew who longs for the Polish earth. As exiles, the Jew and the Pole can join hands in their common love for the distant land and home.

No doubt there are several ways in which to consider the appeal of this story. Exile is a traditional and familiar theme in Chinese literature. Still, it would seem that in this particular case, the notion of brotherhood may have been more important. Divisiveness disappears in common suffering. Two people from different backgrounds, from different walks of life, can—and indeed do—join in their common love for home, which is the nation, the soil, the land where they have their roots. The potency of this message would not have been lost on the Chinese writer. A common humanism, reinforced by a love of the land, mitigates destructive divisiveness.

The last category concerns Jewish existence and, as with the preceding section, consists of only one story. Sholem Aleichem's "Passover in a Village"[60] describes the friendship of two children: one a Jew, the other a gentile. The story is told against the implied background threat of blood libel. Feitel and Fedoka have gone into the hills to share a piece of matzah. Delighted with their treat, their friendship, and spring itself, they stay out longer than intended. Meanwhile, the villagers surround Feitel's house, and the blood libel accusation is in the air. Luckily, all ends well when the children at last return. This story, then, contains sinister overtones of instant violence as well as the precariousness of Jewish existence together with the subtle joys of a spring holiday and friendship.

The fact that no other translations deal with the vicariousness of Jewish existence is not otherwise surprising. Stories of religious persecution would have been meaningless within the Chinese context, except perhaps as they communicate the universality of suffering and oppression. However, it should be suggested that the issues that made Jewish existence intolerable would have remained largely incomprehensible to a Chinese reading public. Moreover, the problems such issues raised for the translator might have been impossible to overcome. In the final analysis, the objectives of this translation literature were less to inform Chinese readers of Jewish life and its problems. Rather, they were to show the communality and concerns of human values in China and elsewhere.

What kind of problems did Chinese translators encounter in translating terms peculiar to Jewish culture? It should be noted first that most translators seem to have chosen equivalent terms with considerable care. Much effort was spent on attempts to convey all such terms in a clear and precise way or to append explanations either in footnotes or in the text. A random sampling based on Chinese translations of English translations will show the different ways in which problems were handled.

The term *rabbi* was usually transliterated as *la-pi*. In "Poland 1919," Shen Yen-ping added the parenthetical explanation that a rabbi was a pastor superintending education (*chang-chiao chih mu-shih*) and in "The Temptation of Rabbi Akiba"[61] that he was a Jewish pastor (*Yu-t'ai mu-shih*). Evidently, Shen understood the educational function of the rabbi in spite of choosing the term *mu-shih*, which was derived from Christian usage. Wang Lu-yen, in his appended glossary to "What Is the Soul?,"[62] reveals a more sophisticated insight by describing a rabbi as a Jewish doctor who explains the law (*Yu-t'ai chiang-fa po-shih*), thus avoiding the Christian implication. On the other hand, the 1957 translator of "A Weaver's Love" discarded the transliteration and translated rabbi as *Yu-t'ai fa-shih*, or Jewish priest.

In "Rabbi Akiba," Shen Yen-ping transliterated Torah as *tu-la*, explaining it as the Jewish teaching of righteousness (*Yu-t'ai chiao-i*). In "What Is the Soul?" Wang Lu-yen also transliterated Torah as *tu-la* but describes it more specifically as the traditional five-part Mosaic code of Hebrew law. The 1957 translator was more precise. In "A Weaver's Love," Torah is translated in the text itself as the Five Books of Moses (*Mo-hsi wu-shu*), and a footnote explains that this is the holy scripture of the Jews. In "Eternal Life," however, Torah is translated in the text as the teaching of righteousness (*chiao-i*), and the footnote describes it as the Five Books of Moses.

Still another way of handling transliterations meaningfully was to add the English term parenthetically after the first mention. Hu Yü-chih did this in "Diplomacy" when dealing with names that were difficult to explain. On the other hand, when neither an explanation nor the original term was added, meanings could be easily obscured. This, for example, was the case when Nan-ming transliterated *Jahrzeit* as *yeh-erh-tsai ti* in "Passover in a Village" without explaining that this was the annual commemorative prayer for a departed family member. The Chinese reader had no way of knowing what father and son were doing in the synagogue.

A more serious problem, however, arose when Chou Chien-jen merely transliterated the term *ḥasīd* in "Srul from Lubartow" as *hu-shih-ti* without clarification. Szymanski, writing for a Polish audience, had the Polish-Yiddish pronunciation of *ḥusid*, which was also retained in Benecke's English translation. Moreover, neither the author nor the English translator explained the term. Quite possibly Chou did not know what a *ḥasīd* was, and the underlying meaning of the story may have been distorted as a result.

Another method, in addition to transliteration, was to either coin a new phrase or choose a familiar term. Pogrom, for example, was translated literally as searching out and destroying (*sou-chiao*) as well as killing (*t'u-sha*) in "A Pity for the Living." A similarly literal translation is used for People of the Book, rendered as *shu-chung ti jen*, and chosen people is clearly recognizable in *t'ien-hsüan chih-min*. Synagogue was translated either as church (*li-pai t'ang*); as *t'ai* in "Winter" and "A Weaver's Love"; or as Jewish church (*yu-t'ai chiao-hui*) in "Picnic."[63] Meeting hall (*hui-t'ang*) was used in "The Passover Guest."[64]

Huang I, the translator of the last story, did make, however, several careless mistranslations. Reb, a form of address commonly used in Eastern Europe, was transliterated by him as *lei-pei*, as if it were part of a name. He translated *kiddush*, the blessing of the wine, as the prayer before eating (*fan-ch'ien tao-kao*) and the Haggadah as a scriptural Bible comment (*sheng-ching hsün-hua*). The translator of "Eternal Life" also misunderstood the nature of the Haggadah. Transliterating the word as *ha-chia-ta* in the text, he explained in a footnote that this is the legendary part of the law. Both translators were apparently ignorant of the fact that reference was made to the Passover Haggadah, or the Passover story.

The word *God* occurred frequently in the Yiddish stories. Generally, the word was translated as *shang-ti*, an ancient Chinese term that can be translated as the Lord on high.[65] The translations from 1957 use *shang-ti* even when such other terms as Almighty, Lord of the Universe, or His Name had been used in the version from which the translation was prepared. Still, some exceptions should be noted. In "In the Storm,"[66] the term is omitted from translation whenever possible. It occurs only once, and then as *Lao-t'ien-yeh*. Chou Tso-jen, it seems, was also reluctant to translate the term. In "Forgotten Souls,"[67] there is only one mention of God in the translation, and the Chinese chosen for it is *fo-shen*, which has Buddhist and native religious connotations.

A few other terms are of interest. In "Three Little Heads,"[68] Shavuoth, the holiday of the giving of the Law, is transliterated as *chien-wu-ssu* and explained in a footnote as an important Jewish holiday that comes fifty days after Passover. In the same story, Sukkoth, the Festival of Booths, is not transliterated but translated as "Festival of Greens" (*mao-chieh*) and explained as the Jewish autumn festival. In "Eternal Life," *tefillin*, or the phylacteries used for daily prayer, is translated as "scripture box" (*ching-hsia*), and their use is described in a footnote. But in the same story, *kaddish*, or the prayer for the dead, is simply translated as "hymns" (*tsan-mei-shih*) without further explanation. The ingenuity of the last story's translator is altogether admirable. For the pious utterance "Blessed be He who gives, and He who takes," he found perhaps a more prosaic but nonetheless suitable proverb: "Life and death are caused by fate" (*Ssu-sheng yu ming erh*). He was undaunted even by *shlemazl*, which became "unlucky one" (*tao-mei chia huo*).

On the whole, the translations are faithful and read easily. If occasionally a translator found it useful to omit a phrase, the general meaning was not impaired. The immediacy of Sholem Aleichem's Yiddish, for example, is frequently recaptured with a Chinese colloquialism. The 1957 translators tended to take their task more seriously by annotating their translations carefully and even supplying references to biblical citations, something none of the earlier translators had done, apart from Wang Lu-yen. Still, a random comparison of Chinese translations with their Yiddish originals shows that in some instances the Chinese departs from the original. This is especially true in translations prepared from Esperanto. Therefore, in so far as all translations were secondary, they could be only as good as the translations from which they were in turn translated.

The major objective of this study has been to show the uses to which literature can be put or the ends it can serve. But literature also has the power to move human beings to new thoughts and new perceptions. Literature, in the sense that it allows a person of a given time and place to participate in the lives of persons of another time and place, is a door to the world, and a bridge. It is pleasing to think that for moments in time, Yiddish literature bridged the gulf that separates culture from culture and man from man. It is pleasing to know that at such moments, a Chinese reader could participate in the joys and sorrows of a people so different and yet in some ways so like himself.

NOTES

1. Wolfgang Bauer, *Western Literature and Translation Work in Communist China* (Frankfurt/Main–Berlin, 1964), 1.

2. This figure includes a series of eight stories that were published in *I-ch'ang huan-his i-ch'ang kung* (Poor and joyous ones) (Peking, 1959), which came to my attention too late for inclusion in this account. It is entirely possible that in addition, some translations have escaped my attention. Chinese bibliographies are notoriously incomplete, and some major journals in which translations appeared, especially in the twenties, were unavailable to me.

3. Concerning the remaining seventeen stories, I suspect that the majority were translated from Esperanto.

4. Shen Yen-ping, *Yin-hsiang, kan-hsiang hui-i* (Impressions, reflections, and reminiscences), 2nd ed. (Shanghai, 1918), 52.

5. There were several Esperanto collections of Polish literature that were widely used by Chinese translators. These are described in my "Poland and the Polish Author in Modern Chinese Literature and Translation," published in *Monumenta Serica*, 1975. Esperantists were not lacking in China since the early years of the twentieth century, and the language has continued, even in recent years, to enjoy some popularity. See Honfan, "Boom in Esperanto," *People's China*, April 16, 1957.

6. The intellectual revolution, as part of the May Fourth Movement, is discussed in Chow Tse-tsung, *The May Fourth Movement* (Stanford, 1967).

7. *Hu Shih wen-ts'un* (Collected works of Hu Shih) (Taipei, 1953), 1:64, 67–70, 73.

8. Chou Tso-jen, "Jen ti wen-hsüeh" (Human literature), in *K'ung Ta-ku* (Empty drums) (Shanghai, 1928). This essay first appeared in *Hsin ch'ing-nien* (New youth) 5, no. 6 (December 1918): 575–584.

9. Chou Tso-jen, *Yü-wai hsiao-shuo chi* (Collection of foreign short stories) (Shanghai, 1920), first published in Japan in 1909.

10. Witold Jublonski, "Mickiewicz w Chinach" (Mickiewicz in China), *Przeglad Orientalisticzny*, no. 20 (1956). It was Lu Hsün (pseudonym of Chou Shu-jen, 1881–1936), elder brother of Chou Tso-jen, who first discovered Mickiewicz in Georg Brandes, *Poland: A Study of Polish People and Literature* (London, 1903).

11. A. Galla, "Pai Mang und Petöfi (aus der Geschichte der Aufnahme der Ungarischen Literatur in China)," *Acta Orientalia* 15 (Budapest, 1962).

12. Lu Hsün, "Mo-lo shih li shuo" (On the power of Mara poetry), in *Lu Hsün san-shih nien-chi* (Lu Hsün thirty year collection), *Fen* (The grave), *1907–1925*, 1937, 53–100. In this essay, first published in *Honan tsa-chih* (1907), Lu Hsün compares the search for a new culture in China with the desire to arouse the people to new life in Europe.

13. *Hsiao-shuo yüeh-pao* (henceforth *HSYP*) 12, no. 10 (October 1912): 2.

14. Apparently no translations whatsoever were prepared from Hebrew-language literature. There are, however, two articles discussing Hebrew poetry. One is Yeh Ch'i-fang, "Ku Hsi-pai-lai shih-yün yen chiu" (A study in ancient Hebrew verse rhymes), *Ch'en pao fukan*, November 1923. The other was a translation by Shen Yen-ping, published under the pseudonym of Ch'ih Ch'eng, "Hsien-tai ti Hsi-pai-lai shih" (Modern Hebrew poetry), *HSYP* 14, no. 5 (May 1924): 1–7. This article was originally written by T. Shipley.

15. Shen Yen-ping, "Hsin Yu-t'ai wen-hsüeh kai-kuan" (Views on Yiddish literature), *HSYP* 12, no. 10 (October 1921): 61.

16. Ibid., 65–66.

17. Li Nien-p'ei in *I-wen* (Translation), September 1957, 105; and T'ang Chen in *I-wen*, July 1957, 88.

18. Ch'en Jen-kuang, "T'an Hsiao-lo-mu Ah-lai-han-mu ho ta ti tso-p'in" (On Sholem Aleichem and his works), *Chung-shan ta-hsüeh hsüeh-pao* (Journal of the Sun Yatsen University), nos. 1–2 (1959): 93.

19. Chiba Kameo, Han, Ching [Shen Yen-ping], trans., "Yu-t'ai wen-hsüeh yü Pin-ssu-ch'i" (Jewish literature and Pinski), *HSYP* 12, no. 7 (July 1921): 3, 7–8.

20. Hai Ching, "Yu-t'ai wen-hsüeh yü Kao-pa-lin" (Jewish literature and Kobrin), *HSYP* 16, no. 12 (December 1925): 1.

21. Shen Yen-ping, "Yu-t'ai wen-hsü chia shin-shih" (A Jewish writer about to die), *HSYP* 13, no. 11 (November 1922): 3.

22. Shen Yen-ping and Cheng Chen-to, "Hsien-tai shih-chieh wen-hsüeh che lüeh-chuan" (Brier biographies of present-day world authors), *HSYP* 15, no. 3 (March 1924): 2; and "Hsin Yu-t'ai wen-hsüeh Kai-kuan," 68.

23. Shen Yen-ping, "Hsin Yu-t'ai wen-hsüeh kai-kuan," 64–65.

24. Chao Ching-shen, "Hsin Yu-t'ai tso-chia Na-ti-erh" (The Yiddish writer nadir), *HSYP* 21, no. 11 (November 1930): 1675.

25. Shen Yen-ping, "Hsin Yu-t'ai wen-hsüeh kai-kuan," 67.

26. This in a translation from Isaac Goldberg, "The Yiddish Drama," in *The Spirit of Yiddish Literature* (Girard, KS: 1925), 50–57. The translation is by Yang Chen-hua, "Hsin Yu-t'ai ti hsi-chü" (Yiddish drama), *Shih-chieh tsa-chih* (The world) 5 (May 1913): 928–933.

27. Shen Yen-ping, "Hsin Yu-t'ai wen-hsüeh kai-kuan," 67.

28. See, for example, *Wan-kuo kung-pao* (Review of the times) 10 (1878): 305b–6a, 418a–49b; 14, no. 11.167 (December 1902): 18a–b; 17, no. 4.196 (1905): 21–22.

29. See, for example, Ko Sui-ch'eng, "Yu-t'ai jen-kou ti fen-pu ho chi min-tsu yün-tung ti kai-kuang" (The scattering of the Jewish people and their national movement), *Tung-fattg tsa-chih* (Eastern miscellany, henceforth *TFTC*) 26, no. 20 (October 1929): 113–123; and Yü Sung-hua, "Yu-t'ai jen yü Yu-t'ai fu-hsing yün-tung" (The Jews and their revival movement), *TFTC* 24, no. 17 (September 1927): 21–28.

30. "'Yu-t'ai hsüan min' tsai Chih-chia-ko shang yen-ku chü" (The "Chosen Jewish People" is performed in an old drama in Chicago), *Wen-i yüeh-k'an* (Literature and art monthly) 4, no. 5 (November 1933): 173.

31. "Yen-chiu Yu-t'ai hsin wen-hsüeh ti san chung hsin ch'u Ying i-pen" (Three newly published translations of Yiddish literature in English), *HSYP* 12, no. 1 (January 1921): 2.

32. Shen Yen-ping, "Hsin Yu-t'ai wen-hsüeh kai-kuan," 60.

33. Shen Yen-ping, "Hsien-tai ti Hsi-pai-lai shih" (see note 14 above), 5.

34. Marian Galike, *Mao Tun and Modern Chinese Literary Criticism* (Wiesbaden, 1969), 80.

35. See ibid., 70–82, for a discussion of the complex aspects of the issue.

36. Joseph R. Levenson, *Revolution and Cosmopolitanism* (Berkeley–Los Angeles–London, 1972), 6–7.

37. Works omitted from the table are two stories by Sholem Aleichem, two stories by Peretz, one story by Asch, and one story each by Taje and Rabinovitch, whose identities as authors I am unable to determine. Also not included in the table are the series of eight stories that appeared in *I-ch'ang huan-hsi i-ch'ang kung*. Special thanks are due to Mrs. Chava Turniski of the Yiddish department at the Hebrew University of Jerusalem for giving invaluable help in identifying a number of stories.

38. For a collection of essays on this topic, see Change Chün-mai, *K'o-hsüeh yü jen-sheng kuan* (Science and the philosophy of life) (Shanghai, 1925). See also O. Briere and Laurence G. Thompson, trans., *Fifty Years of Chinese Philosophy, 1898–1948* (New York, 1965), 29–31.

39. I am not certain whether the story "The Jew's dance," published in 1931, is a translation. It may be a story created on a Jewish theme by a Chinese writer, though it has the ring of an anonymous Jewish folktale.

40. Lu-yen, trans., "Yu-t'ai hsiao-shuo chi" (Collection of Jewish fiction) (Shanghai, n.d.); and "Pin-ssu-ch'i chi" (Pinski collection) (Shanghai, n.d.). According to Chang Ching-lu, "Chung-kuo hsien-tai ch'u-pan shih-liao" (Materials on contemporary Chinese publishing) (Peking, 1957), 1:271, these were published before 1929.

41. "A pity for the living" and "Passover in a village" are signed as Nan-ming. According to Austin C. W. Shu, comp., *Modern Chinese Authors: A List of Pseudonyms*, Michigan State University, Asian Studies Center, Occasional Papers (1969), 44. Nan-ming is Chou Tso-jen's pseudonym; however, on page 76, Mr. Shu attributes the pseudonym to Lu Hsün.

42. Marian Galik, "The Names and Pseudonyms Used by Mao Tun," *Archiv Orientalni* 31, no. 1 (1963): 89–90.

43. Chou Tso-jen refers to this aspect in particular in his preface to *Yü-wai hsiao-shuo chi*, 5.

44. T'ang Chen, trans., "Yung-sheng," *I-wen*, July 1957, 67–83.

45. Hsi Tzu, trans., "Ch'ien-ch'eng ti miao," *I-wen*, September 1957, 83–84.

46. T'ang Hsü-chih, trans., *Fu-ch'ou shen* (Shanghai, 1936).

47. Li Nien-p'ei, trans., "I-ko chih-kung ti lüan-ai," *I-wen*, September 1957, 92–105.

48. Ch'en Ku, trans., "I-ko o-jen ti ku-shih," *HSYP* 16, no. 2 (February 1925): 1–14.

49. On literature of socialist realism, see Albert Borowitz, *Fiction in Communist China, 1949–1953*, Center for International Studies, Massachusetts Institute of Technology (1954).

50. Lu-yen, trans., "Ho-erh-mu-ssu yü Ah-ssu-man," in *Yu-t'ai hsiao-shuo chi*.

51. Nan-ming, trans., "Tz'u-pei" (Compassion), *Yü-ssu* (Thread of talk) 5, no. 12 (May 1929): 647–656.

52. Shen Yen-ping, trans., "Tung," *HSYP* 12, no. 9 (September 1921): 24–33. Also in Shen Yen-ping and Shen Tse-min, trans., *Hsin Yu-t'ai hsiao-shuo chi*, Collection of Yiddish fiction (Shanghai, n.d.).

53. Lu-yen, trans., "Ho-hsia-no-la-p'o ti ch'i-chi," *TFTC* 22, no. 15 (August 1925): 115–122. Also in *Yu-t'ai hsiao-shuo chi*.

54. Lu-yen, trans., "La-pai-i-ko," *TFTC* 21, no. 9 (May 1924): 107–115. Also in *Yu-t'ai hsiao-shuo chi*.

55. Lu-yen, trans., "Pu-hsing," in *Yu-t'ai hsiao-shuo chi*.

56. Hsi Chen [Shen Yen-ping], trans., "Po-lan i-chiu i-chiu nien," *HSYP* 12, no. 8 (August): 1–10.

57. Tung Fen, trans., "Mei ni," *HSYP* 12, no. 8 (August 1921): 21–28.

58. Hu Yü-chih, trans., "Wai-chiao," in *Hsien-tai tu-mo ch'ü* (Contemporary one-act plays) (Shanghai, 1924).

59. Chou Chien-jen, trans., "Yu-t'ai jen" (Jews), *HSYP* 12, no. 9 (September 1921): 4–13.

60. Nan-ming tri, "Ts'un-li ti yü-yüeh chich," *Yü-ssu* 5, no. 13 (June 1929): 677–693.

61. Hsi Chen [Shen Yen-ping], trans., "La-pi Ah-ch'i-pa ti yu- huo," *HSYP* 13, no. 1 (January 1921): 26–32.

62. Lu-yen, trans., "Ling-hun" (The soul), *TFTC* 21, no. 11 (June 1924): 117–124. Also in *Yu-t'ai hsiao-shuo chi*.

63. Chao Chung-ch'icn, trans., "Yeh-yeh," *Wen-hsüeh* (Literature) 2, no. 5 (May 1934): 931–935.

64. Huang I, trans., "Yü-yüch-chieh ti k'e-jen," *Wen-hsüeh* 2, no. 5 (May 1934): 936–940.

65. Milena Vetingerova, "Kuo Mo-jo's Übersetzungen von Goethe's Werken," *Archiv Orientalni* 26, no. 3 (1958): 444, notes that *shang-ti* comes closest to the Christian conception of God, whereas *t'ien* (heaven) has pantheistic overtones.

66. Ch'en Ku, trans., "Pao-feng yü li," *HSYP* 15, no. 3 (March 1924): 1–4.

67. Chou Tso-jen, trans., "Pei-hsing wang-ch'üeh ti jen-men" (Forgotten by luck), *Hsin ch'ing-nien* 8, no. 3 (November 1920): 427–438. Also in *K'ung ta ku*.

68. T'ang Chen, trans., "San-ko hsiao t'ou-erh," *I-wen*, July 1957, 83–88.

CHAPTER 10

Meylekh Ravitch in China

A Travelogue of 1935

Among those who traveled in China, we rarely if ever read about Jewish travelers who wrote for Yiddish-speaking readers. There may not be many Yiddish travelogues, yet they are of considerable interest because of the rather different cultural inclinations of the traveler and the fact that they are directed at a Yiddish readership. Meylekh Ravitch (Zekharia Khone Bergner, 1893–1976) was in China in the first half of 1935, and among his legacy is a travel diary of over one hundred typewritten pages. He was a well-known poet and writer who, according to his own account, was dispatched as a "delegate" by two organizations concerned with occupational training and health (*Israel's Messenger* 1935, 23). He carried a typewriter along, and his impressions of what he saw were apparently recorded at the time. Thus there is a feeling of "immediacy" about the travelogue, of sincerity—often even despair—concerning the human condition. At the same time, one also finds many pages largely unpolished, often repetitious, and whole paragraphs seemingly given to sentimental flights of fancy. The latter does not strike one as extraordinary in Yiddish but does so when cast into English. The bulk of the travel account remains in manuscript form, and Ravitch merely published several articles based on it.

When paying tribute to another great traveler, Peretz Hirshbein (1880–1948), Ravitch (1941) wrote that objective observation such as Hirshbein's must be filtered "through the subjective window of his own soul" (115). Ravitch's travelogue does indeed seem to do exactly that. He apparently enjoyed traveling and, according to his account, had visited forty-four countries by the time he was forty-six years old (Ravitch 1945, 244). Furthermore, he later wrote a number of poems about Harbin, Beijing, Canton (Guangzhou), and Shanghai that were published in a 1937 collection of his poetry, *Kontinentn un Okeanen* (Continents and oceans). These poems, usually based on a sentence or a brief vignette in the travel diary, supply an individualized dimension, often conceived tragically. Small portions of the poems will be cited in this essay.

Not much is known about his life. Although he wrote about himself in two of his four-volume biographies of writers, he tells little about himself in these. We learn, for example, only that he was born in a small Galician town, that he started writing poetry at the age of sixteen, and that he adopted the pseudonym Meylekh from a much-admired poet and Ravitch from the hero of a story of another.[1] He became a vegetarian at the age of eighteen. At some point (he does not state which years, though this must have been before World War I), he attended an Austrian officers' school. Above all, he liked Yiddish literature (Ravitch 1945, 244), and he professed his "belief in [...] the mission (*shlikhis*) of the Jewish people to the peoples of the world, and the mission of Jewish world literature to the literatures of the world" (Ravitch 1958, 386).

Finally, he described himself as having a natural aptitude for order and organization (Ravitch 1945, 243), which led, no doubt, to his holding the position of secretary of the Yiddish Writers' and Journalists' Association section in the Polish association until 1934 and becoming the founder and secretary of the Yiddish PEN section in Warsaw (Rozen 1950, 89; *Israel's Messenger* 1935, 23). He left Warsaw in May 1934 and went to London, where he remained until the end of the year, when he embarked on the long journey to China (*Di Post* 1934). He was in China less than half a year, until May or June—unfortunately, he does not supply dates between Harbin and Shanghai in the travel notes—leaving for Hong Kong from Shanghai. By November 1935, he was in Australia (JNUL, Ravitch Collection, file 2:212).

Before turning to his travels, let me briefly review some facts about China in the 1930s that touch in one way or another on the travelogue. Although Chiang Kai-shek (Jiang Jieshi, 1887–1975) established his Guomindang (Nationalist) government in 1928 in Nanjing, he did not exercise control over most southern and a number of northern provinces. That China continued to be a largely divided country did not escape Ravitch's attention (Sheridan 1975, 183–203).[2] The poet was, furthermore, aware that the Japanese had invaded Manchuria—China's three northeastern provinces—in September 1931; that the Lytton Commission of the League of Nations issued its report on the invasion in 1933; and that in March 1934, Henry Pu-yi became emperor of the state of Manchukuo. While in Beijing he seems to have been also aware of the arrests and executions of Chinese students in 1934 and 1935 (Spence 1990, 413–414).[3] On the other hand, Ravitch was apparently not acquainted with the important events in Communist history that were taking place at the time. One was the Long March, which began in October 1934 with approximately eighty thousand and ended one year later with the arrival of a small remnant in Sha'anxi province. Nor does he mention the Zunyi (Guizhou province) Conference in January 1935 signaling the beginning of Mao Zedong's rise to power.

THE TRAVEL ACCOUNT: MANCHURIA

Ravitch began his journey to China from London on January 28, 1935. The trip to the Trans-Siberian railway in Moscow took him to Denmark, Sweden, and Finland. From there he went to Leningrad, spending an afternoon in the city on February 2. By February 4, he was at last on the Trans-Siberian railway, traveling all together twelve days on trains and two days on ships before arriving at the Manchurian border (JNUL, Ravitch Collection, file 2:370, 2–4, 8, 17, 22).

The long train journey was tedious. Well over six thousand miles, it lasted six or seven days; the railroad led through sparsely populated regions and the endless Siberian wastelands. Between the Yenisei River and the Manchurian border, the train traversed a mountainous region that may have been more interesting, as was undoubtedly the loop around Lake Baikal (Tupper 1965, 408).[4] His poem about the train journey was written at a later time (as were apparently all his China poems), but it captures well the endlessness of the journey. Scenes rush by the window as the train speeds through the wintry countryside. By prefacing a number of verses with "Day," "Night," "Again day," and "Again night," he reminds the reader of the passage of time:

> Again day. Ice-cold, sharp and briefly glittering sun,
> Its beams broken on a red Cossack's rider's lance.

He sees horses, a village, boys and girls on skis, an abandoned church, and a caravan of sleighs, and when the train stops, he sees pictures of Lenin and Marx in a small waiting room:

> Again day. Forests and sun—white porcelain.
> Evening the sun dims like an old copper pan.
> At night his imagination roams freely:
> Night. Far is still Jenghiz Khan's horde
> Far from the wheels of the Trans-Siberian railway.
>
> (Ravitch 1937b, 24–26)

On February 10, he arrived at the Manchurian border, where he boarded the Chinese Eastern Railway. Manzhouli, he commented, was a dead town; there may have been two thousand Jews there, but most had left since the start of the conflict (JNUL, Ravitch Collection, file 2:370, 38). The travelogue makes no mention of Harbin's political situation since the beginning of the Japanese occupation; nor does he mention whom he met there, how he was received by the Jewish community, or about Russian-Jewish coexistence.[5] Rather, he gives several vignettes of Harbin life, and among these, he was especially taken by Harbin's dead and the frequent kidnappings. He was shocked to see two dead Chinese men laid out next to the railroad tracks, and he wrote at length about the Chinese and White Russian kidnappers.[6] The latter, he claimed, were called by the Chinese term *konkboz* and had become the bane of the Jewish population. Kidnappings were mainly carried out, he wrote, by demobilized White Russian soldiers who were worse than the Chinese because they did not have the latter's chivalrous tradition (JNUL, Ravitch Collection, file 2:370, 47–48, 51–52).

The travelogue does not mention the Lytton Commission of the League of Nations that came to Manchuria in early spring 1932 to investigate Japan's conquest and creation of a state. But in a poem that Ravitch wrote subsequently about Harbin, the Chinese dead at the railroad and the commission are brought into juxtaposition together with Japan's conquest. The poem summarizes the political situation in one brief verse:

> Manchuria there, Manchuria here
> And Henry Pu-yi sits already on the throne
> And Japanese ships are anchored
> In Harbin at the river Sungari.

Most of the poem is, however, about Mei Wanfu, the poor coolie from
Chefoo, who seeks his fortune in Harbin only to succumb to a heroin (not
opium) habit. His life and his death are as futile as the task of the Lytton
Commission. Mei Wanfu ends up at the railroad track next to another dead
man, waiting for death:

> Both lie there, playing with them
> is the wind and snow, uncovering, covering, both.
> Here wind plays, there death plays
> with the women and children of Chefoo.
>
> (Ravitch 1937a, 27–30)

Whereas the travelogue conveys a negative impression of the kidnappers, a
long poem about them expresses quite the opposite. *Kidnappers: Song on the
Waters of the Yangzi River* is an outcry over the bitter fate that has caused
them to turn to this kind of life. The poet pities both the victims and the
victimizers—those who have been kidnapped and not ransomed and those
who did the kidnapping:

> Why has one been given everything
> and another given nothing.
> And because he was given nothing
> He went away to the kidnappers.
>
> (Ravitch 1937a, 36–38)

He next went by train to Changchun, renamed by the Japanese Shinkyo
(Hsinking) and established by them as the capital of Manchukuo. The
Changchun travelogue (translated later into English as an article), although
an objective description, betrays an ambivalence about the Japanese efforts
in the city that had been a backwater until the Japanese takeover. Ravitch
describes not only the enormous building activity, especially of office buildings; he also reminds the reader that the new structures are erected with
cheap Chinese labor. Chinese workers have come here by the tens of thousands, "like ants [they] crawl around all day, and even at night, by the light
of huge arc lights, carry there and back chinese [*sic*] baskets on wooden
shoulder yokes, fulfilling a plan of which they are in ignorance" (JNUL,
Ravitch Collection, file 2:212).[7]

   Contrasts between Japanese and Chinese are seen at every turn. Immediately upon arrival in the capital, he discovers that next to the sedate

Japanese chauffeurs, who drive highly polished cars and the latest models, there are the Chinese "droshky" drivers, "their faces black with congealed blood, their eyes reddened by dust storms." He drinks coffee in a Japanese café with a Japanese man who praises it as "wonderful Salvador coffee." Curious as to what makes it special and Salvador, he is informed that Salvador is so far the only country that has extended recognition to Manchukuo in return for an agreement that for three generations, Salvador coffee would be drunk (JNUL, Ravitch Collection, file 2:212, 2–4).[8]

FROM TIANJIN TO BEIJING

Ravitch's journey took him next to Tianjin and then to Beijing. Increasingly he was attracted by the human scene, writing that in Tianjin humanity looked different from the train than from the ground. He claimed that at daybreak, when one sees them labor, one knows that the people have worked all night and not begun at daybreak. Alighting from the train and walking through the concessions, he found the idea of concessions preposterous. In Tianjin, he commented, were the "ideal, classical" concessions. Like a chessboard, each country—British, French, Italian, Japanese, and others—had its concession and its ex-concession, its little piece of land with its churches "as if built for all eternity" (JNUL, Ravitch Collection, file 2:373, 90–92). His eye was, however, taken by the vignettes he observed. At the harbor, he watched the coolies at work, carrying burdens all day long. Three sat in a corner and played cards. One was black because he carried coal, one was red from the bricks he carried, and the third was made white by gypsum. "I stood next to them," he wrote, "and stand already a quarter of an hour, they are not surprised by anything. I stand next to them and think they are like animals who take on the color of the world in which they live" (JNUL, Ravitch Collection, file 2:373, 94–95). This is not meant disparagingly. Rather, the poet pities China's toiling masses, as he will do later in Shanghai, who must labor for a few coppers to feed themselves and their families.

After a brief journey, Ravitch arrived in Beijing, where, according to his account, he spent only a few days. One might expect this visit to have been the high point of the poet's journey, but apparently it was not. He noted that Western influence had contributed aspects to life in the capital, but the foundation remained Chinese. He went to the Forbidden City and described the wonders he saw, but he had trouble telling one palace from the other. He saw the Bell Tower yet commented, "I saw and did not see, and my feelings of seeing and admiring [. . .] in Peking were [. . . (confused)]." That which was seen disappeared at once, and that which was not seen lived on in his imagination (JNUL, Ravitch Collection, file 2:374, 109–110). In Beijing, Ravitch despaired of ever understanding China. He noted the walls—walls around houses, walls everywhere—and expressed his wonder at the symmetry of the city: "Peking is built with a view of the universe. [. . .] Is there another city of that ideal mystery?" (JNUL, Ravitch Collection, file 2:374, 101f.) Nonetheless, as we shall see below, he was more interested in people and how they lived than in edifices and monuments. A visit to the Lama Temple (*La Ma Miao*, also called *Yonghe Gong*, Palace of Concord and Harmony, in close proximity to the Bell Tower; Arlington/Lewisohn 1967, 190–195) was apparently more satisfying. The priest lit incense for the stranger and prayed for him, singing with a "Yiddish melody." He found the Maitreya statue impressive, noting that "with one god I am already secure, now I must still propitiate the Jewish God for my sins" (JNUL, Ravitch Collection, file 2:374, 112).[9] Surprisingly, he did not visit the Temple of Heaven (*Tian Tan*), which was in the Chinese city and in 1935 was in a rather dilapidated state (Arlington/Lewisohn 1967, 105). He did go, however, to the Temple of Confucius (*Kong Miao*), where he commented that the master's teaching had become dogma. Someone must have told him that China's weakness and disunity were due to her military weakness, which led him to cite a well-known phrase about the poor quality of Chinese soldiers (JNUL, Ravitch Collection, file 2:374, 112).

A brief section in the travelogue about a visit to Beijing's National Library led Ravitch to thoughts about students and the fact that their heads "were separated from their bodies"—in short, that they were executed (JNUL, Ravitch Collection, file 2:374, 111f.). However, the long poem of thirty-one stanzas that he wrote later, "He Naiwan and Li Guanyu: A Peking Love Ballad," seems to have been inspired by an additional account as well. Might he have met Harold Isaacs (1910–1985) and his wife, Viola, who were living in Beijing until June 1935 and who may have told him of students' concerns? Although neither man mentions such a meeting, Isaacs, who was then writing his important book *The Tragedy of the Chinese Revolution*, was hardly a friend of the National or local Nationalist governments and would have been a willing informant. Student concerns about Japanese encroachments into North China that led to the ferment later in fall and to the December Ninth Movement—the large demonstrations that surged through the city at the end of the year—would not have escaped Isaacs's attention (Isaacs 1985, 50–58).[10]

In my imagination, I can see the two men sitting at the red table in the Isaacs's modest courtyard in the East City (vividly described by Isaacs) while the latter explained the volatile Beijing situation to the visitor. He may also have told Ravitch about the events of early 1931, when twenty-three communists were executed by the Nationalists in Shanghai, having been arrested at a secret party meeting (see Hsia 1968, 163–233). In Ravitch's poem, He Naiwan's love for the leftist student leader Li Guanyu is fused with the story of the secret party meeting, its betrayal, and the execution of the students.

The poem begins with Naiwan's plea that her parents allow her to go to the university in Beijing. Permission is finally granted, and she arrives in the capital, where her love for Li is combined with her love for China. He sends her a note to come to the highly secret meeting at Five Bridges, and when she receives the note,

> He Naiwan smiles, He Naiwan trembles,
> Today with her books, as trembles a leaf.
> And she vows: Li, Li—for you and your China
> Better hundred times death than betrayal.

But Chiang Kai-shek's soldiers learn about the meeting, and the students are arrested. The next morning they are led to the marketplace to be beheaded one by one,

> And he calls loudly to He Naiwan
> Going next to him quietly like a pigeon.
> Breathing heavily, barely, she says
> —you speak—Li Guanyu—I believe.

Yet despite the brutal story the poet tells and the indifference of society that he points to in the penultimate stanza, he seems also to indicate a glimmer of hope in the last one:

> The crowd is dispersing, the market resumes,
> Only each rickshaw rolling past

Turns aside, lest it smear
Blood on its light rubber wheels.

And He Naiwan's skin through the torn dress
Becomes thinner, greener, as if silky green
Rendering green China's hopes
On the stones of Peking.

(Ravitch 1937a, 39–43)

ON TO SHANGHAI AND CANTON

Ravitch went next by ship from Dalien (Dairen) to Shanghai. During a brief stopover in Qingdao, he marveled at the German look of the city, its houses with their red-tiled roofs—the strange foreign look of an ex-colony. He arrived in Shanghai in April (my guess is that it was toward the end of the month), remaining in Shanghai for six weeks (JNUL, Ravitch Collection, file 2:374, 127). We have no way of knowing precisely when Ravitch went to Canton or why he first went to Hong Kong, taking the train from there to Canton. Nor is it clear whether he left China from Canton, returning from there to Hong Kong.

Remaining six weeks in Shanghai, Ravitch had more to say in the travel-ogue (fourteen pages in all) about the city than about the others, and he also published two articles: one on aspects of life in the metropolis and the other about the Jews of Kaifeng (Ravitch 1936). Regarding the former, he was especially interested in the Sephardim, who he remarked were in Shanghai nearly one hundred years, whereas the Ashkenazim came later.[11] Being, to me, surprisingly color conscious, he described the Sephardim as brown people who, however, had British passports and therefore considered themselves Europeans. Among them were several blonde youngsters who either were adopted (not an uncommon occurrence) or were the offspring of rarer mixed marriages. Silas Hardoon (1849?–1931), though by then dead for more than ten years, occupied him in particular. Ravitch repeated current anecdotes about Hardoon's legendary parsimoniousness, though in fact he owned much rental property in Shanghai. Hardoon's grave, he wrote, was in his garden and was larger than Napoleon's grave. The history of Hardoon is recorded in Chinese, and there are inscriptions in Chinese, Hebrew, and English. Two life-size monuments of Hardoon, one sitting and one standing, are near the grave. Although in his lifetime Hardoon wore Chinese clothing, the monuments show him in Western suits, and on his chest are many Chinese medals (Ravitch 1937b, 10).[12]

The article was written for Ravitch's Yiddish readers, and while it was based on his travel diary, in his notes he also recorded other matters. A night in Shanghai, he marveled, was like a night in Paris, not even like New York. The light screams; the younger civilization is speaking. "Shanghai's night heaven is a rainbow," he wrote, "that was broken and fell into the dark, huge ocean of the night." Lights went up and down in many colors, and in between were Chinese characters. The five hundred Buddhas in heaven, he added, were asking one another in wonder what these lights meant (JNUL, Ravitch Collection, file 2:374, 133). Dance halls were a novelty to the poet. For five Mexican dollars, one could dance one or two minutes. But there was no talk; the girls did not speak European languages. Whereas he obviously described the French Concession and the International Settlement, he did not neglect the Chinese sections of Shanghai. About Zhapei, he wrote that there had been many casualties there in the battles between the Chinese and Japanese three years earlier, referring obviously to the clashes between the Chinese Nineteenth Route Army and the Japanese in January 1932, and the Japanese bombing of Zhapei.

Shanghai's military arrangements caught his attention, "as if the Messiah had already come to earth," and "the lion lies with the lamb in the green pasture." This is because "in uniforms and with guns they come together from all parts of the city and congregate in national companies. Englishmen, Scotsmen, Frenchmen, Americans, Japanese, only no Germans. [...] Instead there are Russians, White Russians." And Jews. This was the only place in the world, wrote Ravitch, where one could see the Jewish military presence with silver Stars of David and guns. The Volunteer Corps of Shanghai had a special Jewish company under the leadership of a British officer (JNUL, Ravitch Collection, file 2:374, 138f.).

But as in Tianjin, it is Shanghai's poor, its beggars and coolies, that he described at length. In a long section about rickshaw pullers, he said that he wanted to write about these poorest of the poor of whom there are several hundred thousand and "their hell on earth is Shanghai." Poetically, as he did not allow himself to write in published articles, he stated, "The world is full of storms, the world is full of worry [...] (and rickshaws are) one of the saddest corners in what is called Shanghai. The world is full of worry, but every human being is a world unto himself and every family is a world unto itself, and every class, and every city, and every nation—a world unto itself worlds in worlds, closed circles, one circle cannot enter into the other" (JNUL, Ravitch Collection, file 2:375, 141). Ravitch's moral indignation cries out from these pages. He did some homework not only on the background of the rickshaw in Japan—a fairly recent invention—but especially on the numbers involved in and dependent on the rickshaw trade, which he figured at 810,000 persons.

In another section, entitled "Pictures from the life of the Shanghai street-dogs on two feet," he wrote that a rickshaw man's day began at 2 A.M. and ended at 2 P.M.: "Once the rickshaw [man] screams high to heaven, and there China screams, he screams from hurt, he screams the scream of his wife and his children [. . .] he screams the scream of hunger and injustice—until they close his mouth" (JNUL, Ravitch Collection, file 2:375, 145–146). His indignation is captured in a vignette that, together with a visit to a Buddhist temple, later became a poem in which he voiced his moral outrage. The vignette is that of a rickshaw man who has stepped on a piece of glass. He nonetheless runs on limping as the glass cuts deep into his foot. The woman in the rickshaw sees what is happening, but maybe she does not see, maybe she does not want to see, or maybe she thinks it is not her business to see, Ravitch wrote. The injured man will not complain because he knows the woman might refuse to pay, a policeman might come, and he could lose his license (JNUL, Ravitch Collection, file 2:375, 145).

A Rickshaw Coolie Dies on a Shanghai Dawn is a poem that relates the story of the man who has injured his foot, but in the poem, he is near death with fever. He takes the only three coppers he has and runs to the Buddhist temple. It is still locked. He pounds on the gate and hears as

> A rusty key turns
> A wooden bolt heavily groans.

The gates to the temple are opened by a yawning servant. The wounded man wants to give Buddha the money and his life. But he wants something in return:

> I want Nirvana. I—worse than a street dog,
> Tore my foot on rusty iron.
> With fever I burn, and no one

Even wants to shoot me compassionately.

Buddha hears, stretches out his hand, smiles again,
Chan Zungui too stretches and smiles at the Buddha.
The first and last smile on his face
Reflected til now only in rain puddles.

Chan dies and the temple servant, grasping Chan's healthy foot, drags him away (Ravitch 1937a, 44–46).[13]

Canton was apparently the last city Ravitch visited in China. However, exactly when he went from Shanghai to Hong Kong, taking the train from there to Canton (as mentioned earlier), is not recorded in the travelogue. From it, we learn that except for the heat, which he found unbearable after a typhoon, the train ride was utterly absorbing. He noted the tropical villages along the way, and he describes them as consisting of pretty houses without windows and roofs in characteristic Chinese style. Dark-gray water buffalo move in the waters, and there are rice fields as far as the eye can see. As he neared Canton, the villages became denser and finally become one large village with no wall surrounding it. As always, he observed the local scene, noting in one of the train stations women baggage carriers—small, thin women with shining eyes as if feverish with hunger. They surround the passengers, and there is one baggage carrier with a child—her advertisement, as it were, "the living part of her need" (JNUL, Ravitch Collection, file 2:378, 161).

A friend picks Ravitch up from the train station, and they go by car to Shameen, the island on which the British and French concessions are located. A half-naked beggar stands in the road, and the driver blows his horn. Ravitch is led to muse over the difference between life and death, thinking that for a Cantonese beggar, death is better. But he is in love with Canton, which he considers the capital of South China. Canton is independent of Nanjing, he notes in his travel diary, although the "dictator" Chiang Kai-shek tries to "talk the world (into believing) that he controls what cannot be controlled [. . .] China." Indeed, Canton is the birthplace of the Chinese Revolution and of Sun Yat-sen: the birthplace of freedom. But, he added regretfully, of Sun's work nothing remains except his statues.

The boat people, those who have never lived in houses, held his interest next. All the water around the island is covered with small boats, perhaps ten thousand of them. He marvels at the changing scene at every step:

"This is how it is described in books and motion pictures," he wrote. And also pityingly, "I walk along the shore already for hours, the eye cannot see enough [. . .] of the hunger and poverty of the people all around." Small vignettes caught his eye, almost small-town Jewish, and he was nearly moved to tears. A mother read a book to her two small children, "5,000 years, 10,000 miles, two gods, water and earth, and despite this, this wonderful similarity" (JNUL, Ravitch Collection, file 2:378, 162–164). He also found a similarity in a pagoda full of kneeling women. The priest (he calls him *ba'al tefilah*, prayer reader) read while keeping time. "The melody is like from the *humash* [the Five Books of Moses], like from the *heder* [where young Jewish boys had their first lesson]," he wrote, "so that I only need to close my eyes and I am in . . . Warsaw on Krokhmalne [Street]" (JNUL, Ravitch Collection, file 2:378, 64).

A nighttime excursion took him and a friend to the floating brothels. He watched the prostitutes on their small boats, their makeup, and their silence. They neither gesture nor call out invitations, he wrote in his travel diary. On one of the boats, he saw a blue-eyed woman and then realized that she was blind. Later he wrote an imaginative poem in verse and rhyme about this woman. Like most of his poems in the collection about far shores he visited, it is tragic in the sense that Ravitch seemed to have grasped the hopelessness of the individual's fate. Whether it is a student caught up in secret longings and the fervor of ideological struggle, a wounded rickshaw man, or a blind women, he understood and expressed in poetry the utter tragedy of their individual existence, the clash of the anarchic urges of the individual and the indifference of society. He begins the poem slowly:

> This is a story of the city of Canton,
> A story of everyday life.
> About the Chinese people on the waters
> Around the Shameen Concession,
> Already twelve generations, perhaps even more,
> They live here, around Shameen.
> The wife works the oars as do the daughters,
> The work of coolies on the boat—in the sun.

The story continues with one boat coolie whose wife bore him six sons and the seventh, a blind girl. She was a beauty, and at the age of eight, the father sells her into prostitution. The woman he has sold her to is not bad;

she feeds the girl, and the girl grows more beautiful each day. At last, an old man takes her for the night. Thereafter, the girl has a vision of Buddha as a young man who comes to take her away. She follows him into the water, and the poem ends with the following verse:

The man was Buddha—
Buddha the lover—
And Ye Naipan—
Went into the water—
By Buddha—
By Buddha alone—
To be loved.

(Ravitch 1937a, 53–57)

Finally, there are two pages in the travel diary about interesting people he met in his Asian travels, among them a woman by the name of Rosenthal, known by her Chinese name He Ro-se. He wanted very much to meet her because he was "also interested to acquaint [. . .] [himself] a little with Chinese literary circles," but especially because her book, *Love and Duty*, sold half a million copies in Chinese after being translated from French (JNUL, Ravitch Collection, file 2:356, 1f.). Although I was unable to discover details about the life of the author, her book was indeed very successful in China in the 1920s and 1930s. Reprinted several times as *Lian'ai yu yiwu*, it was also made into a silent film in 1931 by Bu Wancang (1903–1974) and was shown at the twenty-fifth Hong Kong International Film Festival in 2001.[14]

After Ravitch arrived in Beijing and before he ever went to Shanghai and Canton, he wrote in his travelogue that people say "not to see Peking is not to see China [. . .]. So says the one who searches in China for the legend and not the reality. But China can never be truly seen and it can never be understood" (JNUL, Ravitch Collection, file 2:374, 100). Ravitch's journey was not a quest for legends, and he was unable to describe the reality he encountered. China's vast size, the complexity of the human landscape, the differences among the parts that make up this great country, he realized, could not be reduced to one-dimensional sentences. Perhaps this was one of the reasons he did not attempt to revise and publish the travelogue and why vignettes captured in poetic images were more satisfactory.

But despite the increasing popularity of travel and tourism in the 1930s and the many journalists and writers who roamed the world (Burdett/

Duncan 2002, 4), Ravitch was a different kind of traveler. He does not quite fit the categories of those who were after news stories or who traveled far and wide to observe events unfolding. With his Polish-Jewish background, transplanted into the uniquely cosmopolitan environment of Warsaw, his personal disposition was also different. How he experienced China was dependent on this background and also on the knowledge about China and Chinese affairs he brought with him. These and other individual and social factors determined what he perceived and how he chose to express his perceptions (Brenner 1989, 27).

He was ostensibly a delegate of charitable organizations that had charged him with fundraising activities. He makes no mention of these in the travel diary, and I doubt that he raised any money aside, perhaps, from Shanghai's relatively larger Jewish community. The fact is, however, that Ravitch was a city person, and his journeys took him to cities rather than to villages, which he observed, for example, when he traveled from Hong Kong to Canton.[15] In the cities, he was interested less in important personages or the wealthy of the Jewish communities (described in his published articles) and more in the poor and downtrodden. Time and again, whether it was in Tianjin, Shanghai, or Canton, he recorded impressions about their lives. Time and again, his sympathy—indeed, his concern for them and their future—is evident from the travelogue's pages and expressed in the poems, where he gave them faces and names.

His concern for the poor and especially the coolies was, however, not politically motivated. Ravitch did not seem particularly interested in Chinese politics, and he certainly did not consider the masses of the poor as revolutionaries from whom an uprising could be expected. About the rickshaw coolies in Shanghai, he wrote that even if they and their children go hungry, they will not be the ones who make revolution (JNUL, Ravitch Collection, file 2:375, 147). To be sure, he knew something about Sun Yat-sen and Chiang Kai-shek and about the Sino-Japanese conflict, but his discussion did not go beyond a brief mention. Nor was he particularly interested in finding out more about religious beliefs, whether noted in the travel diary or in the poems; to Ravitch, all Chinese deities were Buddhas.

Apparently, the China journey left neither a lasting nor indelible impression. He made no mention of it in the four-volume biographical dictionary in which he included himself. It would seem that after he had published the poems and articles about China two years following the trip, he was done with the China experience. But even if for Ravitch this was no more than an episode in a large part of a life spent traveling, for us today his travel-ogue, his record that took him beyond his own culture, is valuable. In it, we find not theories about Chinese politics or social change but one person's views of the human condition. In his travel diary, Ravitch does not tell us about the exotic, the strange, and the different in China. The lives of human beings, whether in China's cities or in his native Poland, often did not differ that much from one another. Encountering China, the encounter with the "Other," struck him as strange—and at times as not so strange. Ultimately, he brought to China, it would appear from the travel diary, neither an ide-ology nor an interest in politics but a profound humanism that transcended nationality. This humanism, which animated a portion of the Jewish-Polish intelligentsia between the wars, manifested itself again six-odd years later when, despite the hardships of flight and displacement, Jewish-Polish writ-ers and poets arrived in Shanghai and continued to write in Yiddish.

REFERENCES

Altman, Avraham. 2000. *Controlling the Jews, Manchukuo Style*. In *From Kaifeng . . . to Shanghai: Jews in China*, edited by Roman Malek, 279–317. Nettetal.

Arlington, L. C., and William Lewisohn. 1967. *In Search of Old Peking*. New York.

Bren, Frank. 2001. *A Century of Chinese Cinema: The 25th Hong Kong International Festival . . . and Beyond*. April 6–21, 2001. http://www.senseofcinema.com/contents/festivals/01/14/hongkonged.html.

Brenner, Peter J. 1989. *Die Erfahrung der Fremde*. In *Der Reisebericht*, edited by Peter Brenner. Frankfurt.

Bresler, Boris. 1999. "Harbin's Jewish Community, 1898–1959: Politics and Adversity." In *The Jews of China*, edited by Jonathan Goldstein, 200–215. Armonk-London.

Burdett, Charles, and Derek Duncan. 2002. Introduction to *Cultural Encounters: European Travel Writing in the 1930s*, edited by Charles Burdett and Derek Duncan. New York-Oxford.

Di Post. 1934. "Dikhter Mcyleckh Ravitch ungekomen kayn London" (The poet Meylekh Ravitch has arrived in London). *Di Post*, May 11, 1934.

Gleber, Anke. 1989. *Die Erfahrung der Moderne in der Stadt*. In *Der Reisebericht*, edited by Peter J. Brenner. Frankfurt/M.

Hatong xiansheng yongai lu (*Mourning record of Mr. Hardoon*). [= *Halong xiansheng yangai* n.d.]

Hsia, Tsi-an. 1968. *The Gate of Darkness: Studies on the Leftist Literary Movement in China*. Seattle/London.

Isaacs, Harold R. 1985. *Re-encounters in China: Notes of a Journey in a Time Capsule*. Armonk.

Israel, John, and Donald W. Klein. 1976. *Rebels and Bureaucrats: China's December 9ers*. Los Angeles/London.

Israel's Messenger. 1935. "Ort-Oze Combat Eco-nomic Life in Europe, Interview with Melech Ravitch." *Israel's Messenger* 32 (May 3, 1935): 23.

Jewish National and University Libraries. Ravitch Collection: files 2:212, 2:370,

2:374, 2:375, 2:378. [= JNUL, Ravitch Collection]

Luo Chen [Rosenthal (?)].1924, 1933, 1939. *Lian'ai yu yiwu* (*Love and duty*). Shanghai.

Meyer, Maisie J. 2003. *From the Rivers of Babylon to the Whangpoo: A Century of Sephardic Jewish Life in Shanghai.* New York.

Ravitch, Meylekh. 1936. "Di legende, geshikhte un genoier matsav fun di velt berimte 'khinezishe Yidn'" (The legend, history and exact condition of the world renowned "Chinese Jews"). *Afrikaner Yidishe Tsaytung*, December 31, 1936.

———. 1937a. *Kontinentn un okeanen: Lider, baladn un poeme* (*Continents and oceans: Songs, ballads and poems*). Warsaw.

———. 1937b. "Vi azoy es lebt zikh di por toisnt Yidn fun ale ekn fun der yidisher velt in der grester khinezisher stat, in finefmilioniken Shanghai" (How do several thousand Jews from all corners

of the Jewish world live in the largest Chinese city of 5 million in Shanghai?). *Di Presse*, January 31, 1937, 10.

———. 1941. "Fun di masaoes Binyamin hashlishi biz di masaoes Peretz Hirshbein" (From the travels of Benjamin the Third to the travels of Peretz Hirshbein). In *Peretz Hirshbein* (*tsu zayn zekhtsisten geboirentog*) (*Peretz Hirshbein, on his sixtieth birthday*) by Yovel Komitet (*Oifboi-Grupe*). New York.

———. 1945, 1958. *Mayn leksikon* (*My lexicon*). Vol. 1, Montreal 1945; Vol. 3, 1958.

Rosenthal (?).1929. *Love and Duty: The Story of a Chinese Girl.* 3rd ed. Shanghai.

Rozen, Bes Y. 1950. *Tlamatske 13.* Buenos Aires.

Sheridan, James E. 1975. *China in Disintegration: The Republican Era in Chinese History 1912–1949.* New York.

Spence, Jonathan D. 1990. *In Search of Modern China.* New York/London.

Tupper, Harmon. 1965. *To the Great Ocean. Siberia and the Trans Siberian Railway.* London.

NOTES

I thank Professor Avraham Altman for his careful reading of this essay, his critical comments, and especially his help with Yiddish transcription. My thanks to the Truman Research Institute of the Hebrew University of Jerusalem for their partial support of this research.

1. Ravitch is derived from the protagonist of the story *Offn Yam* (On the Sea), by Lamed Shapira (1878–1948). For Shapira's biography, see Ravitch 1958, 305–307.

2. Sheridan notes that Shanxi, Shandong, Fujian, Guangdong, Guangxi, Hunan, Sichuan, Xinjiang, and so on were barely controlled by Chiang during the years of the Nationalist regime.

3. Spence cites an estimate from 1934 of 300 students and teachers arrested. Between the end of 1934 and March 1935, another 230 were arrested.

4. Tupper notes that in Soviet Russia, there were no longer first- or second-class accommodations, only "soft" and "hard" carriages.

5. A brief description of the Harbin Jewish community is in Bresler 1999.

6. By far the most notorious case was that of Simeon Kaspe, a young pianist who was kidnapped by White Russian thugs in August 1933 and shot by them in December (see Altman 2000, 293).

7. The file is both in Yiddish and in an English translation. Ravitch submitted the English translation to the *Herald* in Melbourne, but I was unable to ascertain whether it was printed. The English title is *A Capital That Was Built in a Night*; the Yiddish title is *Hsinking (sic!)—The Youngest of the Capitals.*

8. Ravitch also traveled to Mukden (Shenyang), which will not be discussed here for lack of space. See JNUL, Ravitch Collection, file 2:373, 69–85, for an account of this journey.

9. Ravitch does not say which statue he saw, and Arlington makes no mention of a Maitreya statue.

10. Cf., however, also Israel/Klein 1976, 20, according to whom 1934–1935 "had been the

quietest year in a decade." Yet I would argue that the students could hardly ignore the gradual moves of the Japanese military into North China, and the arrests mentioned by Spence had much to do with the student unrest earlier.

11. Ashkenazim usually refers to the Jews who spread through Germany and Central and Eastern Europe. The term *Sephardim* was applied to Jews who spread from Spain along the North African coast, the Turkish Empire, and so on and their descendants. The two groups have distinct rituals, differences in liturgy, and some differing traditions. For a recent publication about the Shanghai Sephardim, see Meyer 2003.

12. Hardoon's funeral, eulogies, poems, inscriptions, and so on are reproduced in twelve Chinese volumes, *Hatong xiansheng yongai lu*, n.d.

13. Ravitch wrote one other poem about Shanghai, which has the Russian diaspora in Shanghai as its subject and is especially interesting for taking up a cross-cultural theme.

14. Cf. Bren 2001, 3. Zhu Xilin adapted the book for the screen, and the Lianhua Production Co. produced the film. My gratitude to Thomas Kampen of the Heidelberg University for this and the following information. According to Kampen, *Love and Duty* was published by the Commercial Press in 1926 and 1929, 3rd impression. Rosenthal's Chinese name is also given as Luo Chen or Luo Shen, and a Chinese edition of the book was published in 1934. I am also grateful to Haiyan Lee of Cornell University, who informed me that the book was first serialized in *Xiaoshuo shijie* (World of fiction) and published in book form in 1924, with a preface by Cai Yuanpei (1868–1940). According to Lee, a second Chinese edition was published in 1933. I gratefully acknowledge the help of Kent McKeever of Columbia University, who informed me that another (?) Chinese translation of the book appeared in Shanghai: *Shangwu yishuguan*, 1939. I am more than ever grateful to Joan Hill, who found two English editions in American libraries, one published in 1926 and the other in 1932. I cannot reconcile the discrepancy of dates, as *Love and Duty* is not available in Israeli libraries. Finally, I am especially grateful to Professor Avraham Altman for initiating the correspondence with the above informants and for sharing the puzzlement as well as excitement over Rosenthal's discovery.

15. Gleber 1989 writes, "The culture of the twenties is marked by the city" and "The city as paradigm of the modern determines the experience of . . . the journey" (463).

CHAPTER 11

The Critique of Western Judaism in *The Castle* and Its Transposition in Two Chinese Translations

Following a hemorrhage in August 1917, Franz Kafka's illness was diagnosed as tuberculosis in September. Between 1917 and 1922, Kafka had intermittent leaves of absence from his office and work for which he had little liking. Because of his steadily deteriorating condition, he did not consider himself capable of either prolonged or sustained literary activity and instead wrote a number of shorter works during those five years. In spite of his progressively worsening illness, Kafka began work on *The Castle* sometime in February 1922. He apparently worked throughout the spring until the end of June, but he never completed the novel. In September Kafka wrote to Max Brod that he was unable to "connect" the story.[1]

Whatever the combination of motive, impulse, and inspiration that makes up the creative process, there can be little doubt that the autobiographical moment plays a major role in *The Castle*.[2] By the first half of 1922, Kafka knew that he was already very ill, and in addition, several significant events had occurred that had a shattering impact on his life. There was the complex and unhappy relationship with Milena Jesenská, the engagement and disengagement with Julie Wohryzek, and the increasingly distressing relationship with his father. The last deteriorated markedly between 1917 and 1920, a problem that Kafka felt a need to articulate in his "Letter to My Father" in 1919.[3] When writing *The Castle*, Kafka therefore wrestled with as well as poetically transmuted the events that had so greatly affected him.[4] Aside from these, *The Castle* also contains Kafka's critique of Western Judaism. The immediate impetus for such a critique in the very body of the novel may have been the crisis in his relationship with his father. However, Kafka's attitude toward Judaism—more specifically, the Western or German Judaism of his native Prague—had been evolving for a number of years, ever since his encounter in 1911–1912 with the Yiddish theater from Poland. That Kafka wrote this novel only two years before his death can be understood on one level as the artistic expression of his consuming anguish and on another as an attempt to explore his relationship to Western Judaism.

There are, to be sure, many levels of meaning in *The Castle*. This essay will be concerned only with understanding the premises of Kafka's Jewish discourse in the novel. The first part will outline the issue of Western versus Eastern Judaism in Jewish intellectual discussions, Kafka's encounter with Eastern Jews, and his references to this in his diary and letters. The second part will deal with three major themes in *The Castle*, within which the question of Western and Eastern Judaism is raised, and how they are transposed into Chinese translation. Attention in this part will be directed to translation as an interpretative activity, the assumption being that the skillful translator who transposes a literary work from one cultural context into another does more than translate words and sentences. Translated works pose questions common to both literary and intellectual history by introducing new literary techniques or new subjects and ideas. Translations are usually undertaken in response to a felt need. Translators in this sense are re-creators, and their translated works will be both identical to and different from the original.

These general considerations raise several questions in reference to the translation of *The Castle*. Are the translations indeed re-creations? How familiar might the translators have been with the background against which the novel was written, and how much recognition is there, especially in the People's Republic, of Kafka's Jewishness and its role in his literary works? How well did the translators know the extensive critical literature on *The Castle* and on Kafka's significance in modern Western literature generally?

WESTERN AND EASTERN JUDAISM

In his biography of Kafka, Max Brod, one of his closest friends, pointed out that although "the word 'Jew' does not appear in *The Castle*, straight from his

Jewish soul [Kafka] has said more about the situation of Jewry as a whole today than can be read in a hundred learned treatises."[5] Brod recognized the significance of the Jewish elements in *The Castle* but did not elaborate on them. Among the numerous critics who have commented on Kafka's works and the novel, most have tended to emphasize the religious, or spiritual and mystical, rather than the specifically Jewish elements.[6] Hartmut Binder, on the other hand, stresses that the Jewish content in Kafka's *The Castle* reflects the author's perception of the breakdown of Jewish values and traditions in urban Western Jewish culture.[7] Binder's suggestion is persuasive when considered in the light of Kafka's eager interest since 1917 to master Hebrew and his extensive reading in Jewish history and literature for more than a decade.[8]

Without negating the importance of the search for spiritual value in *The Castle*, there is also the stratum out of which this search developed—namely, the problems that he believed existed in the society he knew, the society of Prague Jewry, of German Jewry,[9] and on a more personal level, the Jewry represented by his father and his father's generation. It will be useful to recapitulate briefly how the assumption that Western Jewry was in crisis came to be a part of Jewish intellectual discourse among a younger generation shortly before and following World War I. Although Kafka was not as active a participant as were, for example, Brod and Martin Buber, he was very much a part of the circles, Zionist and other, that debated this issue. He also was an avid reader of the articles that appeared in such publications as *Die Selbstwehr* (Self-defense) and *Der Jude* (The Jew), and he read Brod and other Jewish writers' literary works, which frequently reflected the problems of Western Jewry.

In his seminal work *Brothers and Strangers*, Steven Aschheim argues that the European Enlightenment and nineteenth-century Jewish emancipation dissolved the older patterns of Jewish solidarity, demanding new Jewish identities as Jewish life became more closely interwoven with specific societies, like German, English, or French. Among German Jews, the drive to become modern demanded assimilation, which, in turn, required that Jews dissociate themselves from traditional culture and especially its external forms, such as the Yiddish language or the long kaftan worn by men. The emancipated and assimilated German Jew who appeared after 1850 was an urban and middle-class phenomenon. The values he internalized were middle-class values, breeding, refinement, gentility, education, and good manners.[10]

This new self-definition was juxtaposed to the Eastern Jew—the "Ostjude"—who was considered to be dirty and boorish, spoke jargon (Yiddish), and believed in degenerate, superstitious, and fanatical Hassidism. By constructing the contrast between the rational, enlightened, clean, refined German Jew and the irrational, superstitious, dirty, and ill-mannered Eastern Jew, the latter came to stand for everything in the Jewish past that German Jews believed they had transcended. Eastern Judaism, especially in its Polish-Galician variety, was identified as an "Asian" Judaism by middle-class German Jews.[11] The dissociation that German Jews felt was both real and psychological. It was real in the sense that Eastern European Jews continued to maintain traditional Jewish culture, living in close-knit societies and gradually changing from within without being allowed to or, for that matter, wanting to enter into the mainstream of the larger Polish or Russian society. It was, however, also psychological in the sense that Eastern Jewish culture was seen in a negative light and was considered backward. The "Ostjude," the ghetto Jew, began to function as a stereotype and foil in order to highlight the Western Jew's modernity.

German Jewish identity and self-understanding underwent a radical change after the turn of the century with the beginning and development of Zionism. According to Aschheim, a second, younger generation of German Zionists—under the influence of Ahad Ha'am's emphasis on cultural Zionism,[12] together with the pervading "volkisch" atmosphere within German society—argued that being Jewish and being German were not compatible. This postassimilationist generation rejected incorporation into German society and looked instead to a national regeneration of all Jewry. They believed that in spite of Enlightenment and emancipation, and in spite of differences among Jews, the Jews were one nation, and they began to see the "Ostjude" in a new light.[13] Radical views of a Jewish renaissance and romantic visions of existence led these young Zionists to the discovery of the Jewish "Volk" in Eastern Europe.

It was there that the real *Volk* existed, not as a pale imitation or an imitative adjunct of a foreign culture, but as a living, pulsating organism with its own forms. "Genuine" Jews were to be found in the East, and for these Zionists, the Eastern Jew became the surrogate for the German nation. Buber's Hasid—vibrant and rooted in human community and religious values—was the Jewish Volkish answer to the ideal figure of the German Volkish movement, the peasant. A new interest began in Yiddish folksongs and Yiddish and Hebrew literature. Earlier disdain turned into idealization.[14]

This idealization—according to which Eastern Jewish existence was seen as whole, total, and unspoiled—was significant both as a critique of German Jewish life and, above all, as a rebellion against German Jewish bourgeois existence: "It reflected the intellectual currents and sentiments of youth increasingly dissatisfied with conventional middle class German Judaism." And when during World War I Jewish soldiers at the front discovered the "shtetl," Polish small-town Jewish life, a real-life dimension was added to the idealization. The *shtetl* became a metaphor for a totality, an organic community, "*Gemeinschaft*, a counter-utopia to values lost in the world of impersonal society, *Gesellschaft*."[15]

To be sure, not all German Zionists subscribed to these views about the "Ostjude." There were dissenting voices, and the "Ostjuden" champions were only a minority in what was, in any event, still a minority movement around World War I. However, this was an extraordinarily vocal minority, and it had a considerable number of adherents in Prague's Jewish intellectual circles, of which Kafka was a part. As summed up by Aschheim, "Whether negatively or positively conceived, idealized or despised, the *Ostjude* was regarded as the 'real' Jew and the living model of *Ur*-Jewishness lost to German Jewry."[16]

Although Kafka was not actually part of the young Zionist circles where these questions were passionately discussed, he, too, shared with Brod, Franz Werfel, and Buber an ever-growing feeling of urgency and concern about the fate of Western Jewry and Western Judaism. At the same time, he was increasingly curious about, attracted to, and also sometimes repelled by Eastern European Jewish culture. The interest began in 1911 with Kafka's introduction to the art of the Yiddish theater. It culminated in an emotional statement of crisis in the 1919 "Letter to My Father."

Evelyn Beck suggests that Kafka's ongoing interest in matters Jewish— history, anti-Semitism, Zionism, Hassidism, Hebrew language—developed after 1912, following his viewing of a large number of Yiddish plays presented by a traveling theatrical company from Poland. Kafka deeply admired these plays, in spite of the fact that some of them were apparently quite corny. According to Beck, a number of elements characteristic of Yiddish drama were later incorporated into his narrative works, and "the Yiddish plays touched some deep emotional response ... [and] the impact of these plays was both immediate and long-lasting."[17]

Kafka apparently missed a few performances, but his diary for 1911–1912 contains frequent and detailed descriptions.[18] He was clearly trying to understand the plays—in many ways, so different from the drama he knew—as well as the cultural background in which the plays had originated and that they, in turn, portrayed. Thus he remarked that even characters like lazy and unproductive members of the community—communal servants, for example—are accepted because they are Jews in a pure way, living effortlessly with religion.[19] Although he was obviously deeply impressed, he was by no means always uncritical of the performances, finding some plays trite or too uniformly similar.[20]

A deep friendship developed between Kafka and the actors, especially with the Warsaw-born Isaac Löwy, from whose stories Kafka learned about Polish Jewish life. In his diary, Kafka recorded such details as customs concerning the ritual bath (*mikva*), circumcision (*brit-mila*), and the importance of schools (*yeshivot*)[21] as centers of unintended intellectual change. Although Löwy may have generalized somewhat too liberally on the basis of his native Warsaw, he accurately described the incipient ferment among Polish-Jewish youths. According to Löwy, the *yeshivot*, no longer bastions of conservatism, were becoming centers of progress. In recent years, poets, journalists, learned men, and political figures were all products of the *yeshivot*, and progressive-minded young men joined them in ever larger numbers.

Kafka probably did not realize the extent to which Löwy personified that moment in Central European Jewish life when so many young men were poised on the brink of irreversible changes. They still knew the old traditions; they had grown up learning the "law" (*Torah*). But even if they rejected neither, they nonetheless began to reach out to the world, to new ideas, to philosophy, to science, and to art. Through Löwy, Kafka gained a glimpse of these momentous changes, and perhaps sensing this, he faithfully recorded everything Löwy told him.[22] But to Kafka, Eastern European Judaism, whether changing or not, was pure, was the real Judaism, was viable; it was everything his Western Judaism was not.

For Hassidism, which attracted but also repelled Kafka, his informant was George Mordechai (Jiri) Langer, a Prague Jew who for a time belonged to the Belzer rebbe's court in Polish Galicia.[23] Langer cut a strange figure in his kaftan and sidelocks among the worldly and emancipated Prague Jews. His tales abounded with the do's and don'ts of Hassidic Jews' lives and the miracles or near miracles Hassidic rebbes can cause to happen.[24] With Langer, Kafka followed the Belzer rebbe and his entourage around Marienbad. Kafka's description of the rebbe's progress through the resort in a drenching downpour has wonderful touches of humor: one follower carries a chair, another a bottle of mineral water in case of thirst, another the glass, and so on. Kafka writes that he looks like a sultan, inspires confidence, and has a childlike interest in everything he sees.[25]

Kafka's response to Hassidism, however, was cool—a visit with Brod to a "wonder rabbi" was not met with much enthusiasm.[26] He was rather inspired by the naturalness of Eastern Jews, which he professed to see in the way they talked, dressed, and related to one another. Jewish refugees from Poland revealed to him an earthy kind of humor.[27] Impressions formed from stories others told him and from his own observations were reinforced by reading. Löwy had introduced him in 1911 to great Yiddish writers like Sholem Aleichem and I. L. Peretz; readings in Jewish history and the history of Jewish literature followed. The biography of Salomon Maimon, which he read in 1917, made him see with incredible clarity the European Jews' dilemma—indeed, his own dilemma—between Eastern and Western Judaism.[28]

The views Kafka developed about his Western Judaism were, however, not merely critical. A note of deep regret often seems present in his remarks. Describing the Orthodox circumcision of his nephew, for example, he wrote that such religious forms and practices had apparently reached an end. The dated practice of circumcision and the chanted prayers were merely of historical interest to these Western Jews, who lived in a transitional time without being aware of it. At a later time, he would use even stronger terms, describing Western Jewry as sick and nourished by medicines[29]—that is, sustained artificially. Unlike Brod and Buber, Kafka never concluded that Eastern and Western Judaism, the *Diaspora* and Zionism, were independent.[30] Perhaps, in part, this was due to a somewhat different constellation in Kafka's intellectual development: conflict with his parents, particularly with his father, combined with a strong distaste for his father's (and, by extension, Western Jewish) middle classness, highlighted the "authenticity," simplicity, and naturalness of Eastern Jews. He did not embrace Zionist ideology, in spite of frequently expressing a desire to go to what was then Palestine and pursuing, often quite intensively, the study of Hebrew.

A strong distaste for Prague's Jewish middle class—its values, way of life, and aspirations[31]—was combined, for Kafka, with an equal distaste for its Judaism. Conversion was not a solution, since Jewish powers, as he put it, continued to live in the baptized Jew.[32] The only solution was to lead an authentic, viable Jewish life, as distinct from a life where Judaism was merely remembered. In his "Letter to My Father," Kafka developed his explanation of the Western Jewish crisis as one of memory versus practice. From the "ghetto-like village community" and its relatively strong Jewish religious life, Kafka wrote, the fathers came to the city. Some Judaism was lost in the army; more was lost in settled urban existence. At first, "impressions and memories from youth were sufficient for a kind of Jewish life," but they were not strong enough to be passed on. They dried up as fathers tried to bequeath them to their children; there was nothing to pass on and nothing (*ein nichts*) to receive. Ultimately, the fathers are to blame, wrote Kafka, because they did not understand that their Judaism had become valueless, that it was only memory, that it was an empty form. Still, Kafka was unwilling to condemn out of hand: his and other families' problem was that they belonged to a transitional generation. His father was to blame, however, for neither understanding nor appreciating his son's search for an alternative Jewishness to his father's.[33]

Kafka associates here the loss of Jewish values and practices with the cessation of Jewish life in the village community. In the urban setting, lifestyles have changed, and as a result, the freshness, the vitality of Judaism as a practice, as a lived value, has ceased to exist. Kafka considers the fathers' generation a transitional one. But transitional to what? It is not easy to see what Kafka had in mind. He did not fully subscribe to Zionism as a genuine alternative to *Diaspora*. Nor did he, of course, think—notwithstanding Langer's serious but rather bizarre attempts—that one could become an Eastern Jew. Aschheim correctly remarks that "German cultural Zionists viewed *Ostjuden* as the embodiment of Jewish authenticity lost to the world of Western Jews, but they also demanded a significant modernization of that authenticity."[34] Kafka similarly did not see a solution to his and his generation's dilemma in Orthodox religiosity, and it is doubtful that he ever shared Brod's or Buber's strong convictions on the importance of community for the practice of Judaism.[35]

Kafka's diagnosis, therefore, does not include a prognosis. He has no solution to the problem of Western Judaism. But even if he saw no way out, he nonetheless continued to probe the question and its complex implications for social life and individual identity in some of his short stories of 1917[36] and especially in *The Castle*, where the problem of Western Judaism found expression in vastly transformed ways.

EASTERN AND WESTERN JEWRY THEMES IN *THE CASTLE*

The crisis of Western Judaism, the attractiveness of Eastern European Judaism lived in tight and self-contained communities, or the middle-class Prague Judaism of his father's generation—all these have a place in understanding *The Castle*. Yet neither singly nor collectively, as Robertson points out, can these topics be considered a "master key" to the novel's hidden meanings, for *The Castle* is surely one of Kafka's impenetrable works. It must be remembered, moreover, that *The Castle*, as he further suggests, is not an entirely successful artistic work. There are inconsistencies, the novel meanders, and characters remain underdeveloped.[37] Since it has remained unfinished, one cannot know what kind of resolution, if any, Kafka intended for the questions he posed. My endeavor in what follows is not to find new lines of interpretation. Instead, I want to determine some specific instances and situations in the novel that reveal Kafka's attempts to express in fiction the precariousness of Western Jewish existence. This will be followed by a comparison of the relevant passages from two Chinese texts—one from the People's Republic of China (PRC), the other from the Republic of China (Taiwan)—in order to understand how successfully the translators transposed these in their translations.

Estrangement and Belonging

Throughout the novel, K. is referred to as a stranger in the village.[38] The villagers identify him as a stranger who, therefore, has or can be expected to have peculiar characteristics. K. also explains himself to others as being a stranger. The peasants belong; the castle population belongs; those "in-between" characters who stand between the castle and the village, like Frieda and the landlady of the Bridge Inn, belong. Only Barnabas and his family no longer belong entirely, though they once did, or thought they did. K. clearly does not belong and never will.

K.'s peculiar kind of estrangement, I suggest, is, however, not a universal alienation, nor is it more narrowly Jewish alienation. Rather, the novel explores varieties of real belonging, the imagined Jewish belonging, and the contradiction that is inherent in the Jew's recognition of his status as a stranger and his tenacious struggle to belong. The novel also explores the attitudes of those who belong toward the man, K., who does not. Is he (the Jew) needed? Can he be useful? Under what conditions can he be allowed to remain? From this point of view, the novel does not portray the Jew, K., as permanently estranged from Christian society (the village) or modern man as permanently alienated from human existence.

As a stranger, K. is ignorant. He does not know local customs and usages, but even more so, as a stranger, he is completely peripheral. He is a nobody. When K. asks the innkeeper of the Herrenhof for permission to sleep overnight, the absurdity of his request that only a stranger would make is pointed out to him (38). The landlady of the Bridge Inn, whom K. informs of his intention to marry Frieda, reminds him that, being a stranger, his family circumstances are unknown (50); he is a nothing, she tells him, and as such, he is "the most ignorant person in the village" (58). Pepi, the barmaid and Frieda's successor in the Herrenhof, says that he is a "nonentity" (280). The stranger comes from a different world, says Frieda (236). He is different, incomprehensible; one cannot believe him (147). She says at another time that his motives cannot be known (152, 274). Olga assumes that he must be suspicious of things happening in the village (216). Included in the superintendent's explanation of how K., the land surveyor, came to be in the village are repeated references to his being a stranger who cannot understand and who cannot know (65, 66, 72).

K. deserves neither respect nor disrespect. His person is frequently a matter of indifference to others. The villagers prefer to keep their distance from K., especially when he interferes in or seems to threaten village order. At their first meeting, when K. identifies himself as a stranger to the teacher (16–17), the latter evinces no curiosity and indifferently goes his way with the children. Lasemann, the tanner, is willing to let K. rest for a while in his house, but he soon informs him that the villagers are not accustomed to visitors (i.e., strangers) and that he has to leave. Quite unceremoniously, he pushes K. out the door into the snow (19–20). For different reasons, but in a similar vein, the innkeeper of the Herrenhof forcibly evicts K. from the inn's passage, since K. had no right being there, "a place where he did not belong" (265). The Bridge Inn landlady advises her husband, according to her account, to keep his distance from K. (55). The peasants may be temporarily interested in what K. is doing or what he is saying (they like the commotion K. produces), but they are not curious about K. as a person (30–31).

Theoretically, the Western Jew can argue for acceptance that brings a tenuous belonging. Although he can become neither a villager nor a member of the castle staff, still he can live in society as a stranger. He can belong in a different sense. By acting unobtrusively, by establishing himself *first as a stranger*[39] and only thereafter confronting the authorities (156–157), by becoming a fellow citizen to the villagers, and by alleviating their suspicions (29–30), K. thinks (as the Western Jew did) that he can belong. To achieve this end, he must employ any and all methods, even if they seem ruthless. K.'s alliance with Frieda, as Frieda so clearly and painfully recognizes, is to use her as a means of reaching Klamm, the castle official, who will assure K.'s acceptance and belonging in the village (148–149). To belong means to become a member of the community. It means to marry, to share with another person daily existence, to be part of a business or professional context, to have personal connections (187). Here Kafka depicts precisely the kind of Jewish middle-class existence his father's generation was striving to achieve. To belong in this fashion is dependent on others allowing it, on others considering it necessary or useful for the stranger to be integrated into the social fabric. But the crux of the matter is that no one thinks it particularly necessary for the stranger to belong, even if Pepi, for one, will admit that people like K., when they appear in the community, can change people's lives (273). Lasemann is doubtful that a land surveyor is needed, although he allows that since K. was asked to come, he is "probably needed" (19). The superintendent tells K. that a land surveyor is most certainly not needed (61). And the teacher remarks sarcastically that the village needs a land surveyor as much as it needs a janitor, the post to which K. was temporarily assigned (95).[40]

But to label K. as a sort of archetypal Western Jew would be doing injustice to the novel's subtle ambivalences. Who this man, K., really is; whether he came by design or accident to this village; and what, in fact, his calling is are never clearly established (10, 12). However, once he has declared himself to be the land surveyor, he uses his calling as his identity. Yet when Klamm affirms what may be a fictitious identity and even embellishes upon it, K. is visibly upset. The second letter from Klamm, which Barnabas delivers, rather than bringing him satisfaction, distresses K. (115–117), although presumably now that Klamm has recognized his work (i.e., his identity), K. will be allowed to remain in the village. The question of personal freedom is also raised in this connection. K. deludes himself when he boasts that he is a free man (13). In his heart of hearts, he knows the senselessness of this illusory freedom (105).

Barnabas's Family

An intricate web connects K. to Barnabas and his family. At first sight, they seem to be part of the village community, but as it turns out, they also do not belong, although their estrangement by ostracism is different from that of K. Until he learns from Olga the reason for the family's fall, K. had hoped that Barnabas, in his capacity as castle messenger, could aid him in reaching Klamm. Olga's long account, however, reveals that because of K., Barnabas and his family hope to change their fate (215).

Amalia's incomprehensible behavior brought on the family's misfortunes. These misfortunes were not only a question of exclusion from communal life; they were also, and perhaps even primarily, the loss of livelihood and the family's subsequent impoverishment. Barnabas's father, who had been a respected artisan, a cobbler, lost his thriving business and home to Brunswick, and this, in turn, led to the complete psychic and physical deterioration of Barnabas's parents. The family's fall was gradual, as if a reprieve were still possible all along; they were only cut off "from the community for ever" when the villagers recognized the family's weakness and failure to deal with their problems (198).

Amalia's inexcusable deed was to reject in an unheard of and unconventional way the advances of one of the castle's officials who had taken a fancy to her. He had sent a servant with an insulting message, summoning Amalia to the Herrenhof. In a dramatic gesture of defiance, Amalia tore up the letter and threw the pieces in the messenger's face. Castle men take village girls if and when they choose—as does, for example, Klamm (185). The girls follow the call, except for Amalia, who, by not heeding it, negated the conventionally accepted relationship between castle and village. The punishment—or "the curse," as Olga says (182)—is not meted out to Amalia alone. The entire family is made to suffer. Although the castle does not act directly against the family, the villagers are aware of the "fall from grace" and respond by ostracizing them. Thus Barnabas's family is also estranged, also does not belong, and Barnabas, like K., spares no effort to find a means of overcoming the estrangement.

This enigmatic and very important portion of the novel (chap. 15) that deals with the fate of Barnabas's family can be explained only in reference to Western Jewry, according to Binder. Similar to Kafka's view of himself, the Amalia figure is seen as weak, as unable to respond to situations of crisis, and as overwhelmed by real life. Amalia perceives reality in terms of black and white, as an either-or, which, Kafka believed, was a weakness in the way Western Jewish youths were raised.[41] Binder furthermore points out that even though Barnabas's family once belonged to the village, they were not peasants, and they had no land. The father was a cobbler, similar to Western Jews whose work as artisans and merchants set them apart from the "Volk." Like Barnabas's family when they were boycotted, they speedily lost their source of livelihood and whatever limited social status they may have had. Olga, for example, earns money by servicing the castle's male servants who accompany the officials to the village.[42] Thus the belonging of Barnabas's family is illusory. Even if the father was an expert cobbler, even if Amalia could sew clothes like no one else, even if their ostracism was at first a loss to the villagers (195), in the end, their presence was not missed.[43] The village needs neither K. nor Barnabas's family. Paradoxically, it is Frieda, who belongs to both the castle (by being Klamm's mistress) and to the village community, who suggests leaving to live elsewhere (132). In response, K. asks this most difficult of all questions: Why do we remain where we are when, in fact, the conditions are not conducive to remaining (133)? Why remain when no one is keeping a person from leaving, though no one is throwing the person out either (75)?

Castle and Village

The castle and village are two worlds in juxtaposition that exist together in mutual dependence. Without ever letting the reader know exactly what the castle represents, Kafka weaves threads of relationships between the village community and the castle by means of officials who descend to the village on business, by means of nonpeasant villagers who serve the officials during their village sojourn, and by means of village messengers who carry messages from one to the other. Whether the castle should be understood in terms of religious-spiritual symbolism or as a psychological construction[44] will not be considered. Rather, I want to suggest that the question of Eastern Jewish authenticity, warmth, and vitality is also expressed here in the comparison between the village community and the town-like castle.

At the very beginning of the novel, both K. and Schwarzer establish the mutuality of the castle and the village (9). Somewhat later, when K. identifies himself to the teacher as someone who fits in neither with the peasants nor with the castle, the latter replies that there is no difference between the peasants and the castle (17). Olga, too, reiterates that the village population belongs to the castle, and a gulf between the two is not supposed to exist. Yet, she adds, while this is generally true, there are certainly exceptions (185).

Although K. has glimpses of the castle, his impression of it remains vague. When he arrives in the village, the castle hill is hidden in mist and darkness (9). The next morning, K. finds that the castle consists of many low buildings "closely packed together" with only one tower, which, he discovers, does not even belong to a church. The stone buildings are not in the best condition (15). Although K. is said to frequently look up at the castle, its exterior is seen uncertainly and only twice. In another place, K. remarks on the castle's stillness, its undisturbedness, without "the slightest sign of life" (97). K. is reminded either of his hometown by the castle or of his memories of his hometown when looking at the castle (15, 34).

Castle life is inscrutable. On his very first day in the village, the Bridge Inn landlord tells K., "You don't know the castle" (13), and later K. is told in no uncertain terms by a peasant that "strangers cannot get into the castle without a permit." A permit will, of course, not be forthcoming, and K. is given to understand that he will never be allowed to enter the castle (25, 27). The teacher assumes that K. does not like the castle because "strangers never do." To K.'s query as to whether he knows the castle's count, the teacher gives him to understand that he has no reason to know him (16).

The castle world is a male world, and the officials, their secretaries, and their servants are apparently bachelors with undisguised sexual appetites once they visit the village.[45] Unlike the villagers, they do not form a community. Olga's account of the officials at work, as related to her by Barnabas, tells of each doing his work in isolation from one another (165, 168–169). This isolation among themselves persists when they take rooms on business in the Herrenhof. Klamm sits alone in a room drinking (41); in their rooms, the officials read aloud or dictate but do not converse with one another

(227–228). The solitude of the castle officialdom contrasts with the family and communal life of the village.

Descriptions of the physical appearance of the village are as sparse as those of the castle. The village houses are lined up in a row along one street (17–18), although K. assumes that there are side streets. Already on his first day, K. encounters a gregarious bathing and washing scene in Lasemann's cottage (18–19). Groups of peasants sit together in the inn, drinking beer, where they collectively manage to annoy him (9, 27, 30–31). The two inns are run by married couples and families (88). The maids too, Pepi and her friends, live together in a room that is warm and snug; they help one another and entertain each other with stories (293–294).

K.'s efforts to fit into this community are doomed to failure. His and Frieda's attempt at domesticity in the hastily vacated maids' room in the Bridge Inn fails, and they set up housekeeping in the schoolhouse, where he has been given the post of janitor (121). But the comfort of home eludes K. here also. Having overslept, K., Frieda, and the assistants are awakened by the lady teacher, who, angered by the domesticity in the classroom, smashes their few belongings (125). Frieda breaks off her engagement to K. and returns to her job as a barmaid in the Herrenhof. K. is unable to reach Klamm or the castle, and he is unable to settle in the village. Each attempt either at gaining confirmation of his existence or at integration into village life only reconfirms K. as the outsider.

The village and town juxtaposition that Kafka mentioned in his "Letter to My Father" thus reappears in *The Castle* in a vastly transmuted form. Whatever other interpretations can be ascribed to the castle, the text also constructs Western Jewry's sterile urban existence. Whatever significance one may ascribe to the village, it also has the *volkisch* elements that the younger generation of intellectuals ascribed to the Jewish *shtetl*.

THE CASTLE IN CHINESE TRANSLATION

Kafka's perception of Western Jewry's crisis and its dilemma is embedded in the three themes outlined above. In order to understand how these extremely subtle and complex themes appear in Chinese translation, two different editions—one published in the People's Republic of China (PRC), the other in Taiwan—were consulted. The first was translated by Tang Yongkuan,[46] the second by Xu Ren.[47]

Neither edition is annotated; the PRC edition has a brief introduction by the translator pointing out the significance of both Kafka and the novel; the Taiwan edition has merely a one-page publisher's preface. Whereas the PRC edition identifies the Muir 1957 Penguin edition as the source of the translation, the Taiwan edition makes no reference to its source. Since it, however, closely follows the Muir text, it can be assumed that this was also used by the Taiwan translator. The fact that the Chinese translations were prepared from the English translation instead of from the original is a distinct problem.

In the German original, the language is razor sharp. Kafka's masterful literary style is almost painfully clear and contrasts with the novel's utterly complex and often obscure content. The Muirs' translation did not—as perhaps no translation can—reproduce a similarly intense style. The Chinese translators' reliance on the English translation is, therefore, a decided drawback. It resulted in translations that preserve none of the sharpness of the original. Xu Ren's translation is more literary and therefore on the whole more graceful but strikes me as far too wordy. In contrast, Tang Yongkuan's translation, though less wordy, seems to me too colloquial. In direct speech, his overly colloquial usages become especially jarring.

More significantly, however, the Chinese translations tend to perpetuate the Muirs' mistranslations, thereby often obscuring portions of the content that are vital to the understanding of this difficult novel. In a literary work where plot and story play major narrative roles, translating from the original may not be as crucial. In this novel, with its insignificant plot and its enormous insistence on ideas, uncertainties, and the relativity of perception, not using the original is a handicap. Hence *The Castle* has not been re-created as faithfully as it might have been.

But this is not to underrate the effort at translating. On the contrary, Tang Yongkuan and Xu Ren must be given high marks for attempting to produce accurate and faithful translations. They have spared no effort to render the text as fully as possible, and no omissions occurred in those portions where the translations were closely checked.

Yet in order to transpose and re-create, even from the English, the complex themes of estrangement and belonging, castle and village, and the Barnabas family's ostracism, greater familiarity with Kafka's background as a Czech-Jewish writer would have been helpful. The translators could have attended more closely to the nuances of language and emphasis, bringing out with greater clarity the several dimensions of estrangement and the intense desire to belong or the puzzling and variously perceived relationship between castle and village. That insufficient attention was paid to the cultural context of the novel is revealed not only in some of the critical literature about Kafka, which will be discussed below, but also by a certain unevenness with which crucial expressions and passages are handled. Although the following may be somewhat tedious, I want to cite a number of examples that both pinpoint and compare where the translators have gone astray and where they have accurately conveyed meanings.

For the word "stranger," *mosheng ren, wailu ren,* or *waixiang ren* are used in both translations. The differences among the three terms are admittedly small, yet within the context of the novel, using one or another term may suggest different connotations, with the first leaning toward "estrangement" and the other two toward "outsider." In the PRC version, the Herrenhof innkeeper remarks, as he should, that "only [someone] like a stranger (*waixiang*) can speak like this" (41)—namely, to ask to sleep in the Herrenhof. The Taiwan version, however, states simply, "Only a stranger (*mosheng*) can speak like this" (41), which is too offhand. Frieda takes a great risk, says the Bridge Inn proprietress, by marrying a stranger (*wailu ren,* 59), in this case underscoring the fact that K. is an outsider. Both texts carefully reproduce the landlady's emphatic coupling in this long speech of K.'s outsider status with his condition of ignorance (*wuzhi*). Pepi refers to K. as a nonentity, which neither version captures accurately. According to the Taiwan text, K. is a worthless person (*bu zuqu de ren,* 339), and according to the PRC text, he is more of a good-for-nothing (*wonangfei,* 362).

But this is not at all what K. represents. It is rather his incomprehensibility to others and, by the same token, his utter inability to understand others that are stated time and again in *The Castle*. In the long passage when Frieda analyzes K.'s (to her) self-serving interest in the child Hans, she also says she cannot understand K. because he keeps things from her: "You come and go, I don't know where or from where" (Muir, 152). In both Chinese versions, this is stated more explicitly and less tersely, with a far stronger overtone of K. hiding matters from Frieda (*qingman zhe wo,* PRC text, 197; *zangzai xinli meiyou dui wo shuo,* Taiwan text, 184). The superintendent, whom K. sees in order to have his official status of land surveyor confirmed, points out repeatedly that K., being a stranger (*mosheng ren,* 81, and *waixiang ren,* 82, 90 in the PRC version; *wailu ren,* 78, 86, or *wailusheng ren,* 79 in the

Taiwan version), cannot possibly understand (*zhidao*, Taiwan, 86; *dong*, PRC, 90).

The blame for K. not having made his way into village society is laid at the feet of Schwarzer, the son of a minor official, who with uncalled-for zeal telephoned the castle authorities on the very night of K.'s arrival at the Bridge Inn. How differently things might have gone for him, muses K. in a lengthy passage, if only he had been given a chance. This passage is beautifully translated in both versions (PRC, 202–203; Taiwan, 188–189). And K.'s perception of himself as a "wandering stranger" (*liulang de wailu ren*, Taiwan; *waixiang liuliang*, PRC) and as someone who has lost his way, at least temporarily (one is tempted here to substitute "wandering Jew"), is sufficiently emphatic in both versions.

K.'s reflections on the circumstances that might have allowed his integration into village society contrast sharply with the opinions of the village inhabitants and are expressed by Lasemann, the superintendent, and the teacher. K., who has stumbled into Lasemann's cottage by chance, is informed by the latter that receiving guests "is not our custom" (*fengsu*, PRC, 15; *xiguan*, Taiwan, 15) and that guests have no use (*meiyou shenme yongchu*, PRC, 15). This is better expressed in the Taiwan version as "We have no use for any guests." The question of whether guests are useful turns into the question of whether K. is needed. Here the PRC version has different connotations from the Taiwan version by stating, "If you have been invited to come, perhaps we need you" (PRC, 16). The Taiwan version conforms to the English: "If there were people who invited you, then perhaps you are really needed" (Taiwan, 15). The PRC translator distorts the meaning because Lasemann means to convey that neither he nor the villagers need a land surveyor, though in an abstract sense, he can allow for such a person to be needed.

The juxtaposition of "need" and "use" is also raised when K. visits the superintendent, who tells K. unequivocally that a land surveyor is not needed, and "there wouldn't be the least use for one here" (Muir, 61). The differentiation between "need" (*xuyao*) and "use" (*yong*) is maintained in the PRC translation (74) and is stated emphatically in two brief sentences. This is not the case in the Taiwan translation, where *xuyao* is used throughout (72) and where the statement loses much of its impact due to the length of the sentence. Both translators reproduce faithfully the teacher's sarcastic equation of a janitor (*kanmen ren*) with a land surveyor and the fact that either is a burden for the village. The PRC translation is, however, more literal as "a burden on our shoulders" (*jianbangshang fudan*, 121) as compared with simply "a burden" (*fudan*, Taiwan, 115).

Klamm's second letter to K., praising the work he presumably accomplished, fell victim to both translators' pens. The Taiwan translation faithfully reproduces Klamm's last sentence, "I will not forget you" (141), which is incidentally an inaccurate rendering of the original: "*Ich behalte Sie im Auge.*" Tang's sentence reads, "I will arrange everything" (*Yiqie wo zi you anpai*, 149), which strays even further.

The fate of Barnabas's family and the reason for their fall are related by Olga in chapter 15, the longest chapter in the book. The fall, to be sure, occurred within the village community, yet Olga's account suggests larger implications and includes the castle as well. It is more than a mere village affair. The Taiwan translator has not grasped the meaning when he describes the ostracism in terms of cutting the relationship (*guanxi*) between the family and the people of the village (242). Olga's crucial statement has a much better rendering in the PRC translation as "cutting us off from public contact" (*shehui gongzhong laiwang*, 260). The Taiwan translator has similarly failed to differentiate between "curse" (*zuzhou*) and "punishment" (*chengfa*). He has translated Olga's statement that because Amalia did not heed the official's lewd summons, a curse was laid on the entire family: "the entire family suffered punishment" (222). The PRC translator, on the other hand, differentiates between the curse (*zuzhou*) and the punishment (238).

Still in connection with Barnabas's family, there is a moving but also very disturbing passage in which the ostracized victim, Olga, excuses the victimizers, the village families. The text conveys the fine line between the two and the ease with which one can turn into the other. The villagers were sorry for the way they acted, says Olga; they felt distressed and uneasy (*nanguo bu an*, Taiwan, 239), but they could not desist. "We would have acted the same," concludes Olga. Both translations capture the spirit of the passage (PRC, 256); however, the Taiwan version is somehow surer in the way in which the victim's malady, the compulsion to understand and to excuse, is expressed.

The castle and the castle's ways are unknowable. The Bridge Inn proprietor informs K. on his first day in the village that K. does not know the castle. Neither translation is on the mark here with "You don't know the castle affairs" (*zhidao chengbaoli de shi*, Taiwan, 7) and "You cannot explain the castle" (*jie chengbao*, PRC, 7). As seen from the village, the castle seems to K. like a small town (*xiao zhen*, Taiwan, 9; *xiaoxiao de shizhen*, PRC, 9), the latter suggesting more specifically a market town. The whole place appears to be rather in disrepair and reminds K. of his "native town" (Muir, 15). "Native place" (*guxiang*, Taiwan, 9) does not convey clearly that K. is originally a townsman. "Native village and town" or "native area" (*jiaxiang de cunzhen*, PRC, 10) also misses the point.

Although castle and village are clearly two separate entities, there is the repeated insistence that the village belongs to the castle or that distinctions between the two do not exist (Taiwan, 1, 11; PRC, 2, 12), as stated by Schwarzer and the teacher. Yet Olga points out that distinctions do indeed exist depending on whether the matter is important. "We're all supposed to belong to the castle" (Muir, 185), she says, which is translated correctly as "we're all considered [*bei renwei*] to belong to the castle." (PRC, 242). In the Taiwan translation, this sentence receives different connotations when it is simply rendered as "we all belong [*shuyu*] to the castle" (226). Because the teacher, on the one hand, and Olga, on the other, perceive the matter of castle and village differently, the correct translating of these sentences would seem particularly crucial.

This cursory but microscopic examination of the two texts reaffirms, I suggest, both translators' inattention to the cultural context within which the novel originated. In the case of the PRC translator, this is understandable. In his introduction to the translation of *The Castle*, Tang states that he began translating it fifteen years ago—that is, in 1964, when Kafka was, for all practical purposes, unknown to Chinese writers. During the years of the Cultural Revolution, access to materials on Kafka was highly unlikely, and even in 1979, when he completed the translation, opportunities for acquiring such materials were still extremely limited. The case of the Taiwan translator is, of course, very different. By the time Xu Ren completed the translation of *The Castle*, materials about Kafka and translations of his works were already available for more than a decade.

On the other hand, there is something truly remarkable about the fact that two translators turned to a writer from a world so different from their own—a world essentially unknown to them—and to a work so strange and impenetrable in meaning. What were the translators' motivations? If we are correct in assuming that translated works serve literary as well as intellectual ends, what kind of impact has and will *The Castle* have in translation, regardless of how it is read or misread? To find the answers, much depends on present and future directions of Chinese criticism.

Since the appearance of *The Castle* and other translations (especially the early "Letter to My Father"), a number of essays about Kafka and his works were published in the PRC. The following will briefly summarize several of these in order to determine to what extent the issue of cultural background and Kafka's Jewishness is raised in relationship to his works.

Chinese criticism generally tends to direct attention to the circumstances of an author's life, and some references to Kafka's life and times have been made in comments on his works that have appeared in China since 1979. Indeed, Tang Yongkuan, the translator of *The Castle*, stated clearly that to study an author includes also studying his life together with his works.[48] Yet most of the writers who discuss Kafka and his works label him an Austrian or an Austro-Hungarian writer, with scant attention to his specifically Czech and Jewish background. Even when he is identified as having been born into a Prague Jewish household, the location of Prague is not specified.[49] Within the context of the development of European literature, whether an author was Czech, Polish, Hungarian, or Austrian (though these were all part of the Austro-Hungarian Empire) makes rather a difference.

Still, it would be unfair to fault Chinese critics for not paying closer attention to Kafka's origin and background. The sources they consulted about the writer, who until 1979 had been practically unknown, were often misleading. One of these, Anthony Burgess, wrote in *The Novel Now* that Kafka was an Austrian Jew born in Prague.[50] More than likely, Mainland writers simply had no access to the better-known biographical works on Kafka, including those by Max Brod, which were apparently available to Taiwan critics.[51]

Instead of cultural background, the critics focus attention on the political circumstances of Kafka's times. Therefore, even if Sun Kunrong, for example, grants that Kafka's last short story, "Josephine the Singer, or the Mouse Folk," portrays the Jewish people, he also sees in this work an accusation against Austria's immoral treatment of the Jews.[52] Tang Yongkuan, though he acknowledges that Kafka's study of Hebrew literature toward the end of his life reflected his love for his ancestral Judaism—stressing, however, that Kafka was not fanatically (*kuangre*) religious—concludes nonetheless that Kafka's works mirror reactionary feudalism and capitalism.

Tang's introduction to *The Castle* contains similar political references, and he is obviously misled by Burgess, whom he quotes, that Kafka's works cannot be understood in reference to either Judaism or Christianity.[53]

The political references appear frequently in connection with the theme of alienation (*yihua*), which most writers attribute to Kafka's works and especially to his story "Metamorphosis." Guo Xianggeng and Dai Jinglun write that Kafka was the first to connect the theme of alienation to the capitalist system. Under capitalism, alienation is the reduction of the self to a thing and a nonperson (*fei ren*). Sun Kunrong similarly relates alienation to the capitalist system, within which the creative human being loses contact with others, becoming a nonperson.[54] In these writers' assessment, then, Kafka becomes a social critic, attacking, in works like *The Castle*, the power of feudalism, licentious and corrupt bureaucrats, or the rigid stratification of society. According to Sun, the various characters of Kafka's fictional works all portray an estranged world (*mosheng de shijie*).[55]

The writers, however, also acknowledge that Kafka's works are mystical and strange, that the symbolic content and Kafka's ambiguous way of writing make access to his work difficult. They agree on Kafka's greatness and importance in twentieth-century letters as the creator of modernist and absurdist literature. Together with explaining Kafka as a social critic of his day, his works therefore also have universal implications. The Chinese translation of Joyce Carol Oates's essay "Kafka's Paradise" was, no doubt, largely responsible for conveying these in addition to creating an awareness of the difficulties, complexities, and pitfalls of studying Kafka.[56] The wide-ranging essay ascribes to Kafka's thought and works religious, spiritual, and psychological implications: mysticism, Zen, transcendence, the conscious mind in battle with the unconscious, and the intellect's struggle with the soul. Kafka's Jewishness is referred to only in passing as allowing him to identify with the spiritual and timeless. The castle, she believes, should be understood as the *Dao*. Tang Yongkuan, who quotes the opening sentences of her essay in his introduction to the translation of *The Castle*, prudently avoids mentioning any of this.

———

This essay attempted to show that Kafka's concern with what he perceived as the sterility of Western Judaism and the more viable but, to him, problematic Eastern Judaism found a fictional expression in *The Castle*. His friends, like Max Brod, who knew him well and who at the time also seriously considered the question of Eastern and Western Judaism, readily perceived this facet of *The Castle's* latent content. The reader of another time and of another place has a harder time of it.

The Castle, like Kafka's other creative works, is richly suggestive. Various interpretations of the whole or its parts are possible, and over the years this novel has stimulated much discussion. Whether one interpretation is more correct than another is not the issue here, nor is it the intention to restore a "lost" meaning. Rather, I want to turn attention to the more commonplace consideration—namely, that a writer's life and concerns bear a relationship to his work and that all serious writing is in some way autobiographical.[57] Thus rather than posing only the generalized problem of alienation in modern society or a generalized quest for meaning that eludes twentieth-century human beings,[58] *The Castle* also presents a very specific discourse with which Kafka and Prague Jewish intellectuals were concerned then and earlier.

The question of Kafka's Judaism is not only noted superficially in the essays briefly discussed above; it is not considered significant as concerns *The Castle*. To be sure, the study of Kafka and his works is still in its early stages in the PRC and was apparently in the first half of the eighties still too dependent on randomly available Western sources. It was also fettered by political considerations that no doubt inhibited them from using the more varied approaches that were open to Taiwan critics.[59] Finally, neither translation, in spite of being meticulously executed, is sufficiently sensitive to those nuances in *The Castle* that are relevant to a more "Jewish" reading. However, from another perspective, the translation of *The Castle* marks a milestone in translating trends, especially in post-Mao China. Similar to the 1920s, when translated literary classics had an important role in shaping the direction of modern Chinese literature, *The Castle* and works like it may very well assume a comparable function.

NOTES

I would like to express my appreciation to the British Library Oriental Collection and the SOAS Library for the use of their Chinese resources. My thanks go to Professor A. Altman of the Hebrew University for his careful reading of the manuscript and for his valuable suggestions.

1. A thorough recapitulation of Kafka's probable starting and concluding dates of writing can be found in Hartmut Binder, *Kafka in Neuer Sicht, Mimik, Gestik und Personenegefüge als Darstellungsformen des Autobiographischen* (Stuttgart: J. B. Metzler, 1976), 346–365.

2. The importance of the autobiographical influences on *The Castle* was first suggested by Max Brod, *Franz Kafka: A Biography*, 2nd ed. (New York: Schocken Books, 1960), 219–221.

3. Chris Bezzel, *Kafka-Chronik* (Munich–Vienna: Carl Hanser Verlag, 1975), 136, 146.

4. Binder, *Kafka in Neuer Sicht*, 365–366.

5. Brod, *Franz Kafka*, 187.

6. For example, Karin Keller, *Gesellschaft im mythischen Bann. Studien zum Roman "Das Schloß" und anderen Werken Franz Kafkas* (Wiesbaden: Akademische Verlagsgesellschaft Athenaion, 1977); and especially Walter H. Sokel, "Zwischen Gnosis und Jehovah: Zur Religions-Problematik Franz Kafkas," in *Franz Kafka Symposium, 1983*, ed. Wilhelm Emrich and Bernd Goldmann (Mainz: V. Hase und Kohler Verlag, 1985), 37–89, who explores the gnostic dualism in Kafka's works.

7. Binder, *Kafka in Neuer Sicht*, 398.

8. Kafka had several Hebrew teachers, including Puah Bentovim, a native Hebrew speaker from what was then Palestine, who came to Prague in 1921. Although he never studied Hebrew in a sustained manner, Kafka had made excellent progress by the time Puah taught him the spoken language in 1922 (conversation with Puah Bentovim-Menczel, July 14, 1988). See also the rather curious article by Clive Sinclair, "Kafka's Hebrew Teacher," *Encounter* 64, no. 3 (March 1985): 46–49, according to which Puah presumably considered Kafka's turning to Dora Dymant a result of her rejection.

9. See Max Brod, *Der Prager Kreis* (Stuttgart: W. Kohlhammer Verlag, 1966), 96–97. Brod considers Kafka a "true son" of Prague, with strong roots in the city as well as in Czech and German culture.

10. Steven E. Aschheim, *Brothers and Strangers: The East European Jew in German and German Jewish Consciousness, 1800–1923* (Madison: University of Wisconsin Press, 1982), 3–9.

11. Ibid., 14, 20.

12. Ahad Ha'am was the pen name of Asher Ginzberg (1865–1927), essayist and philosopher, who proposed a spiritual and cultural Zionism.

13. Aschheim, *Brothers and Strangers*, 81, 89, 100–101. See also Paul Mendes-Flohr, "*Fin-de-Siècle* Orientalism, the Ostjuden and the Aesthetics of Jewish Self-Affirmation," *Studies in Contemporary Jewry* 1 (1984): 96–139. Mendes-Flohr, in particular, stresses "the image of the Jew as Oriental" as a positive image. He also emphasizes Buber's influence on Prague's younger Zionists, particularly in regard to Judaism's renewal. I am grateful to Steve Aschheim for bringing this article to my attention.

14. Aschheim, *Brothers and Strangers*, 102, 120.

15. Ibid., 212–213.

16. Ibid., 252.

17. Evelyn T. Beck, *Kafka and the Yiddish Theatre: Its Impact on His Work* (Madison: University of Wisconsin Press, 1971), ix–xiii, 195–200, 30. It may be difficult today to understand the power that the plays by such dramatists as Avraham Goldfaden or Yosef Latayner could exert on viewers and readers. In the attic of my father's house, there was a box full of these plays—well hidden, my parents thought, from the prying eyes of children. Quite by accident, when I was about eight years old, I found the box and, in time, read every one of the plays. In the midst of this secret reading—which, no doubt, was only half understood—the town's amateur actors' group began rehearsing one of the plays. Like a magnet, the group's rehearsals drew me in until I learned by heart most of the songs and whatever portions of dialogue I could make out. On the day of the performance, I climbed through an open window into the hall and hid under a bench. Fifty years later, the magic of those hours has not dimmed, nor have the songs been forgotten.

18. Franz Kafka, *Tagebücher, 1910–1923* (New York: Schocken Books, 1949). For example, entries for October 5–6, 1911, 79–89.

19. Ibid., October 5–6, 1911, 80; November 1911, 170, 171; December 1911, 210–212.

20. Ibid., October 22, 1911, 111; January 6, 1912, 213–214.

21. Ibid., January 6, 1912, 236–240.

22. This included also Löwy's "autobiography," which, according to Brod, Löwy told in a confused fashion over many evenings. As

recorded from notes that Kafka made, it is not actually an autobiography but an account of Löwy's discovery of opera, drama, and finally, Yiddish theater. See Kafka's *Hochzeitsvorbereitungen auf dem Lande und Andere Prosa aus dem Nachlaß* (Frankfurt: S. Fischer Verlag, 1980), 116–117, 329.

23. Polish Hassidism developed in "courts" presided over by a line of the founder's heirs. Followers identified themselves as adherents of, say, the rebbe of Belz, Lubavich, or some other town. Langer's importance as Kafka's informant on Polish Hassidism is pointed out by Ritchie Robertson in *Kafka, Judaism, Politics, and Literature* (Oxford: Clarendon Press, 1985), 176–178.

24. Kafka, *Tagebücher*, for example, October 1915, 482–484, 490.

25. Franz Kafka, *Briefe, 1902–1924* (New York: Schocken Books, 1958), 141–146, letter to Max Brod, dated July 1916. See also Brod's note 3, 505. Brod had seen a newspaper announcement of the Belzer rebbe's journey to Marienbad, which he sent on to Kafka.

26. Kafka, *Tagebücher*, September 14, 1915, 478.

27. See, for example, ibid., November 24, 1914, 443–444; March 25, 1915, 468. See also Kafka, *Briefe*, letter from July 1923 to Hugo Bergman, 436.

28. Kafka, *Tagebücher*, October 20, 1911, 105; November 1, 1911, 132–133; January 24, 1912, 242. See also Kafka, *Briefe*, 203, letter to Felix Weltsch, December, 1917.

29. Kafka, *Tagebücher*, December 1911, 204–205. See also Kafka, *Briefe*, 417, letter to Robert Klopstock, September 1922.

30. Brod, *Franz Kafka*, 112.

31. His rejection of Felice Bauer is essentially his rejection of her bourgeois aspirations: comfortable apartment, 11 o'clock to bed, heated rooms. Kafka, *Tagebücher*, January 24, 1915, 459.

32. Kafka, *Briefe*, 269, letter to Max Brod and Felix Weltsch, April 10, 1920.

33. Franz Kafka, "Brief an den Vater," in *Hochzeitsvorbereitungen auf dem Lande*, 119–162.

34. Aschheim, *Brothers and Strangers*, 108.

35. According to Brod (*Franz Kafka*, 112–113), Kafka told Buber and Franz Werfel that he had no feelings about community. In December 1917, he told Brod that he had to achieve clarity about ultimate matters, which he had to do alone (166).

36. See, for example, Ritchie Robertson's intriguing analysis of "Beim Bau der chinesischen Mauer" and "Der Landarzt" in his *Kafka, Judaism*, 172–176, 180–184.

37. Ibid., 226–227.

38. I am using Willa and Edwin Muir's English translation of *The Castle*, since the Chinese translations were prepared from this. Page references in the text are to the Penguin Books edition, 1976, which contains the continuation of chaps. 18 and 19–20, translated by Eithne Wilkins and Ernst Kaiser.

39. Italics are mine.

40. Beck and Robertson have suggested that the occupation of land surveyor carries messianic implications. They have argued that Kafka made a pun on two nearly identically sounding words, *mashoah* (a word no longer in common use), meaning "land surveyor," and *mashiah*, meaning "messiah." See Beck, *Kafka and the Yiddish Theatre*, 195; and Robertson, *Kafka, Judaism*, 232–234. See also Rodney Livingstone's review of Robertson in *The Times Higher Education Supplement*, November 1, 1985, 21, who emphatically rejects the messianic interpretation. It must be also rejected on Hebrew linguistic grounds.

41. Binder, *Kafka in Neuer Sicht*, 484.

42. Ibid., 448. See also Kafka's strongly worded criticism of Western Jewry in Kafka, *Briefe*, 319.

43. Kafka's observation has a chilling significance: the disappearance of the Jews from Central Europe and German life during World War II has not affected these countries economically or socially in the postwar period.

44. See Robertson's persuasive argument that the castle represents *das Unzerstörbare* in *Kafka, Judaism*, 236–241; and Binder's equally persuasive interpretation in *Kafka in Neuer Sicht*, 295, 317.

45. See Binder, *Kafka in Neuer Sicht*, 399–419. The only female figure directly associated with the castle is Hans Brunswick's mother, whom K. encounters in Lasemann's cottage (18–20).

Aside from her, Amalia refers to a castle char-woman and her daughter.

46. *Chengbao* (*The Castle*) (Shanghai: Yiwen, 1982). First published in 1980. Chapter 19 was translated by Chen Liangting and chapter 20 by Xu Ruchun (Introduction, 6).

47. *Chengbao* (Taiwan: Yuanjing, 1984). First published in 1979.

48. Tang Yongkuan, "Kafuka—yige yanshi de tiancai" (Kafka—the world-weary genius), *Wenyi yanjiu* 6 (1982): 109.

49. See, for example, the Kafka entry in *Zhungguo da baike quanshu, Waiguo wenxue,* 1 (Chinese encyclopedia, foreign literature, 1) (Beijing–Shanghai: Zhungguo de baike quanshu chubanshe, 1982), 5:505–506.

50. Anthony Burgess, *The Novel Now: A Student's Guide to Contemporary Fiction* (London: Faber and Faber, 1971), 33.

51. For example, Chen Qihong, trans., "Kafuka de shijie" (Kafka's world), *Xientai wenxue* 31 (April 1967): 175–197. Chen translated portions from Max Brod, *Gesammelte Schriften* (1937). Ye Tingfang, the writer of the encyclopedia entry (see note 48 above), supplies the bibliographical entry, Max Brod, *Franz Kafkas Glauben und Lehre* (1948), which is not as useful as Brod's biography of Kafka.

52. Sun Kunrong, "Lun Kafuka de xiaoshuo" (About Kafka's fiction), *Beijing Daxue xuebao—Zhexue shehuikexue ban* 2, no. 96 (April 1983): 47.

53. Yongkuan, "Kafka," 109; and Ruchun, Introduction, 5.

54. Guo Xianggeng, Dai Jinglun, "Wo guo yanjiu Kafuka shuping" (A critical account of Kafka study in China), *Waiguo wenxue yanjiu* 2 (1983): 133; and Kunrong, "Lun Kafuka de xiaoshuo," 46.

55. Kunrong, "Lun Kafuka de xiaoshuo," 49.

56. Her essay was published in Joyce Carol Oates, ed., *New Heaven, New Earth: The Visionary Experience in Literature* (New York: Vanguard Press, 1974), 265–298. The Chinese translation appeared in *Waiguo wenxue* 2 (1980).

57. I have discussed this question in another context in "Scholarship and Autobiography: A Review of Vitaly Rubin's Work on Confucianism," in *Confucianism: The Dynamics of Tradition,* ed. Irene Eber (New York: Macmillan, 1986), 135–154.

58. See, for example, Ronald Hayman, *Kafka: A Biography* (New York: Oxford University Press, 1982), 274–275.

59. See, for example, Xu Jiesheng, "Kafuka de 'Tuibian'" (Kafka's "Metamorphosis"), *Xientai wenxue* 31 (April 1967): 198–205, which perceptively considers Kafka's relationship to his father without, however, exploring what his father stood for in Kafka's view.

CHAPTER 12

Martin Buber and Chinese Thought

By the time Martin Buber (1878–1965) took up his appointment at the University of Frankfurt in the summer semester of 1924, he had published two books concerned with China: a translation of selections from the *Zhuangzi* in 1910 and a translation in 1911 of selections from Pu Songling's eighteenth-century work *Liaozhai zhiyi* (Liaozhai tales). Buber did not know Chinese, nor had he ever been in China, and both works were translated from Herbert A. Giles's English rendition. His interest in matters Chinese continued throughout the 1920s. In the summer of 1924, he gave a series of talks to a lay group, essentially an exegesis, on the *Daode jing* (*DDJ*). In 1925 and 1926, he published two translations (or perhaps retellings) of Chinese stories in commemorative volumes, and in 1928, he commented at some length on Richard Wilhelm's talk at the China Institute. The anti-Semitic excesses of April 1933 also extended to the University of Frankfurt, and he no longer taught at the university in either the summer or winter semester of that year, although he did not leave for Jerusalem until five years later, in March 1938. While teaching at the Hebrew University, he once again turned to Chinese philosophy, translating eight chapters from the *DDJ* in 1942 and translating and retelling several philosophical texts in 1944. Both publications in Hebrew appeared in popular magazines.

Compared to his voluminous writings on philosophical and religious topics, the works on China are indeed sparse and could be easily dismissed. Yet for a number of reasons, Buber's thinking and writing about Chinese thought occupy an important place in his works as a whole. They are integrated into ideas and views that occupied him at various times in his life. Crucial concepts of philosophical Daoism continued to play a role, and equally significant, Buber was the first Jewish thinker who attempted to move Daoist ideas into contemporary philosophical discourse. His contact with Richard Wilhelm (1873–1930) and the activities at the China Institute played a large role in further supporting his interests in China. Finally, Buber's turn to non-Daoist texts after he came to Palestine corresponded to his increasing concern with political and societal ideas and their philosophical underpinnings. The aim of this essay is to discuss several of Buber's philosophical ideas and how he integrated them at various times into his way of thinking.

BUBER THE TRANSLATOR: *ZHUANGZI* AND THE *LIAOZHAI TALES*

Precisely where Buber first came across materials on Chinese thought is uncertain. It may have been while he was a reader for the publisher Rütten and Loening in 1905 (1969, 58). Or possibly it was through his acquaintance with Wang Jingtao, a Chinese-language instructor at the Berlin Seminar for Oriental Languages who introduced him to Chinese thought and literature.[1] Wang clearly collaborated with Buber on Pu Songling's (1640–1715) stories, as will be discussed below. In any event, it was Buber's preoccupation some years earlier with Hasidic materials and their retelling, together with his interest in myth and culture, that played a role in his turn to Chinese materials.

For his German translation of Zhuangzi's works, *Reden und Gleichnisse des Tschuang-Tse,* Buber apparently relied almost entirely on the English translation by Herbert A. Giles (1845–1935).[2] Where his translation deviates from that of Giles, he apparently resorted to James Legge's (1815–1897) more felicitous rendition (1891, 164–232). Buber translated none of the *Zhuangzi* chapters in their entirety, and he sometimes omitted considerable passages even from the selections he had chosen. He generally avoided discursive portions and translated the stories rather than Zhuangzi's explanatory matter set forth in the beginning of a chapter or at points of transition. He did not use Giles's extensive interlinear notes, supplying instead an occasional brief note of his own. Buber translated twenty-two selections from the "inner" chapters, thirty from the "outer" chapters, and only two from the "mixed" chapters.[3] For each selection, he chose his own title.

In his preface to the 1951 edition of the *Zhuangzi*, Buber explained that he made the fifty-four selections from the philosopher's work "at first only for a group of friends." This may explain why the postscript, which is included in the various editions, is but loosely connected to Zhuangzi's text and was, as Buber stated, originally a separate essay. The essay "Teaching of the Tao" is, however, of considerable interest and reveals the extent to which Buber's engagement with ideas of Daoism at the time reflected his own philosophical position. He was, moreover, highly selective in what he chose to use and integrate (Werblowsky 2001).[4] According to Buber, the "teaching" was not an accumulation of knowledge but a means toward a genuine existence of the unified personality. The major theme of the essay is unity (*Einheit*) as the path of the teaching of the unified personality that Buber variously called "der zentrale Mensch," "Erfüllende," or "Vollendete." This person fulfills the teaching in life. He does not bring new elements to it. The three manifestations of the teaching, according to Buber, are the "Chinese teaching of *Dao*, the Indian teaching of liberation, [and] the Jewish and early Christian teaching of the Kingdom of God." Buber thus firmly linked Chinese Daoism to a larger context, seeing the major ingredients of the Chinese teaching as promulgated by Laozi as nonbeing (*wu*) and nonaction (*wuwei*).

Use of the parable to perpetuate the teaching was important to Buber, as he had found in other materials he had worked on. He wrote, "The parable is the insertion of the absolute into the world of events." Yet Laozi's *Daode jing* is not written in parables; it contains images "on the way to parables." It was Zhuangzi, the poet, wrote Buber, to whom came the teaching and who composed the parable. Zhuangzi was the teaching's messenger, the apostle, to the world. The link between master and messenger is, however, not only the teaching. It is also their solitariness, their concealment. According to Buber, we know next to nothing about Laozi's life, and we similarly know almost nothing about Zhuangzi.

When trying to explain *Dao*, Buber returned to the idea of unity, as mentioned earlier. *Dao* is unknowable and unrecognizable; it is not nature, or reason, or energy, as some have tried to explain. *Dao* appears in the world as the undivided, the unifying, the completing force. "Tao realizes itself in the genuine life of the perfected man," wrote Buber; therefore, the unified life of the central human being, in his genuine existence, is the embodiment both of the teaching and of *Dao*. This perfected man is the true ruler who rules by means of nonaction. He does not compel, command, or impose but pays attention to the "natural life of the kingdom" and rules by not interfering.[5]

Buber's translation was the first into German (Wilhelm's did not appear until 1912), and it was widely and enthusiastically praised. Wilhelm von Scholz wrote that the book was full of life and beauty, that it could be understood and enjoyed by even the most nonmystical and unphilosophical person.[6] Moritz Heinemann praised Buber's translation as "full, strong and soft." In Zhuangzi, Heinemann believed, Laozi's *Dao* was reborn.[7] Contrary to Werner Haefcke, who wrote that Buber's postscript was a masterpiece,[8] another critic stated categorically that what Buber had written had little to do with Zhuangzi. He also criticized current German translators who translated without knowing Chinese. While the interest in scientific Sinology was laudable, declared the reviewer, it was necessary to point out the value of translations by someone like Buber, who would want us to believe that he had thoroughly studied the original text.[9]

Although one must agree with the critic who chided Buber for translating from an intermediate language, it is only fair to point out again that Buber's Zhuangzi translation was the German reader's first exposure to the ideas of the Chinese philosopher. In addition, the postscript represented an attempt at integrating Daoist ideas into a larger philosophical discourse and must be seen as Buber's initial engagement with and response to some of the ideas of philosophical Daoism. Far from relegating the work of nearly half a century earlier to the trash bin of history, the reviewer of the 1951 edition wrote that Buber's encounter with Zhuangzi resulted in a "schriftliches Zeugnis von erregender Tiefe."[10] Twenty-odd years later, Maurice Friedman wrote that Daoism remained important to Buber throughout his life. Moreover, *I and Thou*—the "central work to which his thought led, and from which the rest came"—could not be understood, wrote Friedman, unless the Daoist concept of the perfected man together with the concept of nonaction (*wuwei*) is understood. Nonaction signifies noninterference, not passivity, and to Buber it meant "a philosophy of action that makes doing integral with being" (Friedman 1976, 411–426). Jonathan Herman, while also seeing an inherent connection between Buber's Zhuangzi translation and *I and Thou*, believed the latter to be "*a work of interpretation* [italics Herman] as the second interpretive layer of Buber's engagement with *Chuang Tzu*." Herman (1996) argued that instead of searching for influences of the Chinese text on Buber, the I-Thou relation was present in the Chinese text, making Buber's contribution a Sinological one that had been overlooked (168–169). Whether one can or cannot be persuaded by Herman's argument, the fact is, however, that Buber's next engagement with Daoist thought was with the *DDJ* and not with Zhuangzi. But before continuing with the subject of Daoism, let me first consider Buber's other translating project: a collection of eighteenth-century short stories, the *Liaozhai Tales* by Pu Songling, which Buber published in 1911.[11]

What attracted Buber to this collection was, of course, the content, the poetry, but also the philosophical substratum that did not acknowledge, he wrote, the separation between the real and the transcendental worlds. In his preface to the 1920 edition, Buber marveled at the manifold relationships between ghosts and human beings. A ghost could be a friend, a wife or son, and none of this is frightening, he wrote; "it is home, it is life." The order of nature is not broken but expanded; all life carried within it the seed of ghosts (Buber 1920, ix–xiii). In the preface, Buber credits Wang Jingtao for having introduced him to Pu Songling's stories, and indeed Wang had a considerable part in the translating enterprise. He was a lecturer or Chinese-language instructor since February 1907 at the Seminar für Orientalische Sprachen in Berlin, where he remained until December 1911. Wang's interests seem to have been more political than philosophical or literary, which may account for some of the omissions and commissions in Buber's translation.[12] After returning to China, he held some kind of official position in the newly established Republican government.[13]

Buber apparently translated the stories from Herbert Giles's translation,[14] which had appeared in 1880. Either Buber made good headway with translating the stories or Wang had already translated some that were now with Buber, for in August 1909, already Wang inquired how Buber was getting on with the corrections.[15] That Buber translated ten of the sixteen stories he had selected and Wang three or more can be concluded from the following evidence. First, among Buber's papers are drafts of three stories apparently in Wang's handwriting;[16] second, the six stories are not translated in Giles's book.[17] There is no way of knowing the precise method the men used for translating some of the stories. But there is one handwritten manuscript, "Die Musik," in a very rough and partial draft in Buber's handwriting. The nature of the notations suggests that Wang may have been translating from the Chinese text orally to Buber, who was writing down incomplete sentences while occasionally asking questions about some of the terms.

The method is reminiscent of that used by Lin Shu (1852–1924), translator of Western fiction into Chinese.

Giles had not produced felicitous translations of the stories. He had added phrases and sentences, omitted others, and occasionally changed the meaning. Nor did Buber produce felicitous translations of Giles's version, sometimes correcting his mistranslations but then creating mistranslations of his own. Giles omitted Pu Songling's appended comments, which are added to many of the stories. In these, the author raised questions about their significance or said what he thought about the tale he had narrated. Eleven of the sixteen stories have these comments in the original, but none were translated. Why did Wang Jingtao fail to render them even in the drafts? Did he perhaps not understand the philosophical significance many convey? Was Buber aware that they had been omitted? Buber, furthermore, did not use Giles's titles but made up his own, which more or less corresponded to the content of the story, and since many of Giles's titles are also not Pu Songling's, both works have titles different from the original.

Like the *Zhuangzi*, the book was widely reviewed and praised, even if it was not the first translation into German, an earlier one having appeared at the beginning of the century (Gast 1901).[18] Buber's style was extolled,[19] and others declared that the book was one of the most beautiful about love.[20] Hermann Hesse (1877–1961) heaped unstinting praise on Buber's work. This was not a contribution to folklore, he wrote, but the entrance into a heretofore unknown fairy world. He compared the stories to an embroidered Chinese silk carpet with its rich imagery of birds, flowers, dragons, trees, people, and clouds.[21] Paul Ernst echoed Hesse, noting that nothing as exquisite as these stories had ever appeared before.[22]

In 1925, a story Buber translated or retold from the Chinese entitled "Der Wettstreit" was included in a volume honoring E. R. Weiss (1875–1942), a publisher of especially beautiful books (Reichner 1925).[23] It is impossible to trace Buber's source for this story. The same is true for another story, "Schlichtung," that was included in a 1926 commemorative volume for the Indologist Karl Eugen Neumann (1865–1915).[24] Although Neumann was not a Sinologist, Buber apparently did not hesitate to use a Chinese story to honor the man. His comments are significant, for they reveal something about how he regarded his craft as a translator. Most translators and interpreters, wrote Buber, wanted to raise the original speaker on a pedestal and thereby ruin him. They took it upon themselves to extol the individuality of the original and thus distort the truth, not realizing that to capture what is genuine is important. Genuineness differs from originality. Buber's assumption that the truth, the genuine content of a text, can be captured by translators and exegetes is, of course, open to many questions.

Although much later Buber translated and retold small portions from Chinese thought—the *Daode jing,* the *Lunyu,* and the *Daxue*—his activity as a translator ended, for all practical purposes, with the publication of these two volumes and the two brief stories. It was interpretation, hermeneutics, of Chinese texts that would occupy him mostly henceforth, perhaps because he was in search of this genuine content. Before turning to this topic, however, we must ask how to evaluate his translations. There is no question that Buber frequently went astray or mistranslated by using intermediate renditions. Yet "creative mistranslation" can be and often is an advantage. All translations become in one way or another new works—some to acclaim, some to blame. The enthusiastic reviews of Buber's 1910 and 1911 publications are proof that both his *Reden und Gleichnisse* and *Liebes- und Geistergeschichten* were a resounding success, offering German readers a taste of China they had not before enjoyed. One major example concerning the *Zhuangzi* was Buber's recognition of the importance of the parable. No doubt, it was the Hasidic materials he had worked on that made him especially receptive to the ambiguity of the parable. Whatever the reason, he did not attempt to impose consistency on contradiction or clarify where clarity was not to be had.[25] Walter Benjamin's concern with language is important here, for above all, the language of Buber's renditions is outstandingly beautiful and enticing. The translator must discover in the target language, wrote Benjamin (1961), the means of raising echoes of the original (56–69).

Translating is, however, a complex activity in the course of which, suggests Willis Barnstone (1993), the author of the text and the translator set up a dialogical relationship. Writing, reading, and translating form, as it were, a continuum, and all three are translating activities. The writer translates thought into signs, "coded graphic marks," and the reader translates these "back into a mental text." Thought is transformed into writing, writing into reading. The place of the translator is not between author and reader but between the text and reader; the translator writes a second text, which is translated once more by the reader. Like Benjamin, Barnstone too is concerned with the target language: "The true ethical task of the translator is to be a good writer, to produce a work that is clear and beautiful, however close or distant the inspiring source voice" (8, 20, 22, 26)

BUBER THE EXEGETE: THE *DAODE JING* AND "CHINA AND US"

By far the most extensive exegetical work that Buber undertook concerned the *DDJ* in August 1924. Buber gave a series of lectures on the work in Ascona, Switzerland, which were arranged by a lay group interested in Chinese philosophy. The three-week course consisted of two-hour daily meetings with an additional two-hour evening meeting every second day.[26] Participation was by invitation only of no more than twenty-five to thirty persons. Presumably only participants from Switzerland were to be invited, but Buber managed to persuade the organizers to include some of his friends (Rübner/Mach 1990, 86). The lectures are a chapter-by-chapter exposition of thirty-three of the book's eighty-one chapters. Buber's lectures are not preserved among his papers (was there in fact a written text?), nor were the lectures ever printed. What we have today is a typewritten manuscript recorded by one or several participants,[27] which in abbreviated form gives the gist of his talks.[28]

Before discussing a number of Buber's expositions in greater detail, some general observations may be useful. One concerns the popularity of the *DDJ* in Germany. As many as seventeen German translations had appeared since the closing years of the nineteenth century, and Buber must have read some, if not many, of the translations, since he considered the *DDJ*, it will be recalled, the fountainhead of Daoist thought.[29] Thirteen years had elapsed since he wrote the postscript to the *Zhuangzi*; in 1923, he had published his major work, *I and Thou*; Germany had experienced the catastrophe of World War I; and in the summer semester of 1924, he had begun teaching at the University of Frankfurt.[30] Changes had taken place in his life and in Germany's political situation, and the lectures reveal a new understanding of the *DDJ*'s concepts. They establish a still wider philosophical context than did the postscript by comparing the *DDJ*'s concepts with ideas from Jewish, Christian, and Confucian thought. In these talks, Buber created for the *DDJ* a place in his philosophical and religious discourse, and his interpretations of the various chapters, now far less mystically understood, can be considered the first Jewish-German commentary on the *DDJ*. He drew on an august assembly for his exegesis, resorting in his explanations to the Rizhiner rebbe, Goethe, Kepler, St. Matthew, Verlaine, Cusanus, Orcagna, Luther, Spinoza, and Jesus.

For their text, Buber and his devotees used the translation by Friedrich von Strauss und Torney, *Lao Tse's Tao Te King*, published in Leipzig in 1870.[31] It is curious that Buber did not use a more recent translation or even the 1911 rendition by Richard Wilhelm. Although he may not yet have been acquainted with Wilhelm, who returned to Germany only in the summer of 1924, one must assume that he had heard of the man and his translations of Chinese works. But Buber was apparently fond of von Strauss's rendition, and he accepted some of the latter's interpretations, such as that the text was authentic and that it was principally a religious text.[32] He did not, however, accept von Strauss's conclusion that God and *Dao* are synonymous, although he attributed to *Dao* the quality of the divine (*das Göttliche*). Nor did Buber apparently subscribe to von Strauss's notion of an "Urzeit" when all religions were one and when both Judaism and Daoism emerged. The ancient Chinese were, therefore, according to von Strauss, monotheists and not polytheists (von Strauss und Torney 1870, LXIII).

But what was *Dao*, and how to explain it? Buber differentiated between a transcendent and an immanent *Dao*. The latter can be spoken about—it is the manifested *Dao*, the cosmic *Dao*, the Way, he explained in chapter 1. The constant and eternal actualization of *Dao* is in Buber's view creation, and creation is a constant, ongoing process. In chapter 21, Buber cited a phrase from the morning prayer, "renews each day the work of creation." However, he did not suggest dichotomizing *Dao*. Oneness is the important attribute, no longer a mystical and difficult-to-explain concept; rather, completeness is related to the person who participates in the divine, who exists in a higher state of undividedness (chap. 10). According to Laozi, there is no dichotomy of knowing and living, nor is the One real and the many an illusion. Both form an indivisible whole. To Laozi, the world is real and not an illusion as it is to the Vedantist (chap. 7). Buber understood chapter 20 as a description of Laozi himself among the people of his day. He, Laozi, knew the truth, but he lived in a world of lies. The longing for release promised here is also obvious in Greek tragedy. But the most extensive description devoted to the man of *Dao* (the one who has *Dao*, or the "Heilige")[33] is in those chapters that Buber interpreted as *Dao* and the state.

Buber commented on altogether six chapters (29, 30, 57, 61, 78, and 53) that deal with society, the state, and the person who heads it (Eber 1994,

461–462).[34] The state to him meant community (*Gemeinschaft*), but not the community as the collective of individuals. The state was to join people spiritually, causing them to act together. Such a community is not dominated by one person; it is constituted by the relationship its members have to the person in the center. Laozi, Buber argued, considered the political state both a state of human beings and a state of God. The perfection of the human state is for him the state of God (*Gottesreich*), pointed out in chapter 29. This is not nationalism or indication of a "folk." One is born into the folk (*Volk*); it is something given, not something conscious. But the more it is objectified, the more it is fictionalized (chap. 29). Similar ideas would be voiced by Buber at a later time when he tried to come to terms with Zionism. The person at the center was the religious and legitimate ruler. He did not explain specifically from where the ruler derives legitimacy, but he linked kingship to the messianic ruler. This is not messianism, for Laozi does not talk about messianism, but messianic kingship. Buber did not explain what he meant by the difference between messianism and messianic kingship. All messianisms, he commented, are in the final analysis the yearning for a king (chap. 49). It is the king as an intermediary who takes upon himself responsibility and guilt and who steps into the gap that has been created between God and the world (chap. 78).

In the chapters dealing with state and society, Buber did not resort to von Strauss's commentary, and he engaged in free and far-reaching discussions. Von Strauss's comments to these chapters referred to textual matters, but Buber, although noting here and there what seemed to him interpolations, was not especially interested in textual analysis. The lectures on the whole, to him, I would suggest, were to test the *DDJ*'s relevance and applicability to the world of his day. Thus, for example, in chapter 57 he expressed opinions on industrialization and the increase in demands for production and supply. But to require a return to more primitive economic forms, as some would want, would be missing the point. Return (*Rückkehr*) is impossible. Turning back (*Umkehr*) is desirable; only by turning around will people be brought on the way to *Dao*. The best example that social efforts were moving in the wrong direction, said Buber, was Russia, where people were becoming cogs in a brutalizing and senseless machine. Buber's exegetical work in these lectures should not be mistaken for Sinological analysis. This it is not. Rather, Buber's attempt to come to terms with the *DDJ* should be regarded as the philosophical quest of someone who, firmly and existentially lodged in the events of this world, was profoundly engaged in the task of understanding Daoism. The *DDJ*, Buber thought, offered a key toward such understanding. Buber's lecture at the China Institute in 1928, his next venture into Daoism, seems to confirm this.

Richard Wilhelm returned to Germany in September 1924 to take up his chair in Sinology at the University of Frankfurt later in autumn.[35] We do not know whether the two men met then or later, but there is no question that Buber also participated in the activities of the China Institute after its founding in 1926, which probably ceased only in or around 1930, when Wilhelm passed away in March of that year. One would like to think that Buber heard such popular lecturers as Hu Shih (1891–1962) at the China Institute (Wilhelm 1956, 356), and he obviously was very much interested in the Venerable Abbot Tai Xu (1890–1947), president of the Chinese Buddhist Association, who came to the institute with a proposal to establish an international institute for Buddhist research.[36] There were also less-formal social occasions when the two men and others met. Salome Wilhelm mentions a dinner at their home on May 6, 1926; a visit to the Bubers in Heppenheim ten days later; and an evening at the Wilhelms' on July 22, 1929.[37] For Buber, these must have been highly stimulating years in Frankfurt: old friends like Hermann Hesse came to visit at the institute, as did Carl Gustav Jung (1875–1961), who shared Wilhelm's interest in Daoism and especially in the *Book of Changes* (*Yijing*), which appeared in Wilhelm's translation in 1924.

The occasion for Buber's 1928 lecture on Chinese thought, including Daoism—actually a response to one of Wilhelm's lectures, "Bildung und Sitte in China" (Wilhelm 1929/30, 27–35)—was the October meeting of the China Institute. It was an important social and political event held twice a year, in spring and fall. In October 1928, it was attended by prominent personages, including men from the German Foreign Office.[38] Wilhelm had spoken eloquently about the crisis in Europe brought about by the overemphasis on progress and technological achievement. He contrasted these to the Chinese emphasis on continuity of tradition, on connecting the past with the present, on transmitting and teaching. With Confucius, said Wilhelm, Chinese culture became conscious; with him, the center of the collective soul was transferred to the soul of a single person. Now the ideal of Chinese culture became the responsible individual who consciously explored the connections among events in order to be part of them. The relationship to education (*Bildung*) was, therefore, not learning a specific task but learning how to perform it. The teacher was someone who instructed students to think that when they see one corner to know what the other three are about (*Lunyu* 7:8).

Buber agreed with Wilhelm's basic premise of a European crisis (1929/30, 40–43),[39] but more pointedly than Wilhelm, he attributed the problem to a state of general dissolution and a loss of direction.[40] Like Wilhelm, Buber suggested borrowing from Chinese culture, but not from Confucianism. In Buber's view, it was the Daoist concept of *wei wuwei*, acting without acting, that was of value in the current crisis. Buber rejected Wilhelm's premise on two grounds. The first was the easy connection the living maintained with the dead in China as expressed in ancestor worship. The other was the model human being, "the essential person" (*ursprünglicher Mensch*), who was the pure person of antiquity. In China, there was confidence in the past as a time that was right; the past could be fashioned anew at different times. The easy intercourse with the dead, with ghosts of all kinds (Buber returned here to ideas he had developed nearly twenty years earlier when translating the *Liaozhai* stories), was unique to China and altogether lacking in the West. For both these reasons—to which, Buber said, he could add more—he doubted that the West could accept something from Confucianism or Confucian culture. Instead, he proposed that the revolutionary notion of nonaction was more suitable, more acceptable to European sensibilities.[41] Real acting, said Buber, was not organizing, not a show of power, but a resting in oneself (*in-sich-selber-ruhen*) that did not lead to historic success. It was barely perceptible acting, lasting perhaps for generations, until it suddenly became visible, a part of the life of humanity. Acting by means of nonacting, he concluded, provided a point "at which we can be in touch with the wisdom of China."

Buber's talk, poetic rather than prescriptive, invited enthusiastic applause despite its vagueness. To be sure, aspects of Daoist thought were popular in Germany of the 1920s, but still, his rejection of Confucian thought in favor of a very passively interpreted Daoism seems curious, especially since he admitted that his thoughts had taken a decisive turn during World War I (Buber 1982). And as will be seen below, his dislocation from Germany to Palestine in 1938, where he encountered a new and different set of problems, and World War II caused him to turn to non-Daoist writings in search of answers.

ONCE MORE THE *DAODE JING* AND "LESSON FROM CHINA"

In 1942 and 1944, Buber turned again to Chinese texts. Precisely why he decided to translate into Hebrew several chapters from the *DDJ* in the first instance and translate and retell into Hebrew several texts, together with his comments, in the second is not clear. On the one hand, he probably included Chinese materials in his lectures at the Hebrew University,[42] being able to do so because he had brought with him from Germany a number of books on China.[43] But on the other, he may have had a more urgent or immediate reason—namely, the affirmation of his view of Zionism and its present and future tasks. Both differed considerably from that of the Zionist (Yishuv) establishment in Palestine at the time.

In 1938, Buber arrived in a land that was hardly a tranquil haven. His vision of the Zionist enterprise, which he did not hesitate to express, moreover, must have struck many as antagonistic to their aims. In order to understand better why he chose to turn to Chinese thought again and why he decided to confront his Hebrew readers with the selections from the Chinese classics that he did, let me briefly recapitulate some of Buber's ideas. In Palestine, he knew a new state and a new society were in the making. The foundation on which both would develop was an important consideration to him, and he saw himself as a participant in their construction. As he explained in 1941, the goal that he and a group of young people had set for themselves forty years earlier was a Jewish renaissance that he called Hebrew humanism. This Hebrew humanism was not an external transformation; rather, it proceeded from the basis of a person's being (Buber 1963, 732, 737). It was the transvaluation of all values, the rebuilding of public life from the bottom up (Buber 1963, 652).[44]

Buber was not only concerned with the state and society as abstractions; the individual human being and how he changed were important to him. In 1943, he wrote that the regenerative change of a person was not an issue of belief but an issue of being (*Sein*). The new regenerated Jew is the pioneer (*halutz*) who identifies the human aspect of his being with social goals. To live means for this person to live with others (Buber 1963, 262–263). Buber rejected narrow nationalism as politically impractical. Sovereignty was not what interested him. Being more concerned with the daily life of individuals, Buber advocated for cooperation with Arabs on the basis of equality.

Works created by Jews in the country should benefit both the Jewish and Arab populations. The road, he wrote in 1948, was one of work and peace, a peace built on mutual work (Buber 1963, 351). Toward that end, in 1942 he joined a group of like-minded people, the Ihud (Union) Association—headed by Judah L. Magnes, president of the Hebrew University—that declared it was not a political party but stood for the "union of Jews and Arabs in a bi-national Palestine" (Magnes/Buber 1947, 10). Buber's Ihud activities need not concern us further here. What is important is that he did not remain aloof from dealing with political issues. This must be taken into account when we next turn to his writings on Chinese thought during those years.

In 1942, Buber published eight chapters from the *DDJ* (Buber 1942, 6–8). He did not comment on the eight chapters he translated but only wrote several explanatory notes. The eight chapters are 17, 29, 30, 31, 57, 58, 66, and 67; each deals with both the nature of the ruler and how to rule. Chapter 66 recommends that the ruler be behind, for in order to be in front, he should not strive. He should rule with nonaction (chap. 57), and the people will be transformed. Chapter 17 advises the ruler not to obtrude; whatever he does should be unobtrusive, as if the people had done it themselves. The sage (*shengren*), states chapter 29, does nothing and therefore spoils nothing. Chapters 30 and 31 strongly reject the use of arms and armed force. Arms are evil, and the person who has *Dao* takes no pleasure in violence; indeed, the person who is in harmony with *Dao* will not resort to the force of arms. Extremes are to be avoided, that all acting and all states of existence are relative to one another is pointed out in chapters 29 and 58, and chapter 57 discusses the futility of too many laws, prohibitions, or contrivances. They will only engender their opposite.

In 1944, he turned once more to Chinese texts, translating and retelling a number of stories and portions of chapters. The essay entitled "Lesson from China" (Buber 1944, 14–15) is quite likely the earliest discussion in Hebrew of less-well-known Chinese philosophers, aside from Confucius, and is a unique contribution to Sinological literature in that language. It consists of two parts. In the first, ideas on statecraft, social values, and the nature of society loosely connect the five portions. The second part, consisting of selections from the writings of several philosophers, seems not to have a discernable thread tying them together. On the whole, however, the portions Buber had chosen to present to readers in 1944 convey concrete, even timely, messages rather than abstract or esoteric philosophical ideas, and he gave each selection an appropriate title.

Thus the first is entitled "The Government" and deals with the appointment of Shun by Yao because Shun was not only a paragon of filial piety; he was also able to put his house in order. Buber appended to this the following sentence from the *Daxue* (Great learning): "To govern the state it is necessary [first] to regulate the family" (9:1).[45] The second, entitled "Initiative," retells the story of Han Wudi (140–86 B.C.E.), who recommended capable men for service at court. Buber added a sentence that the young emperor recognized that new methods must be used. Both selections were most likely based on Franke's *Die Geschichte des chinesischen Reiches* (65, 297). The next two selections are brief and are probably taken from Wilhelm's (1910) translation of the *Lunyu*.[46] The first is a translation of Confucius's pronouncement of the importance of trust (*xin, Lunyu* 12:7); the second deals with Confucius's famous statement about the rectification of names (*zhengming, Lunyu* 13:3). The fifth selection in this first part is a very free retelling of a story from *Liezi*, which may be based on either Wilhelm's (1911) or Ernst Faber's (1877a,b) translation[47] and is entitled "Politics and Life." Buber's title carries the message he tried to convey—namely, that there must be cooperation between the state and the people. In the state are trained craftsmen—potters, scribes, musicians, carpenters—and all of them possess knowledge those in government do not have. The latter, however, have power, and only when those in power work together with those who have technical know-how can the state function properly.

The five selections in the second part are heterogeneous translations from several sources. From the *DDJ* he chose chapters that he had not translated two years earlier, but he did not render them in their entirety. He presented only a few lines from chapters 81, 12, 20, 52, and 76, using most likely von Strauss's version. From the *Zhuangzi* he translated two stories not included in his 1910 German translation. The first is from chapter 26, its message being that a person ought to do that which is necessary at the time he encounters the need. Zhuangzi tells this important lesson by means of the fish parable: the little fish will die unless he immediately gets some water; he cannot wait for the rivers to be diverted. The second selection is a brief story from chapter 12 about the Yellow Emperor, who traveled north and lost his magic pearl. For both stories, his source was Herbert Giles. A long section was translated from the *Analects*, but since he used only a sentence here and there, it is difficult to know to which chapters he resorted, except for the one dealing with a person's character (*Lunyu* 13:24). The selections from *Mozi* are clearly taken from Faber's translation, the only one available at the time and in Buber's library. The selections deal with universal love and condemnation of offensive warfare, two teachings *Mozi* is best known for.

Jonathan Spence has written, "One aspect of a country's greatness is surely its capacity to attract and retain the attention of others. This capacity has been evident from the very beginning of the West's encounter with China... [and] the apparently unending receptivity of Westerners to news from China, all testify to the level of fascination the country has generated" (1998, XI). In Buber's case, the attraction, receptivity, and response were not a search for the exotic, the "other," of a questing imagination but a genuine attempt to integrate aspects of Chinese thought into his own framework of thinking, on the one hand, and to make aspects of Chinese thought part of a larger discourse, on the other.

His activities as a translator were not merely the relaying of information from one cultural context into another; he was also intent, whether consciously or not, to transmit knowledge. When he retold stories or portions of philosophical texts—"reinvented" them, as Michael Richardson would say—Buber the translator used "the original work as the basis... [and re-created] the text in a way that is not strictly bound to the original" (1999, 268, 273). That he translated not from the original Chinese but from an intermediate language did not disturb him, he wrote in 1925, as long as he believed that he apprehended what was genuine in the text. Like Walter Benjamin, he may have also believed that the target language was the means of raising echoes of the original. Buber's rewriting of Wang Jingtao's fairly pedestrian German prose into beautiful and suggestively modulated language may testify to this.

Despite his warning about interpretation, Buber did not hesitate to interpret and explain facets of Chinese thought, as is obvious in his Ascona lectures and in his later work in Jerusalem. Some ideas—aspects of mysticism and Hassidism that had led him to Zhuangzi—are still noticeable in the *DDJ* interpretations of 1924, but so are others, especially those of statehood and what constitutes a people or community (*Gemeinschaft*). Then as later, he rejected the idea of nationalism or even of a purely secular state. Only a spiritual community, not a collective of individuals, can act together in a state that is a state of God and of human beings. From the *DDJ* he also accepted wholeheartedly the idea of acting by means of nonaction, which he expressed most fully in 1928 in his response to Richard Wilhelm's talk.

Although evidence is lacking, the years at the University of Frankfurt were, no doubt, stimulating (Schottroff 1985, 24),[48] as was his contact with Wilhelm, who also taught at the university, and the activities at the China Institute. Buber did not produce anything on China in the thirties. Yet the translation into Hebrew of several chapters from the *DDJ* and his work on non-Daoist texts in the first half of the forties lead me to conclude that Chinese thought continued to occupy him precisely because of these earlier contacts. The importance of his translations and re-creations cannot be overestimated. Not only were Hebrew readers for the first time exposed to a variety of Chinese ideas,[49] but students at the Hebrew University would encounter ideas in the classroom they had not heard before. Thus more than twenty years before the establishment of the Department of East Asian Studies, ideas on China began to circulate.

Even in this place and at a most catastrophic time in world history, Buber continued to maintain that acting by means of nonaction was the only way. Moreover, at a time when the sound of guns was heard everywhere, Buber strongly rejected aggression and the use of armed force. He did not name names or point at individuals in power, but some may have recognized themselves in portions he translated and stories he retold, and in the selections he chose he left little doubt about the Jewish state he hoped would come into being. In pre– and post–World War I Germany, Buber's interest in Chinese thought was not an isolated phenomenon. His interest is not significant because it is unique. It is unique, however, because then and later he seems to have been the first among Jewish philosophers who appropriated Chinese philosophical ideas and moved these into a specifically Jewish discourse.

REFERENCES

Aescoly, A. Z. (trans.). 1937. *Sefer haderekh ve'orah meyesharim* (Book of the way and way of honesty). Jerusalem: Reuven Mas.

Barnstone, Willis. 1993. *The Poetics of Translation: History, Theory, Practice*. New Haven: Yale University Press.

Benjamin, Walter. 1961. "Die Aufgabe des Übersetzers." In *Illuminationen, ausgewählte Schriften*, 56–69. Frankfurt: Suhrkamp.

Buber, Martin. 1910. *Reden und Gleichnisse des Tschuang-Tse*. Leipzig: Insel.

Buber, Martin (ed.). 1911. *Chinesische Geister- und Liebesgeschichten*. Frankfurt: Rütten and Loening.

Buber, Martin. 1917. *Die Rede, die Lehre, und das Lied—Drei Beispiele*. Leipzig: Insel.

Buber, Martin. 1929/30. "Professor Dr. Martin Buber." In *Chinesisch-Deutscher Almanach für das Jahr Gi Si 1929–1930*, 40–43.

Buber, Martin. 1942. "Laozi al hashilton" (Laozi on government). *Hapo'el Hatsa'ir* 35, nos. 31–32 (May 1942).

Buber, Martin. 1944. "Lekah meSin." *Hagalgal* 1, no. 14 (January 20, 1944).

Buber, Martin. 1953. *Hinweise, Gesammelte Essays*. Zürich: Manesse.

Buber, Martin. 1957. *Pointing the Way—Collected Essays*. New York: Harper.

Buber, Martin. 1962. *Werke*, Bd. 1. München: Kösel.

Buber, Martin. 1963. *Der Jude und sein Judentum*. Köln: Joseph Melzer.

Buber, Martin. 1965. *Nachlese*. Heidelberg: Lambert Schneider.

Buber, Martin. 1966. "China en wij." In *Sluitsen* (Nachlese), translated by van Hengel-Baauw and F. des Tombe, 193–199. Rotterdam: Lemiscaat.

Buber, Martin. 1970. *Kyoiku ron, saiji ron* (Martin Buber on education, on politics). Translated by Yamamoto Seisaku. Tokyo: Misuzu Shobo.

Buber, Martin. 1982. *Das Problem des Menschen*. 5th rev. ed. Heidelberg: Lambert Schneider.

Buber, Martin. 1991. *Chinese Tales, Zhuangzi: Sayings and Parables and Chinese Ghost and Love Stories*. Translated by Alex Page. New Jersey: Humanities Press International.

Eber, Irene. 1994. "Martin Buber and Taoism." *Monumenta Serica* 42:461–462.

Faber, Ernst. 1877a. *Der Naturalismus bei den alten Chinesen, sowohl nach Seite des Pantheismus als des Sensualismus, oder, die sämtlichen Werke des Philosophen Licius*. Elberfeld: Friederichs.

Faber, Ernst. 1877b. *Grundgedanken des alten chinesischen Sozialismus*. Elberfeld: Friederichs.

Fleming, J. 1998. "On Translation of Taoist Philosophical Texts: Preservation of Ambiguity and Contradiction." *Journal of Chinese Philosophy* 25, no. 1 (March): 147–156.

Friedman, Maurice S. (ed.). 1974. *Pointing the Way: Collected Essays by Martin Buber*. New York: Schocken.

Friedman, Maurice S. 1967. *Martin Buber: A Believing Humanism*. Gleanings, NY: Simon and Schuster.

Friedman, Maurice. 1976. "Martin Buber and Asia." *Philosophy East and West* 26, no. 4: 411–426.

Gast, G. (ed.), and Li Te-schun (trans.). 1901. *Chinesische Novellen*. Leipzig: Bibliographisches Institut.

Giles, Herbert A. (trans.). 1880. *Strange Stories from a Chinese Studio*. London: Thos. De la Rue.

Giles, Herbert A. 1889. *Chuang Tzu, Mystic Moralist and Social Reformer*. London: B. Quaritch.

Graham, Angus C. 1989. *Chuang-Tzu: The Inner Chapters*. London: Unwin Paperbacks.

Herman, Jonathan R. 1996. *I and Tao: Martin Buber's Encounter with Chuang Tzu*. Albany: State University of New York Press.

Isay, Gad. 2000. "The Philosophy of the View of Life in Modem Chinese Thought." Ph.D. diss., Hebrew University of Jerusalem.

Jewish National and University Library. *Buber Archive* (JNUL).

Kohn, Hans. 1961. *Martin Buber: Sein Werk und seine Zeit, Ein Beitrag zur Geistesgeschichte Mitteleuropas 1880–1930*. Köln: Joseph Melzer Verlag.

Legge, James. 1891. "The Writings of Kwang-Zse." *The Texts of Taoism*, 164–232. London: Oxford University Press / Humphrey Milford.

Magnes, Judah/Buber, Martin. 1947. *Arab-Jewish Unity: Testimony before the Anglo-American Inquiry Commission for* the Ihud (Union) Association. London: Victor Golancz.

Reichner, Herbert (ed.). 1925. Emil Rudolf Weiss zum fünfzigsten Geburtstag, 12. Oktober 1925. Leipzig: Insel.

Richardson, Michael. 1999. "Translation as Means of Cultural Transmission." In Crossing Cultural Borders: Toward an Ethics of Intercultural Communication Beyond Reciprocal Anthropology, edited by Inaga Shigemi and Kenneth L. Richard. Kyoto: International Research Center for Japanese Studies.

Rübner, T., and Mach, D. (eds.). 1990. Briefwechsel Martin Buber-Ludwig Strauss, 1913–1953. Frankfurt: Luchterhand Literaturverlag.

Rütten und Loening. 1969. Hundertfünfundzwanzig Jahre Rütten and Loening 1844–1969: Ein Almanach. Berlin: Rütten and Loening.

Schottroff, Willy. 1985. "Martin Buber an der Frankfurter Universität." In Forschung Frankfurt, Bd. 3, S. 23–29.

Schottroff, Willy. 1989. "Martin Buber an der Universität Frankfurt am Main (1923–1933)." In Martin Buber (1878–1965), Internationales Symposium zum 20. Todestag, edited by Werner Licharz and Heinz Schmidt. Frankfurt: Haag und Herchen.

Spence, Jonathan. 1998. The Chan's Great Continent: China in Western Minds. New York: Norton.

Strauss und Torney, Victor von. 1870. Lao Tse's Tao Te King. Leipzig: Fleischer.

Wang Jingtao. 1912. Confucius and China: Confucius' Idea of the State and Its Relation to Constitutional Government. Shanghai: Commercial Press.

Welch, Holmes. 1968. The Buddhist Revival in China. Cambridge: Harvard University Press.

Werblowsky, R. J. Zvi. 2001. "Buber and the East Asian Religions." In Martin Buber: A Contemporary Perspective, edited by Paul Mendes-Flohr. Jerusalem: Israel Academy of Sciences and Humanities.

Wilhelm, Richard. 1910. Kung Futse, Gespräche (Lun Yü): Aus dem chinesischen ver deutscht und erläutert. Jena: Eugen Diederichs.

Wilhelm, Richard. 1911. Liä Tsi, das wahre Buch vom quellenden Urgrund. Jena: Eugen Diederichs.

Wilhelm, Richard. 1929/30. "Bildung und Sitte in China." In Chinesisch-Deutscher Almanach für das Jahr Gi Si 1929–1930, 27–35.

Wilhelm, Salome. 1956. Richard Wilhelm, der geistige Mittler zwischen China und Europa. Düsseldorf: Eugen Diederichs.

NOTES

I thank the Truman Research Institute and the Frieberg Research Fund for their partial support of this research.

1. Buber Archive, Jewish National and University Library (henceforth JNUL), Arc. Ms. Var. 350/855:1, postcard from Wang to Buber, April 14, 1909, states that he has Giles's book but does not say which one.

2. Buber's German translation was published in Leipzig, Insel Verlag, 1910. A revised edition was published in 1918, and subsequent editions appeared in 1920, 1921, and 1922. A revised edition was published in Zürich, Manesse Verlag, 1951, and again in 1976. The revision of the transliterations of the 1951 edition was done with Willy Tonn's help. Tonn and Buber had corresponded twenty years earlier; later Tonn fled to Shanghai and after World War II settled in Tel Aviv. JNUL, Buber Archive, 817:8, Tonn letters to Buber, May 22 and 30, 1950. The English translation is Alex Page (1991). The English translation used by Buber is most likely by Giles (1889).

3. Scholars agree that the book we have today was not written by one person and that the contents are drawn from several strands of Daoism. The first eight chapters are considered the "inner" and most authentic chapters, chapters nine through twenty-two are considered the "outer" chapters, and twenty-three through thirty-three are considered "mixed." The outer

chapters may not be Zhuangzi's, whereas the mixed chapters may include some of the philosopher's materials. See Graham (1989, 28–29).

4. This is pointed out by Werblowsky (2001).

5. The above was summarized from Buber's essay, "The Teaching of the Tao," in Friedman (1974, 31–60). In German, the essay was reprinted (Buber 1917). It was also reprinted in Buber (1953) and (1962). The essay was translated into Japanese in Buber (1970).

6. JNUL, Arc. Ms. Var. 350/48-yud gimel, Wilhelm von Scholz, in Münchener Neueste Nachrichten, April 15, 1912. Clipping.

7. JNUL, Arc. Ms. Var. 350/48-yud gimel, Moritz Heinemann, "Anmerkungen zu 'Tschuang-Tse,'" Die Neue Rundschau, May 15 (?), 1911, 712–716.

8. JNUL, Arc. Ms. Var. 350/48-yud gimel, Werner Haefcke, "Schriften- Besprechungen," Ethische Rundschau, March–April 1914.

9. JNUL, Arc. Ms. Var. 350/48-yud gimel, "Bücherbesprechungen," Kölnische Zeitung, March 26, 1911.

10. JNUL, Arc. Ms. Var. 350/48, "Aus der Manesse-Bibliothek," Neue Züricher Zeitung, March 25, 1951.

11. The first 1911 edition was published by Rütten and Loening, as were the 1919 and 1920 editions. The 1948 edition was published by Manesse. Individual stories were published in journals in 1912 and 1913 as well as in collections of stories in 1977 and 1983. One story, "Shuchi" (Book crazy), appeared in a Yiddish rendition in Heynt 208 (September 5, 1937): 10. I thank Itamar Livny for finding this version. The English translation is by Alex Page and is together with the Zhuangzi translation, 111–211.

12. In 1912, Wang published Confucius and China: Confucius' Idea of the State and Its Relation to Constitutional Government, Shanghai, Commercial Press, 1912. The preface is signed Nanking, Bureau of Foreign Affairs. The aim of the book is to show the compatibility of Confucianism with constitutional government, a subject that must have interested Wang already before the Chinese Republican Revolution of 1911. I thank Professor Herman for bringing the book to my attention.

13. I thank Dr. Hartmut Walravens for the information about Wang, personal communication, February 12, 1990.

14. Pu Songling wrote approximately 500 stories, which were widely circulated in handwritten copies in his lifetime. The Liaozhai zhiyi was not published until 1766. Giles translated 164 stories into English. The Liaozhai Tales were apparently popular with Western readers, and a Russian edition of 5 stories appeared in 1868, 2 stories appeared in English translation in 1873, and 14 more appeared in 1874. Wilhelm translated 1 story in 1909 and another in 1910. I thank Dr. Hartmut Walravens for making this information available to me.

15. JNUL, Arc. Ms. Var. 350/855:7, August 1, 1909, Wang Jingtao letter to Buber.

16. JNUL, Arc. Ms. Var. 350/50Bet; the three stories in Wang's handwriting are "Shuchi," "A Xiu," and "Xiao Xie."

17. The six stories are "Shuchi" (Der närrische Student), "Pianpian" (Das Blätterkleid), "Gongxian" (Der Ärmel des Priesters), "Huanniang" (Musik), "A Xiu" (Die Schwestern), and "Xiaoxie" (Wiedergeburt). Apparently, however, Wang and Buber had a disagreement early on about the extent of Wang's contribution to the translating project, which Wang considered equal to that of Buber. JNUL, Arc. Ms. Var. 350/855:2, Wang's letter to Buber, April 22, 1909 (?). A week later, the two signed a contractual agreement, dated April 28, 1909, which states that Wang will be paid 250 Mark for the help he has given Buber in translating the Chinese stories. JNUL, Arc. Ms. Var. 350/855:3.

18. The book contains twelve stories. Four additional stories appeared in 1904 in Die Welt des Ostens. I thank Dr. Hartmut Walravens for this information.

19. JNUL, Arc. Ms. Var. 350/C46, H. Bethge, "Chinesisches," Breslauer Zeitung, November 11, 1912.

20. JNUL, Arc. Ms. Var. 350/C46, W. von Scholz, in Der Tag, April 17, 1912.

21. JNUL, Arc. Ms. Var. 350/C46, Hermann Hesse, "Chinesische Geistergeschichten," Neue Züricher Zeitung, March 25, 1912.

22. JNUL, Arc. Ms. Var. 350/C46, Paul Ernst, in Das Literarische Echo, November 1, 1912.

23. I have not seen the book. Buber's story is reprinted in *Stuttgarter Neues Tagblatt*, October 9, 1925. JNUL, Arc. Ms. Var. 350/C46.

24. The *Denkschrift* was to be published by R. Piper in Munich, but I was unable to find evidence of the book's publication. Buber's story with his comments was reprinted in *Frankfurter Zeitung*, October 18, 1925. JNUL, Arc. Ms. Var. 350/C46.

25. This is especially stressed by J. Fleming (1998). Buber may have omitted Giles's clarifying interlinear comments for these very reasons.

26. JNUL, Arc. Ms. Var. 350/627, W. Rosenbaum's letter of invitation with schedule of topics; 350/627:10–12, Mrs. Rosenbaum to Buber, May 11, 19, and 22, 1924, describes some of the difficulties in coordinating the group.

27. I thank Professor Paul Mendes-Flohr for this suggestion.

28. JNUL, Arc. Ms. Var. 350/bet-45, "Besprechungen mit Martin Buber in Ascona, August 1924 über Lao-tse's *Tao-te-king*."

29. See JNUL, Arc. Ms. Var. 350/87a, "Buber's Bibliothek, Religionskunde, Religionsphilosophie und verwandte Gebiete." Buber had a sizable library of rare and important works on Chinese thought, religion, and Daoism. The notebook lists the books that he brought to Jerusalem.

30. According to Robert Weltsch, Franz Rosenzweig (1886–1929) was supposed to accept the appointment at the University of Frankfurt but had to decline because of failing health. Buber accepted the appointment only reluctantly upon urging by Rosenzweig (Kohn 1961, 419). See also Schottroff (1989, 51). According to Schottroff, he was informed of the appointment on December 8, 1923, retroactive to the winter semester, beginning November 1. I thank Professor Mendes-Flohr for making the article available to me.

31. Von Strauss (1809–1899) was known as a poet and author. He had no formal training in Chinese language and thought. In addition to the DDJ translation, he also translated the *Shijing*, and in 1885, he published a study, *Ancient Chinese Monotheism*.

32. The extremely complex textual history of the DDJ and questions of authorship have been widely discussed in the past thirty years

due to the discovery of both the Mawangdui silk manuscripts and the Guodian bamboo strips with their variant text versions.

33. "Der Heilige" is not a successful translation of *shengren* because it introduces religious connotations that are not implied in the text, but it probably suited Buber, who regarded the text as a religious one.

34. The following portion on the state and its members is in part summarized from Eber (1994, 461–462).

35. I thank Ursula Ballin for the information about Wilhelm, personal communication, April 2004.

36. JNUL, Arc. Ms. Var. 350/902-2, "Aufruf S.E. Tai Hsü." Tai Xu visited Germany as part of a world tour that took him to France, England, Germany, Japan, and the United States. Welch (1968, 59–62).

37. Schriftlicher Nachlass Richard Wilhelm in Bayrische Akademie der Wissenschaften, München, Diaries of Salome Wilhelm. I thank Ursula Ballin for making these entries available to me.

38. JNUL, Arc. Ms. Var. 350/119-5. The event was reviewed in the *Frankfurter General Anzeiger*, October 24, 1928; the *Badische Presse*, November 3, 1928; and the *Frankfurter Zeitung*, October 25, 1928. The latter was accompanied by drawings of several speakers, including Buber.

39. It was reprinted as "China und wir," in Buber (1965, 205–214). The English translation is "China and Us," in Friedman (1967, 186–190); Buber (1957, 121–125). A Dutch translation is "China en wij," van Hengel-Baauw/Tombe (1966, 193–199).

40. The problem of crisis raised by the two men was widely discussed in European philosophical circles by, for example, Henri Bergson (1859–1941) and Robert Eucken (1846–1926). In China, the problem of crisis was also taken up by intellectuals who argued for the importance of spiritual content in modern change. For the arguments of those who championed this view in reference to European and particularly German thought, see Gad (2000).

41. Buber mistakenly attributed the idea of *wuwei* to Mengzi instead of Laozi.

42. JNUL, Arc. Ms. Var. 350/50b-Bet. Among Buber's papers are handwritten notes

on various topics, including Buddhism, Bodidharma, and Huineng (sixth patriarch of the Chan school), which were probably intended as lecture notes. There are also boxes with uncataloged materials that contain pages of notes from the *Lunyu*, the *Liji*, and the *Daode jing*.

43. JNUL, Arc. Ms. Var. 350/78a, "Buber's Bibliothek, Religionskunde, Religionsphilosophie und verwandte Gebiete." Buber's library also included historical works, such as Otto Franke, *Die Geschichte des chinesischen Reiches* (1930).

44. He wrote the essay in November 1939, the anniversary of Kristallnacht.

45. In his quotation, Buber inserted "the ancient rulers."

46. This volume was in Buber's library.

47. Both volumes were in Buber's library.

48. Schottroff writes that the twenties, when he taught at the university, were singularly fruitful.

49. An early Hebrew translation of the DDJ, probably from Wilhelm's German, is by Aescoly (1937). Buber makes no reference to this book and may not have known about it.

CHAPTER 13

Chinese and Jews

Mutual Perceptions in Literary and Related Sources

This essay attempts to show that neither Chinese perceptions of Jews nor Jewish perceptions of Chinese were simple and unchanging. In the nineteenth century, the Chinese viewed Jews as a people who preserved their identity even though they were despised and discriminated against in Western society. New elements were added when Chinese writers explained the Zionist movement as a political as well as a cultural movement. May Fourth writers and translators added still further aspects when translating from the rich literature in Yiddish. The translations of mainly short stories and plays introduced Chinese readers to the simple small-town folk of Central and Eastern Europe whose everyday concerns were not much different from those of peoples elsewhere. The powerful Jew who was allied with international capitalism and a threat to China appeared only during the Sino-Japanese War.

The discussion of Jewish perceptions of China and the Chinese people is limited to those writers who wrote in Yiddish. Published in inexpensive series, these booklets attempted to acquaint Jewish readers, living for the most part in remote small towns, with other cultures. Although not free from stereotyping, they did not stress differences between "us" and the "other." Rather, they aimed to inform and explain. In China, Yiddish poets responded sympathetically to China's problems and poverty. Despite distance and cultural differences, the encounters between Chinese and Jewish writers and intellectuals were in many ways unique.

Attempts to understand the kinds of images Chinese writers developed about Jews present fewer problems than trying to determine how Jewish writers constructed their images of China and the Chinese. Chinese writers began to take note of Jews when Protestant Christianity was introduced to China in the mid-nineteenth century and when translations of and from the Bible were undertaken. Subsequently, discussions about Jews, their condition in Europe, and their search for national identity and expression accompanied translations of poetry and short stories by Yiddish writers in the 1920s and 1930s.[1] These largely informative and sympathetic portrayals, reinforced by the fictional images, gave way to occasional anti-Semitic descriptions, especially in the Shanghai press after the outbreak of the Sino-Japanese War in 1937.

By Jewish writers writing about China, I do not mean Anglo-, French- or German-Jewish writers who wrote for broad audiences in the languages of their countries. The Jewish writers who are of primary interest here—principally because they are not well known outside of small circles—are those who in the first half of the twentieth century wrote in Yiddish for a large Yiddish-speaking audience in Central and Eastern Europe as well as in the United States. They conveyed to Yiddish readers their perceptions of China and the Chinese people both in poetry and in prose. But Yiddish works are, unfortunately, not systematically preserved. Vast quantities of materials from a once flourishing literary culture were lost and destroyed during World War II. The materials for study are therefore severely limited and fragmented.

Mutual Chinese–Jewish perceptions in various accounts and literary works are minor topics within the larger subject of Chinese–Western mutual perceptions. Even so, these are beset by considerable complexities, and the present essay can be no more than a bare outline. In this essay, I will discuss Chinese and Jewish perceptions of one another from their late nineteenth-century beginnings in China and starting in Europe some decades later, through the early 1940s.

THE CHANGING IMAGE OF THE JEW

In a 1997 article, Zhou Xun states that Chinese intellectuals writing in the twentieth century have tended to construct Jews as a racial group with various positive and negative racial characteristics, which they borrowed from

Western sources, including at times the language of anti-Semitism.[2] While it is certainly true that the discourse on race, and Chinese race, was eagerly pursued by some Chinese intellectuals in the first half of the twentieth century, it is equally true that anti-Semitism was not a significant, if any, motivation. Chinese perceptions of Jews were of many kinds, as Zhou Xun has noted, but they were often the result of an undiscriminating reading of limited source materials. Aside from popular notions about Jewish wealth and power, there were other, more dominant voices that simply attempted to explain to readers who these people called Jews were.

Possibly the earliest attempt at conveying images of Jews was in the history of ancient Israel, written in Chinese by the British missionary Robert Morrison (1782–1834); this history of ancient Israel appeared in a block print edition in 1814 or 1815.[3] Morrison did not mention the word "Jew" (*Youtai*) in the pamphlet's brief pages, in which he managed to tell the story from the creation (5,800 years ago) to the crucifixion and resurrection of Jesus Christ. Instead of blaming the Jews for the false charges that led to the death of Jesus, they are attributed to Judea's elders and unspecified others. Morrison's pamphlet was most certainly not widely read, but sixty-odd years later, *Wanguo gongbao* (Globe magazine; also Review of the times) reached considerably more readers, Christian as well as non-Christian. The journal, a missionary undertaking, also published occasional articles about Jews—who they were and what their present condition was. These articles appeared in conjunction with the Bible-translating enterprise, which was an important part of the Protestant missionary effort in China. A dominant theme in these early notices about Jews was that they lived not in their own country but scattered among other countries' populations. Although they had adopted the various ways of their host lands, they were unwilling to be like the native populations; hence they were always perceived as different.[4] Jews were the strangers, people who did not belong, and therefore, in many countries, Jews were discriminated against. This was the case even in countries like England, where Jews made important contributions to the life of the state.[5]

Whether these accounts were written by missionaries or by Chinese converts need not concern us; it is important that they were written for Chinese readers. But next to these were also rather different views conveyed, for example, by Liang Qichao (1873–1929), whose writings were avidly read by students and intellectuals. "Among immigrants to America," he wrote when visiting the United States in 1903, "Jews are the most powerful and influential." And in modern times they are the most famous. Although Jews have lost their country thousands of years ago, they have nonetheless great power and have kept their distinctive strength as a people.[6]

Jews as powerful people were now juxtaposed to Jews as undesirable strangers. Liang's image of Jewish power was of course to convince the Chinese to emulate Jews and was not meant pejoratively. This was not, however, the case at a later time when, drawing on anti-Semitic materials, writers presented Jewish power unfavorably, as will be discussed later.

New elements were added to the perception of Jews when Chinese writers and intellectuals informed their readers about the Zionist movement in the 1920s and when translations of Yiddish short stories and poetry began to appear in widely circulated literary journals such as *Xiaoshuo yuebao* (Short story monthly).[7] Zionism was regarded as a renaissance movement (*fuxing yundong*) with political and cultural implications. It was organized in response to persecution and in order to protect the Jewish cultural heritage. The political goal was to construct a Jewish national state, and the cultural goal was to develop the special characteristics of the Jewish people.[8] After discussing at length how Jews had been subjected to anti-Semitism in Western countries, Yu Songhua, for example, concluded that although the Jewish people had lost their country and were punished, disrespected, and rejected, they nonetheless did not fear difficulties and hardships. Their renaissance movement was devoted to their return to their homeland (*guxiang*).[9]

Yu Songhua correctly perceived the attempt at Jewish political and cultural reconstruction by use of the Hebrew language and its revival in Palestine.[10] Mao Dun (1896–1981), on the other hand, believed that it was precisely when Jews discarded Hebrew—the dead literary language (*wenyan*)—substituting for it the living, spoken language of Yiddish (the Jews' *baihua*), that the Jewish renaissance was set in motion. Similar to what was taking place in China, the revolution of the written language (*wenzi geming*) was the means by which modern Jews would be exposed to the wisdom of their brothers. And he too emphasized that despite having no country and a different religion, Jews nonetheless kept their faith, their customs, and their "Eastern thought."[11] The writers who read, commented on, and translated Yiddish literature regarded the Jews as part of the "weak and small peoples" (*ruoxiao minzu*)—that is, a people oppressed by large, imperialist powers. Among Poles, Hungarians, Armenians, and others like them, the Jews as a people were, however, unique because of having lost their country.[12]

Literary images conveyed in many translations of short stories originally written in Yiddish confirmed these perceptions of Jews who steadfastly and admirably clung to their "otherness." Despite oppression and abuses, they retained their uniqueness and, aware of their rich cultural heritage, were forging a new future. On the literary scene, the powerful and wealthy Jew was now supplanted by several, quite different kinds of Jews. In the stories rendered from English and Esperanto translations in the twenties and thirties, May Fourth and post–May Fourth writers saw social and literary concerns not dissimilar from their own.

Yiddish writers had woven tales about the "little Jew"—the small-town Jew who ekes out a living against all odds and who is often overwhelmed by injustice or simply bad luck. They wrote about the gullible small-town folk taken in by clever swindlers; countrymen taken advantage of by callous bureaucrats; failed businessmen and hardworking artisans. None of the characters trying to cope with life's difficulties in these stories would have been unfamiliar to a Chinese reader.

Sholem Aleichem (pen name for Sholem Rabinovitz, 1859–1916), the master storyteller, superbly conveyed these images. An exotic-looking Jew turns up for Passover and is invited home for the holiday. All are mesmerized by his fantastic stories (as translated by the host, since no one else understands him) only to discover in the morning that he has absconded with the family's valuables, including the rather less-valuable maid.[13] A mother moves heaven and earth to have her son admitted to the Russian high school. Teachers are engaged to tutor him and the husband loses his business over the effort, but at last a high school is found in another town that will accept a Jewish boy. The family moves to another house, he begins to attend classes, and then the unexpected intervenes, dashing all hopes—the students go on strike.[14] David Pinski (1872–1959) sketched a powerful picture of an angry, quarrelsome, and destitute man whose spirit, however, remains unbroken. Jailed after attacking a policeman, he cheats his jailers by hanging himself.[15] Not many of Sholem Asch's (1880–1957) stories were translated into Chinese, but he was a writer whose vignettes of the dark, superstitious side of Jewish society were powerfully effective. A Jewish brothel keeper has an only daughter on whom he dotes;

he protects and educates her to erase the sinfulness of his occupation. He commissions the writing of a scroll of the law (Torah) in the belief that it is a holy talisman that will protect him from misfortune. Tragedy overtakes the simple man, however, when his daughter despite his efforts turns to prostitution.[16]

The Jewish character, not always admirable, is wonderfully satirized in a story by Sholem Aleichem about a Jewish dog. The dog is kicked, stones are thrown at it, its leg is broken, and hot water is poured on it, yet all the dog ever does is cringe and hide; it never fights back. Finally, the dog runs away to another village, where it is ceremoniously welcomed by the village canines, which, nonetheless, are not willing to share their food with the uninvited guest. Desperately hungry, the dog makes its way into the forest, where it meets a wolf, which proposes to dine on the dog. But once again the dog humbles itself, and graciously the wolf allows it to leave.[17] Aleichem's allegory might have reminded Chinese readers of Lu Xun's "Ah Q."

Translations are often undertaken at random when a particular work catches a translator's fancy. This is not the case here, as for most of these stories, it was possible to trace the sources of the translation in collections of stories by various authors. Clearly, they were therefore selected from among a number of available examples. (Yet it should be remembered that only a limited number of collections of stories were available to translators.) Although we can only guess why these and not other stories were chosen for translating from among those available, it can be assumed that one of the major attractions was the way the simple folk and their daily lives were portrayed in them. Neither the protagonists nor the situations are idealized, and in none of these stories is there a "typical" or stereotypical Jew. The great variety of characters alone—only a few are mentioned here—is what makes these Yiddish stories such interesting reading. Thus the literary images of poor shopkeepers, incompetent businessmen, quarrelsome wives, defiant beggars, and many others contrast sharply with the perception of the Jew as a persecuted stranger or powerful and rich.

After the outbreak of the Sino-Japanese War in July 1937, Shanghai's Chinese newspaper readers were able to find yet another image of the Jew: the Jew whose financial power was proving dangerous to China. Translated from Japanese, a number of articles in Xin shenbao (successor to Shenbao)[18] were distinctly anti-Semitic and were, no doubt, a reaction to the influx of Central European Jewish refugees into Shanghai.[19] As a result of the German and Italian expulsion of Jews, went the argument, the Jewish problem had also become an East Asian problem. Those Jews who came to Shanghai earlier had already established themselves in business and amassed capital. Within twenty-five years, the wealth of China's economy might very well gravitate toward Jewish hands, and Jews would then control China. Jewish capital, it was claimed, was behind British designs in Asia.[20] Neither small and weak nor oppressed any longer, Jews were now said to be "in every country and in all countries they are influential in government and have economic power. . . . Jews control the world's resources and as an 'international race' they control the world." The Jews' aim in China was to "Sovietize" East Asia and to do this, they first had to Sovietize China. This was their international conspiracy.[21]

Aside from these propagandistic and anti-Semitic statements (possibly borrowed and modified from the Nazi press), views on Jews, their identity, or the nature of their national aspirations were not antagonistic. Rather, the perceptions of Jews, gained from descriptions or literary sources, often reflected the writers' and translators' ideological positions and concerns in regard to China. By attempting to understand Jews, they were not searching to establish uniqueness for either Jews or Chinese but hoping to form an understanding of the human condition and commonalities among peoples. Something quite similar was taking place among Yiddish writers when they reached out to the larger world.

REFLECTIONS OF CHINA AND THE CHINESE IN YIDDISH WORKS

The only scholar who has studied Chinese images in Yiddish writings so far is Zhang Shouhui (Chang Shoou-Huey), and I am greatly indebted to her pioneering work.[22] Let me begin with the Yiddish poet Meylekh Ravitch (pen name of Zekharia Khone Bergner, 1893–1976) and his poems about China. Ravitch traveled in China sometime in the first half of the 1930s, and he apparently wrote these poems in 1935. He arrived via the Trans-Siberian Railway, making his first stop in Harbin and its active Jewish community. Although he was obviously a keen observer, Jewish acquaintances also were, no doubt, valuable informants. Here I will discuss only two from among several poems that he wrote about his journey. The first is entitled "Lord Lytton of Genf and the Kuli Mai-wan-fu from Chefoo: A Ballad of Harbin." The long poem opens with a succinct description:

Manchuria there, Manchuria here
And Henry Pu-yi sits already on the throne
And Japanese ships are already anchored
in Harbin on the river Sungari.[23]

The poem then moves on to the Lytton fact-finding mission to determine the "truth" while the kuli dies of cold and starvation. Ravitch's poem paints a grim picture of politicians' games in which they are unconcerned with the little people's suffering. China's problems and its misery in the twentieth century assume a universal dimension in this poem. There is no hope. Lytton will inform the world of the "truth"; it will be spring when the Sungari River thaws and soya and cyclamen will flower. But of course, Mai-wan-fu will be dead.

The ironic juxtapositions, so pervasive in this poem, are even stronger in another: "He-nai-wan and Li-guan-yu: A Love Ballad of Peking." This too is a long poem, and its opening verse does not even hint at the tragedy that is its focus:

He-nai-wan weeps day and night
on her silk covered bed.
Father weeps and mother with her,
Nai-wan, what do you want, speak.

The girl weeps because she wants to go to Beijing, to the university, where Li Guanyu is a student and a member of the student committee. Emphatically, even if melodramatically (although the Yiddish reader would hardly notice), the poem blends the girl's love for Li with her love for China:

Katai, Katai, this land, young and beloved!
And secret and quieter: Li-guan-yu. . . .

Further on, he continues:

Katai, ancient and forever young!
Li-guan-yu!! He waits already as agreed . . .

But the clandestine student meeting ends tragically when the students are betrayed by Chiang Kai-shek's spies and are arrested. One by one, the twelve are beheaded in the marketplace:

And He-nai-wan's skin through the torn dress
becomes thinner, greener, as if silk-green.
It renders green the hope of China
on the stones of Peking.[24]

The setting in this poem is more "Chinese" (there are frequent references to silk, even a laughing Buddha) than in the previous poem. However, the theme—revolution and/or love, together with love of the motherland—suggests once more a larger dimension. Love versus revolution was a well-known theme in Russian literature and was used by Chinese writers like Ding Ling, Mao Dun, and Xiao Jun in their works before Ravitch set foot in China. The choice of subject, therefore, might very well indicate that Ravitch had contact (and if so, probably in Shanghai) with Chinese writers. The events described in this poem—a student meeting, a betrayal, an execution—might actually be a combination of two real events: the March 18, 1926, student massacre in Beijing and, closer to the poet's visit, the execution of a group of communists in 1931, of whose secret meeting in Shanghai the Guomindang authorities had been informed. More than likely, Ravitch learned about these events, especially the latter, from Chinese informants.[25] The perception of China conveyed in these and other poems is of a country in turmoil, a deeply troubled place of poverty and injustice. And yet there are also its youths, its young people who love and who sacrifice their lives for their country. The poet made no attempt to embellish or "Orientalize" his portraits; he wanted to bring his readers neither an exotic China nor a mysterious Orient. But China had been perceived quite differently several decades earlier.

There is one early account of a small booklet from 1910 in the "Home Library" series, which is aimed at a broad audience. The author, Akiba Flayshman, freely mixed fact and fancy, which were probably gleaned from Russian sources. Together with his factual description of borders, population, and geography, he also proposed that the Chinese were different from other peoples because they were separated from the rest of the world by high mountains, a huge desert, and an ocean. The Chinese are described as smaller and weaker than other peoples, not good-looking, and superstitious and backward. Their devotion to the dead was a major characteristic of their religious life, according to Flayshman. No doubt for the Jewish reader's benefit, he added that the Chinese believed that every person had three souls: one that goes after death to heaven to give an accounting; a second that remains with the body; and a third that lodges permanently at home.[26]

Another popular but more ambitious account was published in the inexpensive series "Countries and Peoples" and was adorned with many apparently hand-drawn illustrations. An example of Chinese writing was printed upside down. Aside from a highly confused account of Chinese history, the authors repeated some of Flayshman's stereotypes, adding several of their own—namely, that Chinese liked peace and quiet and cannot be hurried. Chinese opposed violence; men, when forced to become soldiers, deserted at the first opportunity. From a Jewish point of view, desertion was, however, not necessarily negative. Jewish men were not enthusiastic soldiers either in the czar's or in the Habsburg armies. Possibly betraying the authors' socialist inclinations is the following interesting comment. They stated that Chinese were satisfied with less compensation and were unwilling to struggle with other workers for better conditions. Like Flayshman, the authors commented unfavorably on Chinese facial characteristics, noting particularly their yellow color and "crooked" eyes.[27]

These and other accounts stressed the differences between the Chinese and themselves, their strange religious beliefs—indeed, the absence of religious faith—or the odd nature of the Chinese writing system. Yet there were also features Chinese and Jews had in common. Mencius, for example, was said to be similar in spirit to the Jewish prophets.[28] It behooved Jews, moreover, to shed their provincialism and narrow-mindedness, argued A. Almi (pen name for Elihu-Khayim Sheps, 1892–1963). But Almi had a great advantage over Yiddish writers who lived and worked in Eastern Europe. In New York, where he published in the anarchist paper[29] *Fraye Arbayter Shtime* (The free workers' voice), he had access to English works about China and her culture and literary traditions and was able to write, "We have surrounded ourselves with a Jewish 'Chinese Wall,' and at most, we sometimes smell the air of Berlin, Paris, and there the world ends. China, India? For this one must be crazy. But especially that large world, China with more than four hundred million [people] . . . should be certainly of the greatest interest to the genuinely cultured person who searches for himself or the world, or both; who wants to find something." And he especially admired the way in which philosophy and poetry were interrelated.[30] We might note here that this larger vision was also characteristic of the poet and writer Yeho'ash (S. Bloomgarden, 1872–1927), most likely the first translator of a Chinese story into Yiddish in 1912, who also encountered Chinese literature in New York.[31]

Mordekhay Holzblat's biography of Confucius in another inexpensive series, "The Life and Works of Great Men," designed for a broad readership, was a rather ambitious undertaking. Apparently based on a Russian source (a note on the title page reads "freely adapted from K. M. Karyagin"), the author also supplied a sketch of Chinese history and culture until Confucius's time, retelling the life of the sage in great detail. This includes many legendary materials, such as the meeting between Confucius and Laozi, when the latter presumably lectured Confucius on the necessary conduct for becoming a sage. Summing up, Karyagin and Holzblat professed their admiration for Confucius, who, above all else, was concerned with the welfare of the people and who recognized the usefulness of religious ceremonies "as a means for bringing peace to the kingdom and for benefiting the people."[32]

A number of intellectuals and writers came, together with the large influx of Central European refugees, to Shanghai after November 1938. Their poetry and prose appeared in the Yiddish pages of the Shanghai Russian newspaper *Nasha Zhizn* until 1943.[33] Regrettably, between then and the end of the war, probably due to Japanese censorship, the editor thought it prudent to restrict printed matter to unequivocally innocuous topics. Otherwise, no doubt, more poetry and prose would have appeared in its Yiddish supplements. Several pieces before 1943 registering the newcomers' reaction to Shanghai and its Chinese population are of considerable interest.

Thus, for example, expelled first from Poland, then Lithuania, and most recently from Japan, a poet entitled his dismay at the Shanghai scene "Three Countries Spat Me Out." He laments bitterly,

> On a humid day,
> When Japanese tie up their nose
> And step with wooden feet
> Japan has spit me out
> Into Shanghai.[34]

Shanghai's stark reality, its contrasts of abject poverty and wealth, and its rampant commercialism, both attractive and repellent, were captured by yet another poet. Rainbows of neon lights invite the eye, advertisements urge people to buy, and jazz music and drunken laughter are heard while outside stand hungry Chinese and "a man is harnessed—[like] a horse." In this city, even "China's daughters" are for sale.[35]

Although these poets knew they had been saved by unexpected turns of fortune, Shanghai was a strange, lonely, and isolating place for these tender-hearted poets. The moving poem "A letter . . . ," by the well-known Warsaw poet Yosl Mlotek (1918–2000), has this first verse:

> A word, a word from me—I will come certainly
> To me the great world's strange and tight
> Each night on firmaments I write
> A feverish letter to you, "I'm lonely . . ."[36]

Perhaps because they themselves were down and out in this great metropolis, the poets were not attracted by Shanghai's glamour or its cosmopolitanism. The little people, kulis, rickshaw pullers, and neglected children are what they saw and for whom they expressed their sympathy. In a masterful vignette, Ya'akov Fishman describes an elegant couple who sits at a cafe window drinking coffee. A beggar stands outside looking at them while they "sip and look, sip and look." The three depart—the couple to the taxi—but the poet asks, Where will the beggar go?[37]

The direct encounter with Shanghai and China produced rather different images than those that had been gleaned from earlier written accounts. Whereas the latter emphasized the "otherness" of the Chinese and how place and history contributed to their being different, the former, due to direct contacts, was predominated by the tragedy of poverty, homelessness, and loneliness. Earlier accounts, in attempting to convey information about China and the Chinese, also tended to perpetuate the stereotypes of their sources. On the other hand, the firsthand encounters with China called forth neither fanciful notions nor contempt for Chinese ways (as was often the case with other Westerners) but rather a compassionate, a commiserating, and not a patronizing response.

Perceptions of one another by both Chinese and Yiddish writers were of many kinds. The myth of the rich and powerful Jew was accompanied by a greater emphasis on the Jew without a country who, despite vicissitudes and discrimination, retained his identity. Chinese writers of the twenties emphasized that above all, and notwithstanding their dispersion among the nations, Jews evolved a sense of renewal and nationhood. It is hard to say how widespread the dangerous and scheming perception of the Jew in fact was, but it is very doubtful that these wartime accounts expressed Chinese anti-Semitic convictions. Clearly, however, whatever the images of Jews conveyed to Chinese readers, they necessarily also reflected the Chinese writers' perceptions of their changing historical conditions.

The case was altogether different from those writers who wrote for Yiddish audiences. They, more than Chinese writers, were hampered by the lack of sources in languages they could read. The example of A. Almi, referred to above, is instructive. Living in America, he was able to read and appreciate Chinese poetry as well as Chinese thought in English translations. Although certainly more Yiddish works on China or dealing with Chinese themes must be examined, the conventional myths about China and the Chinese found in Western literature and so ably described by Jonathan Spence[38] were apparently avoided by Yiddish writers. That is not to say, however, that all Yiddish writers mentioned in these pages were immune to stereotyping or to stating dubious truths. Yet when all is said and done, it strikes one as remarkable that in the first decades of this century, intellectuals at opposite ends of this earth would turn toward one another for no special reason except to get to know who the other was. And is it not equally remarkable that writers and poets, gazing at one another from afar, or later from close up, would respond for the most part sympathetically (and creatively) to each other's human condition?

NOTES

I gratefully acknowledge the partial support of both the Truman Research Institute and the Frieberg Research Fund of the Hebrew University of Jerusalem. I thank Professor A. Altman for his thoughtful comments.

1. Yiddish was spoken and read by the great majority of European Jews since the Middle Ages as a kind of lingua franca. Written with Hebrew letters, the language consists of Hebrew, Old French, Old Italian (Loez), Slavic, and German components. Medieval German of the Middle Rhine area was the most important of these, supplying approximately 85 percent of the vocabulary together with its grammatical structure. Yiddish is still spoken by a small number of Jews around the world.

2. Zhou Xun, "*Youtai*, the Myth of the Jew in Modern China," in *The Construction of Racial Identities in China and Japan, Historical and Contemporary Perspectives*, ed. Frank Dikoetter (London: Hurst, 1997), 53–74.

3. *Gushi Rudi'ya guo lidai luezhuan* (Historic account of ancient Judea), Harvard-Yenching Library ABCFM collection, 1814. There is some confusion about the date. It is listed as 1815 (?), but according to his wife, Eliza Morrison, it was published in 1814. See Eliza Morrison, *Memoirs of the Life and Labours of Robert Morrison* (London: Longman, 1839), 1:381.

4. "Lun Youtairen sandun buyi benxin" (On the forced and unchanging scattering of the Jews), *Wanguo gongbao* (hereafter *WGGB*) 10 (1878): 305b–306a.

5. "Wuguo zhi min zhi zhuangtai" (Attitudes toward a people without a country), *WGGB* 17, no. 4 (1905): 21a–22b.

6. Liang Qichao (1966), "Xindalu youji" (Record of my travels in the New World), *Xinmin congbao*, supplement (1903): 49–52 (Taiwan reprint), vol. 9. Liang was in the United States from May until October 1903. He traveled widely in the East and the Midwest and as far as California. The term *minzu* presents some problems. It is often translated as "race," but "people" or "people as a nation / nationality" seems closer to Liang's usage here. The term *zhongzu* was not used by Liang or by the other writers cited below.

7. On Yiddish literature in Chinese translation, see I. Eber, "Translation Literature in Modern China: The Yiddish Author and His Tale," *Asian and African Studies* (Jerusalem) 8, no. 3 (1972): 291–314. The following discussion is largely based on this essay.

8. Yu Songhua, "Youtairen yu Youtai fuxing yundong" (The Jewish people and the Jewish renaissance movement), *Dongfang zazhi* (hereafter *DFZZ*) 24, no. 17 (September 1927): 21–28. In a frequently quoted letter, Sun Yatsen called the Zionist party "one of the greatest movements of the present time." Letter addressed to N. G. B. Ezra, Shanghai, April 24, 1920, General Zionist Archives, Jerusalem, MS. Z4/10153.

9. Yu Songhua, "Youtairen," 21–22, 28.

10. Ibid., 25; Yu Songhua, "Balisi difeng Yalabaren yu Youtairen de minzu yundong" (Palestine's Arab people and the Jewish national movement), *DFZZ* 25, no. 8 (April 1928): 33–34.

11. Shen Yanbing (Mao Dun), "Xin Youtai wenxue gaiguan" (Views on Yiddish literature), *Xiaoshuo yuebao* 12, no. 10 (October 1921): 60, 61, 65–66.

12. The translated literature of several other "small peoples"—Poles, Irish, Black Americans, and Jews—is discussed in I. Eber, *Voices from Afar: Modern Chinese Writers on Oppressed Peoples and Their Literature*, Michigan Papers in Chinese Studies 38 (Ann Arbor: University of Michigan, Center for Chinese Studies, 1980). Partitioned Poland and Hungary, formerly part of the Austro-Hungarian Empire, gained their independence after World War I.

13. Huang Yi, trans., "Yuyuejie de keren" (The Passover guest), *Wenxue* 2, no. 5 (May 1934): 936–940.

14. [Wang] Luyan, trans., "Zhongxue xiao" (Gymnazya), in *Youtai xiaoshuo chi* (Collection of Jewish fiction) (Shanghai: Kaiming, n.d. [1926]).

15. Chen Gu, trans., "Yige eren de gushi" (Tale of a hungry man), *Xiaoshuo yuebao* 16, no. 2 (February 1925): 1–4.

16. Tang Xuzhi, trans., *Fuchou shen* (The God of vengeance) (Shanghai: Commercial Press, 1936).

17. [Wang] Luyan, trans., "Labaike" (Rabchik), *DFZZ* 21, no. 9 (May 1924): 107–115.

18. Started by a Japanese journalist as the Chinese translation of *Shanhai godo*, the daily began publication in 1938.

19. The Japanese and other powers' reaction to the refugees' arrival in Shanghai is discussed by A. Altman and I. Eber, "Flight to Shanghai, 1938–1940: The Larger Setting," *Yad Vashem Studies* 28 (2000).

20. "Zhongguo he Youtai wenti" (China and the Jewish problem), *Xin shenbao*, September 29, 1939, 2.

21. Chen Qian, "Shijie dongluan yu Youtai zhi guoji yinmou" (International turmoil and Jewish conspiracy), *Zhongguo gonglun* [Beijing], February 1940, 14–15, 23. The article is accompanied by a lurid drawing of a skeletal figure. For the communist danger, see also "Chise Youtairen lai Huhou, bai E shangji beiduo" (After Red Jews come to Shanghai, White Russians are deprived of their livelihood), *Xin shenbao*, December 18, 1938, 2.

22. Chang Shoour-Huey, "China und Jiddisch, Jiddische Kultur in China, Chinesische Literatur auf Jiddisch," in *From Kaifeng . . . to Shanghai: Jews in China*, ed. Roman Malek (Saint Augustin, Germany: Monumenta Serica Institute and China-Zentrum, and Nettetal, Germany: Steyler Verlag, 2000), 479–495.

23. Meylekh Ravitch, *Kontinentn un Okeanen* (Continents and oceans) (Warsaw: Literarishe Bletter, 1937), 27–30. The Lytton Commission of the League of Nations came to Manchuria in

early spring of 1932. Its report later in the year condemned Japanese aggression, whereupon Japan withdrew from the league in March 1933.

24. Ibid., 39–43.

25. A brief discussion of both events is in Jonathan D. Spence, *The Gate of Heavenly Peace* (New York: Viking Press, 1981), 193–198, 230–232. In Shanghai, twenty-three young people were executed, among them Li Weisan and He Mengxiong. Is it a coincidence that Ravitch surnamed his two heroes Li and He?

26. Akiba Flayshman, *Di Khineser, zeyer lebn, emune un zittn* (The Chinese, their life, belief, and customs) (Warsaw: Verlag Yiddishn Tages-blat, n.d. [1910]), 1–2, 12, 21–22.

27. Mordekhay Birnboim and D. Kassel, *Khine un Manchurien, Mongolien, Tibet, Korea, un andere* (Warsaw: Yiddish, 1918), 6–17.

28. Ibid., 63.

29. I am indebted to Professor A. Altman for this information.

30. A. Almi *Khinesishe Filozofie un Poezye* (New York, 1925), 6, 60. See also Chang, "China und Jiddisch," 7–8.

31. Yeho'ash translated "The Soul of the Great Bell" from Lafcadio Hearn, comp., *Some Chinese Ghosts* (1887), who is better known for his many books about Japan. The story is included in Yeho'ash *Fun der welt un yener* (Of this world and the other) (New York: Oifgang,

1913), 147–168. Yeho'ash encouraged, in turn, another writer to translate Hearn's entire volume of six stories. See Bernard Witt, trans., *Khinezishe legenden* (New York, 1930). In the preface, Witt pays tribute to Yeho'ash's love of world literature.

32. Holzblat Mordekhay, *Konfucjus, zeyn lebn un tetigkayt* (Confucius, his life and activities) (Warsaw: "Record," n.d.), 44, 86.

33. Other Yiddish pages were published in at least two papers of the émigré press, and there was even one weekly, *Yediyot* (News), specifi-cally for Polish refugees. Most of these papers were ephemeral, and more research is needed to determine the length of their runs. I wish to thank Violet Gilboa of the Judaica collection of the Harvard College Library for making several single issues of these papers available to me.

34. E. Simkhoni, "Drey Lender hobn mikh oisgeshpign," *Unzer Lebn* 20 (Yiddish supple-ment of *Nasha Zhizn*), September 12, 1941.

35. Yosl Mlotek, "Shanghai," *Unzer Lebn* 38, January 23, 1942.

36. "A briv . . ." (A letter . . .), *Unzer Lebn* 99 (47), March 26, 1942.

37. Ya'akov Fishman, "Miniaturen," *Unzer Lebn* 40, February 6, 1942.

38. Jonathan D. Spence, *The Chan's Great Continent: China in Western Minds* (New York: W. W. Norton, 1998).

CHAPTER 14

Learning the Other

Chinese Studies in Israel and Jewish Studies in China

In recent decades, the study of each other's culture and the like has been a rapidly developing field in both Israel and China. A number of universities have established departments and/or centers, and student bodies for the BA degree or advanced degrees are increasing every year. Although the initial attraction to learn more about each other may be due to popular notions about the "exotic Orient" in Israel and Jewish "wealth and power" in China, this soon gives way to more serious considerations. There are the demanding studies of each other's languages and of ancient and more recent histories. The scholars active in the field not only are engaged in writing works on topics of their expertise but also are translating philosophical and literary works in an effort to bring treasures of the past and the present to a wider public. Student exchange programs between the two countries are important in supporting scholarly endeavors. Finally, library acquisitions in a number of languages are an important part of the development of Chinese and Jewish studies in both countries.

CHINESE STUDIES IN ISRAEL

In 1969, the Hebrew University of Jerusalem was the first university to initiate a three-year program in Chinese and Japanese studies leading to the BA degree.[1] Some years later, MA and PhD degrees were added. Until 1985, student enrollment in the department was fairly low. The rigorous language program together with circumscribed employment opportunities discouraged many young people from joining. It also must be remembered that Israeli students begin studies after army service and are therefore more career oriented than their average counterparts elsewhere.

The situation changed drastically after 1985, when enrollments increased and fewer students dropped out of the program. By 1992, after the establishment of diplomatic relations between the two countries, enrollments rose rapidly. Employment became possible, and today several graduates are teaching in the department; others are active in the Foreign Service or in China-related business enterprises as well as similarly specialized careers. Currently, five PhD candidates are writing dissertations on such diverse topics as urban development in China, Chinese philosophy, and the exile press in Shanghai.

The Frieberg Center of East Asian Studies, established in 2006, has an important function together with the department. Louis Frieberg's[2] generous support has made it possible to support research on China, grant postdoctoral fellowships, and especially expand the Chinese-language library. It is the last that has benefited dissertation writers by providing local access to major Chinese research works.

An important goal of the faculty has been to provide instructional materials in Hebrew. Among those that should be mentioned here are the excellent grammar by Dr. Lihi Yariv-Laor for language courses and the early history of China edited by Professor Yitzhak Shichor for introductory history courses. Of singular importance is the publication of the *Four Books* of Confucianism, comprising *The Analects* by Confucius, *The Great Learning, The Mean*, and *The Mencius*. Translated by several hands, these basic philosophical works are the backbone of Chinese thought, and no student of Chinese history and culture can manage without them. Mention must also be made of the important translations from Chinese literature by Amira Katz-Goehr, which are used as supplementary readings in courses on Chinese history. All these works are, of course, also available to the public at large in attractive editions that include short stories by Feng Menglong (1574–1646) and Lu Xun (1881–1936). Besides such materials in Hebrew, the faculty of the department also engages in research on topics of their specialization, publishing these mainly in English. There is the impressive work by Professor Gideon Shelach on Chinese archaeology and by Yuri Pines on pre-Confucian thought.[3] Retired faculty of the center continue their research and writing, while a documentary history of Jewish refugees in Shanghai is currently under way.

The Department of East Asian Studies was established at Tel Aviv University in 1985. As in Jerusalem, the major thrust is language, culture, and history; despite its name, the department also includes Indian studies. However, its fairly large faculty offers a wider range of courses than is the case in Jerusalem, and there is a great emphasis on philosophical traditions. Strong institutional support and generous budgets made possible considerable library development. Another significant development was the establishment of the Confucius Institute in 2007. Under the directorship of Professor Meir Shahar, the institute hosts lectures and conferences in addition to offering courses on various aspects of Chinese studies. Professor Shahar has written widely on Chinese religion both in Hebrew and in English. In distinction to Jerusalem, the department's strength is philosophy, and as a result, several significant works on Chinese philosophy were published by professors Yoav Ariel and Galia Patt-Shamir.[4]

In 2002, Haifa University established its Department of Asian Studies, granting at first only the BA degree. In recent years, the curriculum has been expanded to include the MA degree. Unlike Jerusalem and Tel Aviv, Haifa University's department concentrates more on modern developments in Asia without, however, neglecting language instruction in both Chinese and Japanese. Its faculty is still small, but considering the fairly recent establishment of the department, its library acquisitions are impressive. Under the able leadership of Professor Rotem Kowner, a Japan specialist who has published widely on the Russo-Japanese War (1904–1905), we can look forward to Haifa University's department as an important center of modern Asian studies.

Besides the three universities discussed above, courses on China, including language, are also taught at two other universities in Israel—the Technion in Haifa and Bar-Ilan in Ramat Gan; however, whether these will eventually develop into departments remains to be seen. All together there are at present more than one thousand students enrolled in courses dealing with Asia, and of these, around three quarters, if not more, are studying Chinese. This number may significantly increase, as a new department is being planned for 2011 at a northern teachers' college.

JEWISH STUDIES IN CHINA

Unlike Israeli universities, which have departments of area studies, Chinese institutions offer courses on Jewish studies in the various departments of their discipline. Thus students take courses on Jewish history, philosophy, Hebrew, and related subjects in several departments. Ten Chinese institutions currently grant degrees in Jewish subjects.[5] In addition, there are six centers or institutes of Jewish studies—at Beijing University, Nanjing University, the Shanghai Academy of Social Sciences, Shandong University, Henan University, and most recently Sichuan University.[6] At several of these centers, instruction in aspects of Jewish studies is offered and major research and translation projects are initiated and carried out. The development of Jewish studies at Chinese universities is indeed remarkable if it is remembered that for the most part this phenomenal growth has taken place after 1992 and the establishment of diplomatic relations between the two countries.

Impressive accomplishments can be chalked up for Beijing University. Hebrew language teaching began there in 1985, when a Hebrew language and literature program was established in the Department of Oriental Studies.[7] At the present time, three faculty members are teaching language courses at the BA and MA levels, and students can take Hebrew studies as their major. Many graduates of the program have successful careers in government posts, the Xin Hua News Agency, and the like, while others are pursuing graduate degrees abroad. Although doctoral students are as yet not enrolled, Professor Chen Yiyi, the director of the Institute of Hebrew and Jewish Studies—a research institute—has guided several MA theses. Many departments, such as political science or philosophy, are offering related courses, and students have the opportunity to understand Jewish studies in a larger context. An expert on the Bible, Professor Chen's course on the scriptures is taught as a core course.

Under the able guidance of Professor Xu Xin, the Institute of Jewish Studies at Nanjing University has emerged as one of the major centers of Jewish studies in China. Founded in 1992, it offers both BA and graduate degrees. The institute was renamed the Diane and Guilford Glazer Institute of Jewish Studies after a generous donation made possible the construction of a new building dedicated in 2006. Many projects are under way, both MA theses and PhD dissertations. Attesting to the stimulating leadership of the faculty, they include a variety of important historical and religious topics, among them the function of synagogues, the German Reform movement, or Christianity's separation from Judaism.

The Center for Jewish Studies in Shanghai was established in 1988, before diplomatic relations took effect. Its dean is Professor Pan Guang, and it is part of the Shanghai Academy of Social Sciences. Like Nanjing, this is an active center, engaged in research and publishing. Its research, dealing with a variety of topics, also includes extensive work on the Jewish refugees in Shanghai who were sheltered there during World War II. The center sees its mission, in the words of Professor Pan Guang, as "constructing a Chinese framework for . . . Jewish-Israel studies in China."[8]

The Center for Judaic and Inter-religious Studies at Shandong University was established in 2003 and is also a very active center. Its director, Professor Fu Youde, has been guiding the excellent research and teaching programs with impressive results. Its graduates have been accepted abroad at major universities, and visiting scholars from abroad have found receptive audiences among the students.

The Institute of Jewish Studies at Henan University in Kaifeng was established one year earlier, in 2002. That such an institute should exist precisely in the city where the historic Jewish community once flourished for several hundred years since the twelfth century is certainly appropriate. The guiding light has been its director, Professor Zhang Qianhong, who is a prolific scholar. The institute has been aimed from the start at teaching and research; its scholars abroad have been frequent lecturers, and the institute's faculty lecture frequently at other Chinese universities. Although PhD degrees are not granted, students can enroll in MA degrees. There is also an annual essay competition on a Jewish topic open to all university students. Much effort has been devoted in recent years to expanding the still modest library resources on Judaism.

The most recent center, the Center of Judaic and Chinese Studies, was established in 2006 at Sichuan University. Its director is Professor Fu Xiaowei. The center aims to clarify the misreading and misrepresentation of Jews and Judaism that all too often occurs in popular books and is pervasive among the public at large as well as university students. Its ambitious translating program promises to make a major contribution to the availability of works in the Chinese language.[9]

A significant innovation in the past five years has been the annual workshop on the Holocaust. The workshops have attracted many graduate students from history departments. It is significant that by such means a wider student body can be reached beyond those majoring in Jewish studies.

Scholars active in the institutes and centers maintain a vigorous writing, translating, and publication schedule.[10] Only a few works can be mentioned here. The journal *Jewish Studies* has been published annually since 2002, while *World History* also contains essays on Jewish issues. In addition to the journals are the important publications by Professor Chen Yiyi on the Bible and Old Testament.[11] Professor Fu Youde has a number of outstanding works on Jewish philosophy, including a translation of Maimonides's *Guide for the Perplexed*.[12] Then there is Professor Xu Xin's pathbreaking contribution, his *Encyclopaedia Judaica*, published in 1998 by the Shanghai People's Press. This work especially, translated from the English *Encyclopaedia Judaica*, is a major resource in Chinese.[13] For obvious reasons, Chinese readers are particularly interested in the historic Jewish community of Kaifeng and the modern Jews of Shanghai. Professor Pan Guang at the Shanghai Institute has devoted attention to the latter in several publications in English as well as in Chinese.[14] The institute at Sichuan University is planning an ambitious literature translating program of Jewish fiction pioneered by Professor Fu Xiaowei's earlier translations of works by Isaac Bashevis Singer (1904–1991), who was a Polish-born novelist writing in Yiddish.

The accomplishments in both countries as described in this brief survey are remarkable. If one believes, as I do, that one of our most important tasks is to foster understanding between peoples, no matter how remote, then this is exactly what is taking place. How fortunate are we that we can read some cherished literary works in the original or in translation; that we can learn one another's languages; that we can find out more about heroes and villains in our respective histories. If, as teachers, we can bequeath the sense of curiosity and wonder to our students, the curiosity that we ourselves felt when we first studied another culture, then we shall have accomplished our task. In Professor Lihong Song's apt words, "Judaism is becoming more and more tangible and concrete, and I am increasingly curious, with my nose pressed to the glass looking in, to its colours, smells and breath."[15]

NOTES

1. The earlier history of Hebrew University's East Asia department is discussed in I. Eber, "Sinology in Israel," *Revue Bibliographique de Sinologie* (1969), 29–35.

2. Born and raised in Mielec, Poland, he has been a benefactor of the department since 1991. He envisioned already then a potentially close relationship between China and Israel with the university as a link.

3. Gideon Shelach, *Prehistoric Societies on the Northern Frontier of China: Archaeological Perspectives on Identity Formation and Economic Change During the First Millennium B.C.E.* (Oakville: Eqinox, 2009), and Yuri Pines, *Foundations of Confucian Thought: Intellectual Life in the Chinqiu Period (722–463 B.C.E.)* (Honolulu: University of Hawaii Press, 2002).

4. Ariel Yoav, *K'ung-Ts'ung-Tzu: The K'ung Family Master's Anthology: A Study and Translation of Chapters 1–10, 12–14* (Princeton: Princeton University Press, 1989), and Galia Patt-Shamir, *To Broaden the Way: A Confucian-Jewish Dialogue* (Lanham: Roman and Littlefield, 2006).

5. Lihong Song, "Some Observations on Chinese Jewish Studies," *Contemporary Jewry* 29, no. 3 (2009), 195–214. My information is based on the online version without the pagination.

6. There is apparently also a Center of Jewish Studies at the Heilongjiang Academy of Social Sciences, but not much is known about it and its work. This is regrettable because the Harbin Municipal archives contain valuable materials from the Russian Jewish community, one of the major Jewish communities in China in the first decades of the twentieth century.

7. For information at Beijing University, I am indebted to Professor Chen Yiyi, to whom I want to express my gratitude.

8. For more information on the Shanghai center, consult its very informative website, http://www.cjcs.oreg.cn.

9. Fu Xiaowei, "Chinese Views of Jews and Judaism and the Mission of CJCS," *Points East* 25, no. 1 (March 2010), 12–14.

10. A useful as well as critical bibliographic survey about the topics that have engaged Chinese scholars is Izabella Goikhman, *Juden in China: Diskurse und ihre Kontextualisierung* (Berlin: Lit Verlag Dr. W. Hopf, 2007).

11. For example, Chen Yiyi, *The Hebrew Bible: An Introduction Based on Textual and Archaeological Data (Till 586 B.C.E.)* (Beijing: Kunlun Press, 2006).

12. Among these are Fu Youde, *A History of Jewish Philosophy* (Beijing: Renmin University Press, 2008), and *Essays on Jewish Philosophy and Religion* (Beijing: Chinese Academy of Social Sciences, 2007).

13. This is not to neglect Xu Xin's important *History of Jewish Culture* (Beijing: Peking University Press, 2006).

14. Pan Guang and Jian Wang, *Jews in Shanghai Since the 1840s: An Oriental Page in the Annals of the Jewish Diaspora* (Beijing: Social Sciences Academy Press, 2002).

15. Lihong Song, "Intellectual Autobiography," paper presented at AAJR 2009 Workshop for Early Career Faculty in Jewish Studies, Berkeley. Quoted by permission of author.

Chapter 1 first appeared as "Overland and by Sea—Eight Centuries of the Jewish Presence in China," *Chinese Journal of International Law* 4, no. 1 (2005): 235–256. Reprinted by permission of Oxford University Press.

Chapter 2 first appeared as "Chinese Jews and Jews in China, Kaifeng–Shanghai," in *Religion in China: Major Concepts and Minority Positions*, ed. Max Deeg and Bernhard Scheid, 65–89 (Vienna: Verlag der österreichischen Akademie der Wissenschaften, 2015). Reprinted by permission of the Austrian Academy of Sciences.

Chapter 3 first appeared as "Flight to Shanghai, 1938–1939 and Its Larger Context," in *From Kaifeng ... to Shanghai, Jews in China*, ed. Roman Malek, 417–432 (Sankt Augustin: Monumenta Serica Institute, 2000). Reprinted by permission of the Monumenta Serica Institute.

Chapter 4 first appeared as "A Critical Survey of Classical Chinese Literary Works in Hebrew," in *One into Many, Translation and the Dissemination of Classical Chinese Literature*, ed. Leo Tak-hung, 5–31 (Amsterdam: Rodopi, 2003). Reprinted by permission of Koninklijke Brill NV.

Chapter 5 first appeared as "The Peking Translating Committee and S. I. J. Schereschewsky's Old Testament," *Anglican and Episcopal History* 67, no. 2 (June 1998): 212–226. Reprinted by permission of *Anglican and Episcopal History*.

Chapter 6 first appeared as "Translating the Ancestors, S. I. J. Schereschewsky's 1875 Chinese Version of Genesis," *Bulletin of the School of Oriental and African Studies* 56, Part 2 (1993):

219–233. © School of Oriental and African Studies, University of London 1993. Reprinted with permission.

Chapter 7 first appeared as "Bridges across Cultures: China in Yiddish Poetry," in *China and Her Biographical Dimensions, Commemorative Essays for Helmut Martin*, ed. Christina Neder et al., 277–284 (Wiesbaden: Harrassowitz, 2001).

Chapter 8 is reprinted with permission from *Sh'ma Now*, originally published in a December 2010 (41/675) issue on China and the Jews.

Chapter 9 first appeared as "Translation Literature in Modern China: The Yiddish Author and His Tale," *Asian and African Studies* (Jerusalem) 8, no. 3 (1972): 291–314.

Chapter 10 first appeared as "Meylekh Ravitch in China: A Travelogue of 1935," in *Transkulturelle Rezeption und Konstruktion, Festschrift für Adrian Hsia*, ed. Monika Schmitz-Evans, 103–107 (Heidelberg: Synchron, 2004).

Chapter 11 first appeared as "The Critique of Western Judaism in *The Castle* and Its Transposition in Two Chinese Translations," in *Kafka and China*, ed. Adrian Hsia, 41–72 (Bern-Berlin: Peter Lang, 1996). Reprinted by permission of Peter Lang.

Chapter 12 first appeared as "Martin Buber and Chinese Thought," in *Wege und Kräuzungen der Chinakunde an der J.W. Goethe Universität*, ed. Georg Ebertshäuser and Dorothea Wippermann, 23–49 (Frankfurt/Main: IKO–Verlag für Interkulturelle Kommunikation, 2007).

Chapter 13 first appeared as "Chinese and Jews, Mutual Perceptions in Literary and Related Sources," *East-West*

Dialogue 4, no. 2 (June 2000):
209–227.
Chapter 14 first appeared as "Learning the
Other, Chinese Studies in Israel
and Jewish Studies in China," *Mei
Occasional Papers*, no. 17 (September
2010): 1–7. Reprinted by permission of
MEI@ND.